How Colleges Change

Higher education is in an unprecedented time of change and reform. To address these challenges, university leaders tend to focus on specific interventions and programs, but ignore the change processes and the contexts that would lead to success. Joining theory and practice, *How Colleges Change* unmasks problematic assumptions that change agents typically possess and provides research-based principles for approaching change. Framed by decades of research, this monumental book offers fresh insights into understanding, leading, and enacting change. Recognizing that internal and external conditions shape and frame change processes, Kezar presents an overarching practical framework that can be applied to any organizational challenge and context. *How Colleges Change* is a crucial resource for aspiring and practicing campus leaders, higher education practitioners, scholars, faculty, and staff who want to learn how to apply change strategies in their own institutions.

Adrianna Kezar is Professor of Higher Education at the University of Southern California, USA.

How Colleges Change

Understanding, Leading, and Enacting Change

ADRIANNA KEZAR

Routledge
Taylor & Francis Group

NEW YORK AND LONDON

First published 2014
by Routledge
711 Third Avenue, New York, NY 10017

Simultaneously published in the UK
by Routledge
2 Park Square, Milton Park, Abingdon, Oxon OX14 4RN

Routledge is an imprint of the Taylor & Francis Group, an informa business

© 2014 Taylor & Francis

Library of Congress Cataloging in Publication Data
CIP data has been applied for.

ISBN: 978–0–415–53205–1 (hbk)
ISBN: 978–0–415–53206–8 (pbk)
ISBN: 978–0–203–11506–0 (ebk)

Typeset in Minion
by Swales & Willis Ltd, Exeter, Devon

Printed and bound in the United States of America by Sheridan Books, Inc. (a Sheridan Group Company).

Contents

Acknowledgements

I would like to thank Dan Maxey for helping to copyedit the book and for his work on the book graphics. I really appreciate his time and effort to help make this book come to reality! I also want to thank Rozana Carducci for reviewing and providing feedback on an early version of the book.

I also wish to thank Peter Eckel who I have written with for many years on the topic of change and Jaime Lester, Tricia Bertram Gallant and Melissa Contreras-McGavin who I enjoyed writing about grassroots leadership with. I would like to thank Cecile Sam for having me think about the importance of ethics as it relates to change. Lastly, I would like to thank Jeanne Narum and Susan Elrod for connecting me to STEM reform work and faculty networks aimed at scaling changes in higher education.

Illustrations

Figures

Tables

Preface

The following is excerpted from a scene in the 2012 film *Lincoln,* featuring a discussion between President Abraham Lincoln and Senator Thaddeus Stevens over plans for passage of the proposed 13th Amendment.

> LINCOLN: A compass, I learnt when I was surveying, it'll—it'll point you True North from where you're standing, but it's got no advice about the swamps and deserts and chasms that you'll encounter along the way. If in pursuit of your destination you plunge ahead, heedless of obstacles, and achieve nothing more than to sink in a swamp, what's the use of knowing True North?
>
> (*Lincoln* 2012)

I open this book with a line spoken by President Abraham Lincoln in the film *Lincoln* to demonstrate the importance of understanding the complete change process, not just the direction or vision. Most change agents believe that once they have a vision or idea for change the major work is done, that implementation is nothing but an afterthought. This book is about the swamps, deserts, and chasms that Lincoln refers to on the journey to change.

My goal for this book is to explain how change works in an engaging style. One of the most read books on higher education is *How Colleges Work* by Robert Birnbaum (1991). Through vivid case descriptions, a review of the literature on higher education, and a systems framework, Birnbaum tries to capture the complex ways that colleges make decisions within a professional bureaucracy with distributed power and a frequent sense of chaos. Many observers quip that higher education decision-making is opaque and hard to understand or track. The descriptive archetype campuses Birnbaum reviewed help the reader to envision varying campus cultures and the way that decision-making emerges differently based on the context. This helps the readers to understand how context shapes the way higher education operates. Good decision-making depends on the expectations and norms within the setting. Birnbaum assists readers to see that decision-making is much more complex than is often understood by connecting decision-making to politics, history, culture, external factors, stakeholder influences, and embedded structures such as shared authority.

In a similar vein, this book examines another topic that is often difficult to comprehend—how change occurs on college campuses. Like Birnbaum, I draw on an extensive literature base to support my arguments, but also try to bring vivid illustrations that make the issues more concrete and real for readers. I share the assumption with Birnbaum that change in higher education, like decision-making, requires an understanding of institutional and sectoral context. Additionally, this book provides a systems view of change, recognizing that complex processes require an understanding of the internal and external conditions that shape and frame these processes. My hope is that this book will be as inviting and informative as *How Colleges Work*, which helped to inform the perspective of many higher education leaders today. This book attempts to create praxis—joining theory and practical examples in harmony to create better understanding. Few books are able to successfully join theory with practice and make concepts accessible to policymakers and practitioners, yet still complex enough for scholars. I hope this book achieves that level of blended theory and practice. The book also presents a framework for change to make the ideas more inviting for change agents.

While improving decision-making may have been a strong imperative in the 1980s, I argue that leaders in this century need to have a facility for being change agents. Campus leaders today need to do more than just make sound decisions, they need to re-examine the work that they do in order to be relevant in the future and to maintain core functions and the integrity of higher education. Higher education is at a crossroads for undergoing fundamental changes. Carnegie Foundation President Vartan Gregorian has called for a presidential commission to be formed to examine the future of higher education, noting several changes that need to be implemented to align the system with the new economy, globalization, and technological advances. Decision-making can support this goal of change, but too often it has reinforced the status quo. The key question of the current time is how to create the needed changes to support a new enterprise—one that does not look like the past and hopefully looks better than the present state of the enterprise, which many feel is in decline in terms of quality, learning, and meeting changing needs (Slaughter and Rhoades 2004).

Defining Change

Before describing the approach to this book, its goals, and main contributions, it is important to define change, the main topic of the book. Most scholars of change have moved from the view that change is only an episodic event (e.g. infrequent, discontinuous, and intentional) to the notion of continuous, incremental change (e.g. ongoing, evolving, and cumulative) punctuated by episodic, dramatic changes (Poole and Van de Ven 2004). Some have even argued that we should alter the language from organizational change to organizational becoming, because alter suggests a static state that an organization reaches while becoming suggests an ongoing notion of change that is more authentic to organizational realities (Tsoukas and Chia 2002). Higher education scholars like to emphasize that, as institutions, higher education should maintain traditions and not shift continuously with whims, trends, or public pressure (Birnbaum 1991; Kezar 2001). There is truth in that critique and view of higher education, but it also masks the ongoing nature of changes that are happening continuously.

Scholars use a variety of terms to describe change and reviewing some of these definitions can help make clear what I am referring to throughout this book. When campuses respond to external forces, this is adaptation; when campuses unintentionally switch from one practice to another, mimicking others in the enterprise, this is called isomorphism; and, when campuses implement a new program or practice, this is called innovation. Or, scholars focus on organizational change—noted as bringing a positive outcome for the overall organization. Leaders and change agents tend to focus on innovation—creating something new. But, leaders need to consider the external environment more—the sphere often labeled adaptation or isomorphism. When leaders are more responsive, change is seen as adaption; when they are more passive, such as when mission drift toward research and away from teaching occurs, it is isomorphism.

I like to speak about change in the more general sense and have change agents consider that they are responsible for watching out for isomorphism, leading as thoughtfully as possible through adaptation processes, carefully choosing innovations and reforms, and considering how all these various types of changes tax the organization and its human and financial resources. Yet, a general discussion of change in past literature has masked these key variations of change. It is important to note that the use of the umbrella term in this book includes all aspects. So, change = isomorphism, adaptation, organizational change, and innovation or reform. It is also important to consider that paradigms (i.e. underlying assumptions about change) and theories relate to different definitions of or ways to think about change. Change is not a singular concept, but a multi-faceted concept that has evolved over time as scholars have sought to better understand it. Change is also contested in terms of what it is—its very nature.

A Note about These Definitions and the Way I Conceptualize Change

I tend to identify change as those intentional acts where a particular leader drives or implements a new direction. In fact, people are drawn not only to intentional changes, but innovative ones that draw upon new and creative ideas (Tierney 2012). Innovation, as noted above, is a particular type of change where a new concept, program, or intervention is introduced and implemented on a campus. But not all changes that leaders make or encounter are innovations. While innovation is certainly helpful for organizations and we need more of it, change agents need to be attentive to various kinds of changes that emerge within organizations. Some will threaten their creative and innovative ideas. Campuses can devolve, for example, which represents another type of change—they can lose enrollments, experience declines in funding, poor relationships can form between the faculty and the administration, the curriculum can lose cohesion, and poor reputations can emerge. These are changes, but not the ones that we often focus on—decline is another type of change that we need to aware of. Campuses are constantly undergoing changes. The process is continuous—sometimes it is more cumulative or less intentional. Yet, change agents need to be aware of these types of change, as well. In Chapter 1, I will describe campuses responding to wartime conditions (during World War I and II), which illustrates how sometimes campuses are adapting to external changes. Change is an unavoidable part of organizational life. The more we understand it, the better we can negotiate, resist, and facilitate it.

Main Arguments and Goals

In the rest of this preface, I will describe some of the major underlying assumptions and arguments developed within this book. I will also note the primary audiences for which the book is intended. As I will describe in Chapter 1, major changes will be required of higher education leaders, but there are several indicators that suggest leaders will not be well prepared. What are some of the key mistakes leaders make that lead to failed change efforts?

1. Ignoring the Change Process or Being Driven by Implicit or Tacit Theories of Change

One of the most significant challenges is that leaders[1] tend to focus on interventions and programs (e.g. service learning or STEM reform), but ignore the change process. Campus leaders are often trying to solve a specific problem or meet a need. So, when they have concerns about how ethics is taught to students, for example, they may decide that service learning will help address concerns. Change agents typically think they are done acting once they have chosen a teaching strategy such as service learning and ignore how they will get faculty to teach in new ways. If they pay attention to the change process at all, leaders often have implicit theories of change that are overly simplistic and not grounded in research on change. For example, change agents believe that others will automatically accept a good idea when presented with *proof* that it works. Another simplistic notion is that changes can be mandated in higher education. The book highlights the problem of an unrecognized implicit theory of change and the need for leaders to use research to develop an explicit approach to change.

2. Ignoring Context

Another related challenge is that leaders often ignore the external and organizational contexts, as well as facilitators that could help with change implementation. In general, there is a lack of analysis of the organization, its readiness for change, an initiative's fit or suitability, and alterations that may be necessary in order for a plan to work well within a specific context. A focal point of the book is to help change agents and leaders understand the importance of the external and organizational contexts for successfully creating any type of change.

Another mistake related to ignoring context is that change agents often overlook the ways in which culture and context shape their choice of tactics. While this mistake relates to the second point about organizational context, this focuses more on how change agents are more successful when they adopt strategies that fit into the culture of the institution for which they are trying to make change. For example, trying to develop an institution-wide policy is a change that is unlikely to work well within the context of a campus with a highly decentralized culture.

3. Simplistic Change Models

If leaders and change agents articulate an explicit theory of change (and as they operate off of implicit theories) they tend to adopt a single approach or strategy. A dean might feel that planning is the most important tactic. A department chair may feel that restructuring is always the best way to make change. However, successful change agents use multiple approaches to create change that are matched to the type of change desired and the context within which they are pursuing it. Too often, books on change promise that a linear, four- or five-step process will work, regardless of the context or type of change. Earlier books on change in higher education do not serve leaders well because they are based on simplistic strategic planning models of change—develop a vision, create a plan, assemble an implementation team, garner resources, then evaluate (Kerr 1983; Lucas 2000; Steeples 1990). Most characterizations of change processes are simple, linear, and miss the importance of organizational context. Multiple strategies are needed for change, which have been found to be essential within the multidisciplinary research base (Collins 1998). As a recent critique of the change literature noted, even though most authors claim that they have a recipe for change, the process is far too complex for any single approach to work within every situation and context (Burnes 2011). Still, the literature keeps reinventing this myth. For example, Kotter (1996) presents an eight-stage process for creating change that includes creating a sense of urgency, developing coalitions, developing a vision, and identifying short-term wins. While the eight stages are helpful, they present a model that is too simple, linear, and generalized to utilize in every change situation. Instead of repeating this mistake, this book helps change agents to understand how they can design customized approaches that fit their context and the type of change they intend to make.

The book will highlight the need for change agents and leaders to be savvy in applying multiple strategies and tactics for change. My research documents how leaders often approach change in naive ways (e.g. by not grounding changes in research or relying on simplistic approaches), as well as the value of being trained to understand research-based principles of change. In large, national research projects, I have documented how campus change projects are advanced when leaders are instructed on more complex ways to approach change. In summary, the book attempts to unmask some of the problematic assumptions that change agents typically make.

The work presented here attempts to help leaders overcome common mistakes by providing a research-based, macro framework for conceptualizing change as a complex process and designing a change process that is customized to suit a particular organizational challenge and moment. The overarching perspective taken is that change agents need to learn to be adaptable, creative, and have a host of strategies and tools at their disposal. The situations surrounding change vary and are dynamic, so a linear set of approaches is not going to work well in most situations. Others have critiqued the change literature in similar ways for being overly simplistic and linear, most notably Collins (1998). Most recently, a December 2011 special edition of the *Journal of Change Management* focused on the 70 percent failure rate of organizational change efforts historically. The special edition, titled *Why Does Change Fail and What Can We Do About It?*, suggests that a significant reason for the high failure rate is the overly simplistic models of change that have been advocated over the years that declare there is the one best way to create change. The various studies in this special edition demonstrate a much higher success rate for change agents who use more complex approaches within change initiatives. Furthermore, the edition also examines faulty assumptions around top-down organizational change, demonstrating that power struggles and lack of empowerment also feed into the high failure rates, which is also a theme in this book.

4. Not Grounding Change in Research

Furthermore, books on change in higher education are not grounded in research. Instead, they are often collections of practitioners' stories about how they created change, distilling generalized principles from anecdotes and unique situations. This book will review the latest research on key concepts that have been identified as facilitating change such as organizational learning, sensemaking, social network analysis, and organizational culture. In recent years, our understanding of how change occurs has advanced in critical ways that help us to understand perennial problems such as resistance, scalability, and high failure rates for change initiatives. Many scholars have noted that the high failure rates (upward of 70 per-cent in most studies) of change initiatives should be a caution for change agents and have them consider that they need greater advice and insight. Change is too disruptive a process to engage in with these high failure rates, and poor change efforts can lead to poor morale, disengagement by employees, and wasted time and productivity. This book will be one of the first research-based explorations into the topic. Leaders in higher education will be much better served by a book on change that moves beyond untested advice communicated in personal stories and anecdotes and focuses instead on research-based principles of change.

It is also important to note that studies of change agents who have undergone formal study and then used theory and research to later guide their practice noted several advantages over colleagues who did not have similar training:

1. They felt more comfortable because they could assess and understand the drivers and contexts of change, as well as the reasons for resistance, which helped them feel more empowered to move forward;
2. They felt better able to communicate their strategy to others and have others join them in their change efforts; and,
3. They were better able to match change strategies to change situations with greater confidence.

(Andrews et al. 2008)

Research suggests that change agents learn more from broad explanatory theories about the larger story of how change unfolds as a unique human and organizational dynamic than particular change techniques often emphasized in training sessions in leadership or management courses. The participants in their study rejected pre-scriptive models as helpful and instead found that "theories which enabled them to make sense of and contextualize change situations in which they found them-selves" were most helpful (Andrews et al. 2008: 311). Experienced change agents learned that each change situation might require a different response. Thus, a will-ingness to be flexible to contextual conditions was key to change agents' success. Additionally, knowing multiple theories of change allowed leaders to respond to situations that differed and they were able to harness ideas as needed to fit the situation. This approach to change sees theories not as prescriptions to be enacted unreflectively, but ideas to be considered based on contexts.

Based on a desire to help leaders overcome these mistakes and to provide better information than previous publications, there are four main goals:

1. Present major insights into the change process based on the synthesis of theo-ries of change;
2. Present an overarching framework for conceptualizing change based on these theories/research;
3. Provide detail on special research topics that are very important to executing change such as organizational learning or social networks; and,
4. Review existing models of change that have been put into practice in higher

education such as the Project Kaleidoscope's Leadership Institute; the Center for Urban Education's Equity Scorecard; Achieving the Dream; The Campus Diversity Initiative; and National Survey of Student Engagement's benchmarking efforts; and what can be learned from these initiatives.

Organization

The book is organized into three parts.

Part I—Thinking Differently about Change—contains two chapters that set the context for the rest of the book. Chapter 1 begins by explaining the reasons for change in the current context as well as how the current context shapes change processes. Chapter 2 outlines the main concepts and theories about change that will be applied throughout the rest of the book. Many of the later chapters build upon Chapter 2, so the book is best read sequentially, however, the chapters in Part III are meant to stand alone, so they may be read and are easily understood in isolation.

Part II—A Multi-faceted Framework for Understanding Change—contains six chapters and reviews the reflective framework for analyzing change situations. Chapter 3 focuses on the type of change, as well as how an analysis of the type of change can help leaders to design a strong strategy. Chapter 4 delves into one important type of change—second-order or deep change—and examines two theories from the social cognition school of thought, sensemaking and organizational learning. Chapter 5 reviews various contexts—social/economic, external organizations, institutional culture—that all shape change processes and may also function as levers or barriers for change. Chapter 6 reviews the notions of agency and leadership; it explores how different actors have different agency, which can shape strategies or approaches to change. Chapter 7 summarizes how the type of change, context, and agency can be analyzed together to generate creative approaches to change situations. Five unique cases are presented and analyzed using the elements of the framework. Chapter 8 reviews common obstacles that emerge as change processes unfold, as well as a three-stage model of the institutionalization of changes.

Part III—Challenges for Change Agents in Our Time—contains two chapters exploring some of the perennial struggles of change agents such as scaling up changes and the ethics of change. These chapters provide additional resources for addressing challenges that have long vexed change agents.

Audience and Uses of the Book

I consider change not from the viewpoint of administration or management and I consciously use the term *change agent* throughout the book to signal that anyone can create change. So much of the change literature comes from a managerial perspective and assumes that guidance should only be intended to help administrators put in place their vision or set of interests, providing a view of the organization from the top down within the organizational hierarchy. This book hopes to discourage change processes emerging from this top-down perspective and instead conceptualizes change as a multi-level leadership process with changes emerging throughout the organization at different levels (Sturdy and Grey 2003). Thus, the audience is broader than for many books on change, looking at the roles of all organizational stakeholders.

As a result, the audience for this book is quite expansive, ranging from board members and presidents, provosts, deans, and department chairs; to faculty; to student affairs practitioners; to staff across all units and divisions on campus; to graduate and undergraduate students and change agents across a host of areas in higher education.

The book may be used as:

1. As a guide for change agents and practitioners working in higher education institutions;
2. As a textbook for leadership and management courses in higher education and student affairs; and,
3. As a scholarly book on change for the field.

This book will be a great resource for higher education leadership or administration courses where faculty and students are discussing the importance of change and how to create it. Also, the student affairs curriculum often includes a leadership or management course aimed at creating change. Almost all graduate students register that they come back to obtain their doctoral or masters degrees because they want to create changes in higher education and are frustrated with some aspect of their current role. Higher education programs often teach sections of courses or whole courses on issues relating to change because students have this strong desire to learn about how to be effective change agents. Therefore, this text is important for consideration as a textbook in higher education programs.

However, while this book could be used as a textbook, as it has theory to inform students, it is meant to be a guide for practitioners. As noted throughout this preface, change agents and leaders on campus too often rely on their own experience or peers' perspectives for change strategies and approaches. This book can be used in leadership institutes, academies, and professional development aimed at change agents such as directors of centers for teaching and learning, department chairs, or staff with a vision for change. This book will offer guidance that can help improve the success rate for change initiatives. I also hope the book will encourage leaders to think about the types of changes being made and the ethics behind their choices. As was noted earlier, the book will aim to achieve praxis by bringing in solid research to support practical implications for change agents. It will be squarely based on existing theories and includes a review of significant research about change.

As a scholarly book on change, various change theories are summarized to introduce scholars to this area of research. Also, this book offers several new insights into change such as the approach of grassroots leaders, the role of sensemaking and organizational learning, the potential of social network analysis, ethics and change, and information about the importance of context-based approaches to change. However, readers who are purely interested in theories about change and want a primer that reviews the multi-disciplinary research base are encouraged to access my prior work—*Understanding and Facilitating Organizational Change in the 21st Century* (see Kezar 2001).

Before I start describing *how change works*, it is important to understand why change is important in the academy and the particular context for change in today's unique environment, which is the focus of Chapter 1.

Part 1

Thinking Differently about Change

The first part of the book focuses readers on understanding why change is necessary and encourages them to think differently about the change process through an exploration of theories of change that emphasize aspects that are often not visible to change agents. Part I also establishes the main assumptions and theories that undergird the framework presented in the second part of the book.

Chapter 1 explains why change is needed in higher education, as well as how today's context is unique. Chapter 2 reviews six theories of change that can help leaders to think differently and expand their ideas about change. These six theories will also inform the framework presented in Part II of the book.

one
Why Change?

One should be leery of people who describe changes or crises in higher education as being unprecedented. Some critics today note that higher education faces unparalleled crises and issues and that it is facing a revolution or devolution (Christensen et al. 2011). Yet, significant changes have occurred throughout the history of higher education. For example, there were the debates about changes to liberal arts education around the Yale Report of 1828, the Morrill Act of 1862 introduced vastly different institutional types, massive growth and changes in the student body occurred following World War II and the introduction of the G.I. Bill (Servicemen's Readjustment Act), and the introduction of federal financial aid made it possible for many more and different types of students to enter higher education. As this list suggests, though, many major changes within higher education have come from the outside, rather than resulting from intentional changes made internally. Higher education has always faced changes (some quite dramatic) that shaped the character and mission of the enterprise. Yet, the multitude of directions for change and the lack of capacity (e.g. fiscal and human resources) to meet today's changes present challenges and threaten to overwhelm leaders, requiring more and perhaps even different ways of thinking and reflecting on problems and change than have been common in the past. While higher education may not be at the crossroads of a revolution, the enterprise will be required to shift in significant ways and is already undergoing many changes.

Furthermore, the context in which higher education operates has changed in complex ways that need to be engaged by change agents. This is a time when skills in change agency are critical to the health and success of the higher education enterprise. This chapter examines why leaders need to engage with the change process, as well as the particular challenges we face in this era. I also suggest that the context for change is shaping the way change can and does occur— *the nature of change processes is itself being altered*. Thus, being a change agent today is different. Change agents can engage social media and technology, which were lesser factors or levers in the past. Change agents also need to be more accountable and transparent as there is less trust in higher education as a sector. Leaders need to recognize that the deeper interconnection of higher education to the larger social and economic goals of the public makes them less independent than in the past and more vulnerable to external forces and demands. In addition, change agents need to do more with less based on the financial situation that most campuses face as a result of the global recession. These are just a few of the circumstances that make the context for change different. And, the context will continue to change over the years and leaders need to be constantly scanning the environment; continuous adaptation is needed.

Why Leaders Should Engage Change, Rather than Being Passive Recipients

While history suggests change is a common facet of higher education, history also helps us see why it is important to the vitality of our colleges and universities that leaders engage change. Sometimes change agents are creating changes that are of their own making—implementing a strategic plan, rethinking the curriculum, or implementing a new program. However, just as often changes may not be of our own making (e.g. enrollment declines, financial stress). We are often less likely to think about these types of changes. In this book, when I speak about engaging change, I am referring to both types of changes. Higher education leaders ignore external pressures or organizational devolution at their own peril. And, to some degree, I argue a lack of attention to managing external forces is what has happened in the last 20 years among administrators, faculty, and students. Campus leaders can impact and shape the nature of changes and whether they will support or upset campus operations. Take the response by campus leaders in World War I and World War II, for example. In World War I, campus leaders felt that the military was intruding on campus operations and that supporting the military was not part of their public mission. Thus, as military efforts were moved onto campuses, it created chaos and obstruction. However, during World War II, academic leaders on campuses were proactive and decided to invite dialogue about the ways campuses could support the military; they created new programs such as area studies and language programs that were aligned with their missions, but also supported military efforts. As a result, they actually increased their access to resources and capacity, rather than depleting them. The military presence became complementary and did not disturb campus operations, as it had in earlier times. Academic leaders can shape outcomes differently through their responses (or lack of responses). Another example is more contemporary.

In the last 20 years, higher education leaders have largely *not* responded to changes in the public policy environment around funding and public support rather than thoughtfully adapting to them. Campuses have believed that state money would return to former levels and that public support would rebound, but such changes have not occurred and conditions have gotten worse. Without responding to declining funds, campuses will face increasingly difficult decisions and a worsening climate and set of conditions within which to make changes.

But, responding to changes may not always mean supporting them, as seen in the examples of the military presence on campuses during the two world wars. Sometimes the best response is to resist changes that may threaten the campuses' mission and ability to best operate. For example, in the last 20 years, campuses have adopted corporate employment models of contingency, moving to a workforce wherein 70 percent of the faculty have no consistent employment or connection to campuses. They also encounter working conditions that make it difficult for them to teach and contribute to the core mission of the institution. In fact, higher education has become a "poor" employer to these faculty members, offering low pay with no benefits, short-term contracts with precarious job stability, unsystematic hiring processes, and little, if any, orientation or support. Few, if any, campus leaders resisted this change in faculty composition and practices; instead they mimicked this new approach to employment that was prevalent among corporations and increasingly among their peer institutions as a way to deal with shortfalls in state revenues. So, resisting contingency and considering other employment options may have been a more appropriate response.

Some argue leaders did not intentionally create this change in the faculty. In Chapter 2, I will examine theories of neo-institutionalism that look at how organizations engage in massive changes, often with limited intentionality (Cross and Goldenberg 2009). Yet, the change in faculty composition did occur and there was little, if any, leadership to alter this change—to resist it. So, change agency is engaging change proactively, whether to support or resist it. While implementing changes that leaders see as necessary is critical, change agents cannot ignore alterations that are happening around them, as well. They also cannot ignore the enterprise by always focusing only on their own campuses. Leadership and change agency mean thinking systemically about changes. Appropriate change agency also means knowing about the context and external environment for change.

Change in This Era

The environment for change is different today for several key reasons:

1. Connection of higher education to the global economy;
2. The greater public investment and sense of accountability;
3. Increasingly diverse students who engage campuses differently;
4. The corporatized campus environment;
5. For-profit higher education, competition, and marketization;

6. New knowledge about how people learn;
7. Technology; and,
8. Internationalization of campus.

These issues also suggest and reinforce the imperative to change. While this brings up a litany of recurrent issues that are described when people suggest the urgency to change, I attempt to examine these as more than just drivers for change. I also examine how these issues change the context for change and create a new era in which change occurs, which no other source has examined. I do not wish to suggest these are the types of changes that higher education should be engaged in; rather I mean to describe how they are creating pressures for change and creating a new context for change. In fact, I hope that leaders will instead choose changes and initiatives that are based on evidence and research.[1] Too often, changes chosen are merely a response to political and other external pressures, rather than being guided by the mission of learning, knowledge creation and public service.

Connection of Higher Education to the Global Economy

The primary and overarching shift that shapes many of the other conditions below is that higher education has become the gateway for entry into the knowledge economy. As the labor market has shifted from industry and lower-skilled jobs to positions that require critical thinking and higher-order skills, a college education will be required for most high-paying jobs in the future. Also, innovation is key to global economic development. While this has been an important part of the context for the last 50 years, competition in terms of innovation has become intensified as more nations are providing resources toward creating an educated workforce. Thus, other countries are working to educate more individuals in order to create the potential for driving innovations that will allow them to compete in the global economy. Many reports cite how the number of college graduates in the United States has been declining in recent years (often due to our high dropout rates as compared to other countries), which may impact our global competitiveness (Christensen et al. 2011). These trends have resulted in the introduction of President Barack Obama's 2020 College Completion Goal plan, which intends to double the number of college students, and efforts such as the Lumina Foundation's Goal 2025 to increase the percentage of Americans with high-quality degrees and credentials to 60 percent by 2025. To meet these ambitious goals, higher education needs to respond and change in new ways, as there is limited, if any, new funding coming to incentivize such growth.

In the eyes of policymakers, higher education leaders have been uneven in responding to these goals, often unwilling to consider new delivery systems such as hybrid and online learning or rethink course creation or size in order to increase access more quickly (Christensen et al. 2011).[2] The nationwide dropout rate is over 50 percent and we have not made progress on changing this outcome. And while most of these national reports speak to goals in the next decade, this is likely

an even longer-term challenge the enterprise will face. The challenge of continued massification needs systemic solutions that address high school completion,
K-20 partnerships, rethinking remediation, and greater investment in the community college sector. Furthermore, costs have skyrocketed and tuition has increased
approximately 6.3 percent annually for the last three decades (Christensen et al.
2011). Tuition and fees went up 274 percent from 1990 to 2009, faster than any
other good besides cigarettes. Affordability is a major concern among policymakers and impacts goals for access.

This trend makes the change process different, as well, because individual campus decisions are now tied into the overall economic decision apparatus of the state
and federal government. Many higher education leaders continue to operate in
isolation; they do not realize that they are more intimately a part of a much larger
capitalist-industrial complex. While this shift has been taking place since the 1950s,
it has intensified with changes in the global economy and competition over the last
two decades. Also, changes to address completion and greater access require making
partnerships and working more across sectors (e.g. working with K-12 and community agencies), as many of these challenges cross the boundaries of sectors. The
change context requires more collaboration among higher education institutions,
across sectors, and also within institutions themselves (Kezar and Lester 2009).

The Greater Public Investment and Sense of Accountability

In the past 40 years, the federal and state governments have increased their funding substantially for higher education, primarily through federal financial aid,
but also through state grants to students and research funding through government agencies such as the National Science Foundation and National Institutes
of Health. Higher education was able to undergo substantial growth and spawned
new sectors such as for-profit education because of the increased availability of
financial aid, which boosted the number of students who could take advantage of
higher education.

Due to the increases in funding, however, federal and state policymakers began
to feel that they should have greater say in institutional operations—particularly
those they saw as being central to their investment—such as functions affecting
student retention, transfer and completion, and employability. Also, they started
to require conformity to new legislation and regulations on issues of equity and
civil rights such as the Americans with Disabilities Act, Title IX, and laws protecting employees from sexual harassment. Federal and state governments have
continued to call for greater accountability and transparency as a condition of the
government's investment by requiring assessment of student learning outcomes,
for example. Government entities want assurances not only that students are
learning, but that they are acquiring the right type of knowledge to be successful in
the information economy.

Because higher education has historically enjoyed financial support with limited
public accountability, campus stakeholders have not always been quick to address

calls for change on campus from outside. Many different public opinion polls show that the public worries about college affordability and access, particularly in states like California, where many students are being shut out of classes and institutions. There is greater public scrutiny, rising calls for transparency and accountability for outcomes, and a growing demand for using new means for assessment. The lack of action from higher education leaders or institutions in addressing growing concerns may result in sharper declines in state funding, as higher education is increasingly seen as the problem, rather than part of the public policy solution. Thus, the collective lack of response for the need to change, and lack of acumen about how to do so effectively, may lead for a decline in our perceived value as a social institution.

All of these forces mean change is much more strongly associated with accountability, and again that higher education no longer can be considered to be an independent actor, but one tied to the demands that accompany public investment. Still, this change is not so simple. Even though much more federal and state money has been going into higher education over time, recently declining state budgets and states' ability to provide incentives have resulted in academic leaders calling for greater freedom from state regulation, accountability, and control. So, while there are increased expectations around accountability, there are also proposals to release public higher education institutions from accountability due to the declining role of public funds in their budgets. State investments have simply not kept pace with rising expenses. Campus revenue streams have been further hampered by the recession, which negatively impacted campus endowments and also alumni giving to higher education.

Increasing accountability concerns also are connected to the emergence of other new stakeholders that see higher education as being accountable to them. While Kerr documented the phenomenon of increased stakeholder interest back in the 1960s in his book *The Uses of the University*, the number of these stakeholder groups has continued to grow at an exponential pace, creating new pressures for institutional leaders to manage associated with their various expectations and demands. Corporations, foundations, community agencies, and civic organizations, to name a few, all have legitimate claims to shape the purpose and direction of higher education.

This also affects the change environment. Previous campus administrators might have defined a change agenda largely on their own or with a focus on internal constituents (Kerr 2001).[3] Today, administrators, as well as other campus change agents, need to consider a broader array of stakeholders and balance different views and priorities in their decision-making. Leaders need to think of meaningful ways to help the faculty to understand that a change in requirements for general education may not be as critical as partnering with local schools to create greater alignment within the curriculum to ensure greater access. Policymakers also need to better understand that pressures to graduate more students might actually undermine quality and outcomes for a great number of students. For all groups involved in shaping the future of higher education, there is a greater need to understand the perspectives of a diverse and widening range of stakeholders than has been the case at any time before. Internal and external groups need to have a more expansive and inclusive dialogue, increased interaction, and cultivate their capabilities for understanding each other's perspectives.

Increasingly Diverse Students Who Engage Campuses Differently

Higher education now educates many more students than it has at any point in our history. As the enterprise has grown substantially, many new types of students have been introduced to campuses (e.g. first generation, adult learners, physically challenged, and a greater diversity of racial, ethnic, socio-economic, gender, and international populations) that have different needs. And, the student bodies of the future are going to continue to be increasingly diverse, with the fastest growth occurring among Hispanic students. However, although we are becoming increasingly diverse, we still have poor retention and graduation rates among these groups, particularly for low-income and racial minority students. According to the 2000 Census, 16 percent of all Hispanics, 21 percent of all African Americans, and 15 percent of Native Americans earned a college degree, as compared to 35 percent of Caucasians and 49 percent of Asian Americans. Also, graduation rates for Hispanic students are 45 percent and 31 percent for African Americans, but are 58 percent among Caucasian and 65 percent among Asian American students at Division I colleges. The perception is that institutions have been slow to address the different needs of these populations, which has partly led to these low completion rates for Hispanic and African American students.

The higher education literature in the 1980s and 1990s, in particular, highlighted the need for campuses to change to embrace women, racial minorities, low-income, and adult students (Hurtado et al. 1999). We know what to change to help varying populations succeed, but actual changes have often not been implemented. And, even as we have not addressed historical changes, new changes continue to emerge all the time. For example, in more recent years, rather than moving through a single institution from matriculation to graduation, as was common in the past, students *swirl* between multiple institutions, sometimes attending as many as three or four institutions at the same time. Also, now we have veteran students coming to campuses who have unique needs ranging from post-traumatic stress disorder to depression to re-entry into non-military life. Campuses are finding they need to not only boost counseling services, but prepare counselors for the unique needs of veterans. It is also important to connect veteran students so they have like-minded peers to interact with.

Rethinking structures and support for students from different backgrounds is an area that campuses have made some advances in. For example, there has been great success with engaging women and adult students, while other groups have not been successfully involved in higher education, including low-income, first generation, and racial minorities, particularly African American males

(Touchton et al. 2008). Part of the concern is that higher education institutions have not worked in partnership with K-12 systems to align standards, helped teacher educators in being successful in supporting diverse students, created environments that support college going within high schools, or examined campus transition processes. Furthermore, higher education tends to add on single programs or services to help students, rather than fundamentally rethinking the structures and culture to support new students.[4] While there are complexities to this issue because students are also responsible for their success, this remains a major challenge for higher education. We do not do particularly well with new student populations, which are the same populations President Obama has targeted in his goals for doubling enrollments.

An increasingly diverse faculty and staff have also accompanied the growing diversity of the student body. While efforts have not been as pronounced as some would like, the faculty and staff are increasingly reflecting the diversity of the broader population in terms of gender, race, and socio-economic status. The changing face of campuses provides a different environment for change now than in the past. There are, perhaps, fewer shared interests, or at least perceived interests, among campus stakeholders due to the increased diversity. There is also a great variety of experience and background, making communication and creating a shared vision much more complex. When the majority of the faculty and staff came from similar economic and social backgrounds, there was a greater sense of alignment of interests and ease in understanding each other. Thus, change can be even more difficult, with greater opportunities for misunderstanding and resistance. Often, change agents are unprepared for engaging people from diverse backgrounds, to truly listen and understand different perspectives, make complex decisions, and create change processes.[5]

The Corporatized Higher Education Environment

The corporatization of campuses is another overarching issue affecting why change is needed, as well as how the nature of change has been altered. Thirty years ago, most would agree that campuses operated as professional bureaucracies, where faculty and administration shared the responsibility for decision-making and campus operations. Also, campuses enjoyed greater public support and state budgets provided steady funding for higher education. Yet, as state budgets declined, campus leaders began to look for new ways to raise revenues (e.g. grants, licensing), promote entrepreneurialism (e.g. new programs aimed at generating profits such as online programs and certificates), decrease costs and provide flexibility in uncertain budget times (e.g. non-tenure-track faculty), and centralize decision-making so that administrators have greater control over spending, planning, and priorities. The enterprise, many argue, began to focus on business operations more so than the academic core (Burgan 2006; Rhoades 1996). The faculty became seen as workers, rather than professionals. As a result, administrators began hiring non-tenure-track faculty, both full and part time, often at poverty-level wages and with no benefits, little or no input into campus affairs, evaluation and professional development, or any form of support such as orientation, office space, or instructional resources (Kezar and Sam 2010). This shift is fundamental to the values and priorities of campuses. Academic and professional values have been pushed to the side in planning and governance; conversations and decision-making focus largely on business related to funding, marketing, branding, enrollment growth, and maximizing productivity (Slaughter and Rhoades 2004). This has also resulted in an erosion of shared interests and trust between faculty and administrators. While this certainly varies by campus context or sector, it can be seen across all institutional types.

The environment for change in higher education has also been altered because increasing numbers of administrators and non-academic managers now control and dominate university life (Leicht and Fennell 2008). Formerly, administrators were drawn from the faculty ranks and had strong norms that were related to internal understandings of the organization. Increasingly, administrators are not coming up through the ranks of faculty and have less familiarity with internal norms and are more greatly influenced by external pressures, particularly around those that provide resources and prestige. Even traditional groups that have had a vested interest such as parents and alumni are changing their roles and see themselves more as customers or controlling interests. In the past, administrators provided a buffer between parents, students, donors, research funders, and professors, trying to maintain institutional norms that supported a certain set of values around the professionalization of labor, autonomy, tenure, academic freedom, and foregrounding educational and intellectual values. Leicht and Fennell (2008) argue that today administrators engage each constituent's interests as legitimate and work toward accommodating them, rather than buffering the institution from their influence. Thus, the environment for change within college and university campuses has grown in complexity with more stakeholders' interests being engaged and more competition among values (i.e. entrepreneurial versus academic interests) than in the past, and more corporate and entrepreneurial values guiding leaders.

As a result, many argue that a corporatized work environment means that change processes take place on campuses where shared interests and vision have generally been lost between faculty and the administration (Leicht and Fennell 2008). Trust is limited between staff, faculty, and administrative groups. Faculty, as change agents, are increasingly limited as they are increasingly employed off the tenure track with limited power, although in Chapters 6 I will speak to the potential of even those with very limited power to create change. Campus leaders often see themselves as being in competition with other campuses, so they are less collegial and share very little information. All of these conditions make some changes more difficult and problematic than in earlier eras when there were greater shared interests, more capacity for leadership among faculty, and stronger relationships across and between campuses, which saw themselves as part of a collective enterprise and not just competitors for enrollments and funding. Corporatization allows changes to flourish that lead to revenue generation, such as online programs, new fields that obtain grants, or internationalization and global program development, at the expense of other important efforts such as retention or increasing diversity. Thus, the corporate higher education environment appears to affect the type of changes that can flourish and which changes will be more difficult to pursue because they do not align to corporate values.

For-profit Higher Education, Competition, and Marketization

Closely linked to the corporatization of higher education is the dramatic rise of for-profit higher education. Once a relatively small sector, it now serves 13 percent of postsecondary students, the same number as not-for-profit private higher education. While the sector is plagued with challenges related to illegal recruitment practices, student debt and default, seemingly unfulfilled promises of employment, and questions about the quality of education offered (i.e. students actually taking required credits, students completing assignments or being graded appropriately, pressures for faculty to pass students), it continues to attract more students. As Kinser (2011) notes, there are many for-profit institutions that do not engage in illegal and unethical practice, but because there are no actual studies or ways to empirically understand the magnitude of the problem, these problems taint the entire sector. The sector is attempting to respond to new legislation passed to address fraud associated with gainful employment, requiring for-profits to prove they are successfully placing students in jobs when they graduate. For-profit institutions are also being compelled to respond to the 90/10 rule, which requires them to derive 10 percent of tuition revenues from sources other than federal financial aid.

For-profits may not represent competition for traditional higher education since existing institutions, particularly state schools, often cannot meet the capacity that is demanded of them. Also, for-profit cost structures remain similar to traditional higher education, so unless they can be priced much lower, then they will not place competitive pressure on traditional higher education. However, for-profits have brought a different operating model that appears to be shaping traditional, not-for-profit colleges and universities. For example, the non-tenure-track faculty model, curriculum approach (e.g. pre-packaged and standardized), and governance structures (e.g. no shared governance), and a focus on the bottom line that is increasingly reflected in operations are being mimicked more and more often. The for-profit and not-for-profit models are increasingly similar.

Another aspect of the for-profit sector that is increasingly present in traditional higher education is competition between campuses for students, whether for enrollments or attracting the best students to increase prestige. This encourages campuses to funnel money into campus facilities, merit scholarships, and new services and programs that they believe will entice students to enroll and draw attention to the campus, often at the expense of providing affordable access or providing for faculty support or salaries. While for-profits may not compete for students with most sectors of higher education beyond community colleges, as they tend to draw on different populations at present, they have accelerated a paradigm of competition within the traditional higher education sector.[6]

In addition to the for-profit sector increasing a sense of competition in what has become a higher education marketplace, institutional ranking systems have been used more aggressively within the corporatized university environment, increasing competition among traditional higher education institutions (Pusser and Marginson 2012). Increasingly, new ranking systems are being created worldwide and institutions are allowing these to shape their decisions about quality, performance, and goals and priorities. As certain criteria or characteristics are identified as factoring into rankings, they are increasingly affecting decision-making and priorities on campuses. While one might make the argument that rankings are particularly important for elite campuses that tend to be ranked at the top of the list, the criteria used within these global rankings also become de facto measures of quality and aspiration for all other institutions, even those that are not ranked or appear at the bottom of the rankings. Thus, these ranking systems have come to drive change processes in particular ways toward greater selectivity, higher costs, an increasing emphasis on research and publication, and more attention to improving reputation through marketing.

The rise of the for-profit model and marketization of higher education also shapes the context for change by reinforcing the corporate values that are taking hold of public and private not-for profit campuses. Since one sector has shown it can succeed and grow by using these approaches, this places pressure on the others to consider these practices to compete. The rise of the for-profit sector and its emphasis on online learning platforms and standardized curriculum is also believed to have shaped traditional higher education by having introduced a disruptive technology that may make it possible to fundamentally rethink various core assumptions about higher education (Christensen et al. 2011). The new sector may make more fundamental changes to institutions of higher education possible or more amenable. The history of higher education demonstrates that each time a new institution type (e.g. metropolitan universities, community colleges) is introduced, it shapes the broader enterprise in some way. Yet, these changes have usually not shaken the core assumptions as this one is predicted to do.

New Knowledge about How People Learn

Studies from cognitive and neuroscience are demonstrating that people learn differently than we once thought (Zull 2011). Pedagogical and curricular practices on campuses are generally informed by passive banking concepts of learning, wherein faculty feed information to learners who accumulate knowledge on a blank slate that develops over time into compartmentalized storehouses of knowledge the student can draw upon to address problems and create new knowledge. This resulted in a largely lecture-based format for delivering content and discrete course offerings. While pedagogical studies existed in the past that questioned this lecture and knowledge delivery approach, scholars and many external stakeholders such as the National Science Foundation have been persuaded that we need to integrate new concepts into our teaching and learning practices. Compelling new research evidence suggests that active learning approaches can help people develop deep learning.

Research also demonstrates that learning of discrete facts, rather than synthesis, is much less successful and that curriculum and pedagogies that emphasize integration of content, existing schema, and the like are critical to student learning (Zull 2011). Integration is important, not just across subject matter, but with daily life and experience. Thus, the typical emphasis on abstraction is a poor practice for learning. Students learn better when their existing knowledge is scaffolded and explicit connections are made between content areas. Additionally, the connection of emotions to learning has been prominently demonstrated (Damasio 1994), leading to recommendations about how to engage students in approaches that address or connect to their emotions, such as service learning. These studies also suggest that racism or sexism impacts the creation of a safe learning environment.

Without going into all the details about findings of recent cognitive science, studies have reinforced the need to rethink curricular structures and values, pedagogy, classroom spaces and architecture, and student–teacher interactions. Many campuses are making changes that address these new findings about the importance of integration and synthesis (e.g. senior capstones or learning communities), by creating problem-based and experiential models that activate learning for students and capitalize on students' interests and emotions through self-created majors, student-driven assignments, and service learning courses. This powerful base of research from cognitive science provides a strong foundation for change. While there have been many calls for change in the past, there often was less compelling evidence about why and fewer supporters. Now, with major funders and powerful outside groups championing this research, it is a strong driver of change.

Cognitive science research challenges the direction of higher education toward passive, lecture-focused forms of online learning (particularly MOOCs) and discrete, modularized curricular models championed by for-profit higher education, technology enthusiasts, and encouraged through corporate values of efficiency, scale, and productivity. It demonstrates the dangers of adopting untested learning models, which are moving farther away from practices that support learning, rather than toward them. This research may provide a counterbalance to the corporate values permeating many campuses.

This new understanding about how people learn may also be used as a lever for creating change and to shape the dynamics of the change process. The research from cognitive science reinforces why vision development, communication, appealing to emotions, and understanding fears to help mobilize people for change can be leveraged for change, just as it is used to improve the learning environment. Campus change agents need to think about not only a powerful rationale for their changes, but ways they can appeal to people's emotions. While people have often spoken of fear as it relates to change, it is only through more recent studies of change that we realize people's resistance often has to do with their lack of understanding about the change itself—their own need to learn is really the impediment, not just a psychological fear or attachment to the status quo. This is why the later chapter on sensemaking and organizational learning (Chapter 4) is so important to creating change.

Technology

Technology is also partly responsible for or connected to different ways that students are learning. Video games, Facebook, blogs, and Wikipedia will all be integrated into campus learning experiences in the future in some way. In fact, many of them already are being included. Through social media and the Internet, students have greater access to people and information than ever before to enhance their learning, as well as distract their concentration (Christensen et al. 2011). For good or for ill, technology is increasingly a part of the world and campus life. Students spend more and more time engaged with technology and are demanding more access to campus services and courses via the Internet. Twenty-five percent of students took at least one online course in 2008 (Christensen et al. 2011). While for-profit institutions often use an online learning platform, so too do many traditional institutions. Some institutions (e.g. Massachusetts Institute of Technology (MIT), Carnegie Mellon, Open University, Tufts, University of California Irvine, University of California Berkeley, and Stanford) are even using technology to offer free or open source courses. While they do not offer degrees for completing these courses, they are beginning to offer badges and certificates that suggest students who have passed these courses have acquired or developed some level of skill, as a result. In addition, other efforts such as Udacity (an outgrowth of free computer science classes offered through Stanford University that currently has 15 active courses funded by venture capitalists), Peer 2 Peer University (a three-year-old, online institution where students learn together at no charge using materials found on the web), Coursera (which utilizes a combination of free courses offered by traditional universities), edX (an open source course program run by Harvard and MIT), University of the People (a tuition-free, online institution that offers degrees in select areas) offer courses and degrees for free through online learning environments, and MOOCS, *massive online open courses* that are offered via the web. These current efforts build on many existing and successful efforts, such as the University of Maryland's University College and Pennsylvania State University's World Campus that enroll 100,000 students and are particularly adept at reaching adult students and individuals without close access to a campus.

Much as cognitive science research is driving changes in teaching and learning, powerful foundations such as the Bill and Melinda Gates Foundation and Lumina Foundation are providing funding to promote the use of new technologies for increasing access to higher education. Gates has funded many hybrid models of teaching through their next generation learning grants. Important innovations have emerged from the National Center for Academic Transformation, which has created modules for the most popular 25 introductory science, social sciences, and humanities courses that can be delivered through online delivery systems, take in more students, require less teaching time, and reduce course costs through greater economies of scale. Thus, innovations may drive down costs and address the affordability issue that many consider has skyrocketed in higher education. The best of these efforts use active forms of learning (through flipped classrooms) and synthesize knowledge, practice found to support learning in cognitive science, but many models do not.

Campuses have typically engaged in technological change more easily because of the revenue potential, although new technology systems have not always delivered the desired outcomes. Some online programs launched by major universities have lost money, rather than turning a profit. Online programs often end up requiring more time from faculty, not less. Also, the infrastructure costs often turn out to be extremely expensive, and since technologies are evolving so quickly, as soon as a campus installs one set of software or hardware, changes are made that require upgrades. These continuous costs take away from desired profits that led to the decision to make the investment in the first place. While instructional technologists argue that new systems can drive costs down in the long term, they emphasize that technology should be pursued for its pedagogical value, not because of cost, as lowering costs may not always be an attainable outcome. Unfortunately, many campuses are attempting to use technology to generate additional revenues by increasing the numbers of students served, often using less effective models of online learning instead of using technology in rich ways (Christensen et al. 2011). Also, Clark (1983) has demonstrated that technology is merely a medium, which does not enhance the value of learning in any way on its own, but may be used to try to accommodate greater access, for example. So, leaders need to carefully engage technology and understand its potential, but also its limitations.

In terms of its role in change processes, technology has increased opportunities to establish connections across what were formerly more discrete or closed boundaries. Increasingly, groups of like-minded people who care about service learning, sustainability, or diversity are able to form social movements and support groups via the Internet and use online tools to support changes. Technology will be particularly helpful for less powerful groups that do not have resources and power to draw upon, but who can use free platforms online to mobilize and create change from the bottom up. Technology also allows change agents greater influence to shape change processes by making communicating easier. For example, websites like change.org allow change agents to post their concerns and rally large numbers of people, many of whom they may not have been able to reach using more conventional tools, in support of a desired change. There are currently many education initiatives posted to sites like this. Increasingly, these sites and the capabilities they offer to change movements will shape and influence the direction of change on campuses.

Internationalization of Campuses

Higher education is no longer limited by national boundaries. Students are increasingly likely to be taking courses taught from multiple countries over their college career, potentially at the same time. They will also be interacting with students from other countries, so they may be influenced by their ideas and concerns. Faculty and staff from American institutions are also stepping out into the world in new ways, working on branch campuses abroad or through online programs that serve students across the world. The curriculum and pedagogies will need to be re-examined as they are applied in educating students with different cultures, nationalities, and experiences. Students need to be prepared for their international experiences by developing a more global perspective as they go through college. This is an area with significant revenue generating potential for many campuses, so institutions' expansion beyond their state and national borders has occurred quite rapidly. While it has been easier to create political will around international efforts, this does not mean that all efforts have been successful.

This internationalized context also means that campuses are considering who are their potential collaborators and competitors on a global scale. More and more, we are seeing partnerships form among campuses located in different countries, not only for instruction, but also for research. Also, as institutions think more broadly about who are their competitors, they are thinking about peer institutions in other countries. World rankings systems are continuing to evolve, reflecting this new global educational environment. This has resulted in not only the growth of international branch campus and partnerships, but also the proliferation of a global online for-profit industry through the Open University or Kaplan.

Internationalization also impacts the context for change. Campuses will increasingly be impacted and pressured by international organizations, trends, and policies that will shape their future directions and potential for success. Treaties such as the General Agreement on Trade in Services (GATS) and the policies of international financial organizations such as the Organisation for Economic Co-operation and Development (OECD) or World Bank shape campus governance indirectly, but need to be more explicitly acknowledged in planning (Bassett and Maldonado-Maldonado 2009). In addition to the global ranking systems mentioned above, pressure is building to standardize higher education degrees and curriculum so students can easily move between institutions in different countries. For example, the Tuning Project is implementing objectives of the Bologna Process in Europe and Latin America.[7] Internationalization is leading to new global standards and tests such as the Assessment of Higher Education Learning Outcomes. Thus, this international context presents another series of forces and sources of pressure that higher education leaders will need to proactively address and consider, rather than allowing these pressures to shape and change campuses.

What to Change within the Current Context : Public purposes versus corporatization

These drivers for change point to challenges that most campuses today are grappling with in one way or another because they are such major, overarching forces influencing higher education in the United States and globally. However, each individual campus is also faced with issues that are unique to its specific context that need to be addressed (e.g. needs of their local community, workforce development demands, engaging particular populations). In fact, as I will describe in later chapters (Chapters 3, 4, and 6), deciding which changes are necessary requires careful consideration of the campus history, culture, mission, and strategic opportunities. These meta-drivers also are part of the context, wherein some changes might be much easier to initiate and implement than others.

Today's environment favors revenue generating change approaches. As a leader, there are two ways to think about this issue. One approach is to implement more changes that emphasize or prioritize revenue generation, including the expansion of online programs, increasing enrollments for programs where there is a market, and developing programs abroad as these are easier to make happen. Yet, each time a leader makes the decision to focus on potential for revenue generation, the overall enterprise continues to move steadily in one direction at the expense of other aspects of institutional mission. Leaders can work toward changes that may be more difficult to achieve in this environment and actually cost money to implement, but also improve the quality of instruction or student experience, while also helping to meet the broader mission of higher education. Addressing diversity and equity issues can affect the sense of community and relationships on campus. Considering the quality of the curriculum and how it incorporates innovative pedagogies or teaching strategies (e.g. service, collaborative, and engaged learning) and the ways students are supported toward transfer or completion can improve higher education. Institutions can also examine the nature of the student experience and the skills students are acquiring. They can rethink the nature of the faculty work, hiring more full-time, dedicated faculty and supporting their career development. Collaborating with other scholars (Kezar et al. 2005), I have described this challenge as maintaining the historic public good of higher education in the face of mounting market pressures.

Robert Zemsky and colleagues (2005) have argued that institutions need to try to do both by being market savvy and mission centered. Unfortunately, many campuses take an unbalanced approach, pursuing the easier changes that are most commonly rewarded in this new context (Toma 2011). Even though Zemsky and colleagues had confidence that campuses could pursue this middle road, the lack of a clear plan or sense of direction among campus leaders for pursuing both goals usually means campuses still end up emphasizing revenue generation at the expense of supporting the mission.[8] Campus leaders need to more clearly articulate this middle-road approach if they are to successfully pursue a balanced strategy that provides the rewards and incentives associated with each path. It takes a very courageous and systemic style of leadership to recognize the substantial pull of revenue generation, while also understanding the need to emphasize the mission and priority of the public good. Thus, this context for change means that leaders need to carefully consider the set of changes they are pursuing and how they will shape the very character and nature of their institution and the broader enterprise, for better or for worse. Leaders are used to thinking about changes discretely to solve individual problems. Yet, given the current revenue generating and corporate context of higher education—there is a need for advancing a change agenda that has a much broader scope, tying individual institutional changes to a broader vision for the future of the enterprise.

Will higher education be an enterprise that supports the public good through service and outreach, broad-based admissions processes, rich liberal arts curriculum and better supporting student learning by building a dedicated faculty with a role in shared governance? Or, alternately, will higher education look to our counterparts in for-profit education, which we resemble more and more all the time, by instead focusing mostly on revenues, enrollments, growth, outputs, employing a casual faculty, and maintaining strict managerial control of the curriculum, pedagogy, and admissions processes? When I began my career in higher education, there was a stark contrast between our work for the public good in non-profit higher education and the operations and goals of for-profit organizations. Now, there are few characteristics that differentiate these two sectors. For some, this is an indicator of progress. For me, it marks a decline in our commitment to the public purpose of higher education, a distortion of our historic role, and a call to act to engage in important change. I am not harking back to some idealized image of a golden past. In the past, there was less access and diversity; the enterprise was more exclusive in previous eras. But, I know there is a way to focus on academic values, diversity, and quality while also maintaining financial solvency and efficiency. However, this necessitates systemic thinking by change agents. The final chapter of this book (Chapter 10) provides an extended discussion about the ethics of change, further delving into the question of what changes to pursue and how to make such determinations.

There is a troubling discourse emerging as it relates to change. This discourse suggests that higher education institutions must integrate a series of changes for their survival and global economic competitiveness, highlighting how fierce the competition is and will be (Christensen et al. 2011; Erwin and Garman 2010). This discourse is typically advanced by pro-management scholars (who may be unlikely to recognize themselves as being pro-management), as well as by proponents of efficiency, innovation, technology proliferation, revenue generation, and prestige generating changes (Christensen et al. 2011; McRoy and Gibbs 2009). Individuals who hold this perspective suggest that higher education needs to radically transform, discarding its traditional structure and culture. They perceive anything short of wholesale transformation as a sacrifice of the potential of disruptive technologies like online learning. These proponents see what they would describe as tinkering throughout the enterprise as potentially leading to its demise. This discourse relates to and supports the corporatization emphasis noted earlier in this chapter (pp. 10–12).

While I think technology, innovation, and efficiency are worthy goals, they have become overemphasized within the discourse and actions of leaders on college campuses, often deterring institutions from being attentive to their primary missions of learning, research, and public service. Also, within the pro-management discourse, innovation has often been tied to a more narrow set of institutional goals focused on either efficiency or access. Both are worthwhile goals, but they should not be pursued unilaterally without giving attention to the plethora of goals higher education institutions serve.

We need to have more dialogue and discourse about the underlying assumptions of these innovation-, technology-, and efficiency-oriented changes that are so strongly argued for, but that are accompanied with limited supporting evidence and research. There are some strong core ideas, but they are too often uncritically accepted by proponents and typically do not actually realize their claimed benefits (e.g. cost savings). There is, of course, discussion that change is not necessary at all, which is similarly misguided. Organizations can always improve, adopting better practices that emerge through research and dialogue. While institutions need to be cautious about change to be attentive to their long-standing missions, adaptation of best practices is important.

This book does not advocate for any specific types of changes, although some very promising areas and avenues currently exist, including undergraduate research, service learning, senior capstones, problem-based learning, self-guided instruction, revised remediation programs, and multicultural initiatives. These areas are supported by research and have been found to promote student learning. Change agents should be familiar with and examine the fit of these emerging ideas for their institutions.

Summary

The rest of this book will argue for an approach to implement meaningful changes within higher education. But, the question of "how" is always coupled with the questions of "what" and "why." This chapter reviewed a set of meta-drivers and forces that suggest why changes are necessary within higher education. Also, as leaders, it is important to not only know how to create changes, but to carefully reflect on the nature of changes that are so often championed and supported. The ideas in this chapter are meant to help leaders frame the way they think about the vision and direction for their institutions in this new era. It calls on leaders to engage in ethical reflection on the nature of changes being proposed on various campuses.

In this chapter, I also paint a picture of the unique context within which change agents are operating. Higher education, as an enterprise, is facing greater pressure to change and there are growing calls for accountability. There is a widening range of stakeholders, who may not trust the historic commitments and assumptions that are a part of higher education. While it would be easy to allow the external environment and pressures to create the direction forward for higher education, this would not benefit the enterprise. Neither will ignoring the many pressures for change. Leaders need to understand the landscape and various forces, balancing them with their historic institutional missions, niches, and strengths.

This chapter also argued for how the new context shapes the process for change, pointing out how change agents will need to be aware of international forces and allies, the increasing diversity of stakeholder perspectives, the potential for developing networks through technology, or the demands for accountability that are characteristic of our time. Having contemplated why change is needed, it is now time to consider some underlying assumptions about change.

two
Theories of Change
Change Agent Guides

In this chapter, I will review the main theories of change that have been articulated through six schools of thought. These six schools of thought and their related theories, which are typically represented in the literature on higher education and across various other disciplines, will be referred to again as I describe the framework for change in Part II of the book. They are:[1]

1. Scientific management;
2. Evolutionary;
3. Social cognition;
4. Cultural;
5. Political; and,
6. Institutional.

These various schools of thought and the constellation of related theories have guided the study of change. Each provides key insights for understanding change. When taken collectively, they provide the most complex view of change. I will compare all these theories using a common set of characteristics—their assumptions of why change occurs, how it occurs, what are the outcomes of change, types of change, context of change that is the focus, key metaphors, examples, strategies, benefits, and criticisms or limitations. A chart comparing these various theories is presented in Table 2.1. While this chapter provides an overview of these theories, they are described in greater detail in subsequent chapters. It is not expected that you should possess a full knowledge of each theory by the end of this chapter, rather a broad understanding of the major concepts that each theory has to offer. Details on each specific set of theories of change can be found in the following chapters:

- Scientific management: Chapter 6;
- Evolutionary: Chapters 3 and 5;
- Cultural: Chapter 5;
- Political: Chapter 6;
- Social cognition: Chapter 4;
- Institutional: Chapter 5.

Additionally, to highlight their use in subsequent chapters, the theories have been italicized when they are applied.

Why learn about theories of change? The theories and related schools of thought are not important in themselves. So the goal is not to memorize them, but instead to take the insights offered through the theories to inform your mental model or schema about change. Over time, these ideas will become underlying assumptions that unconsciously drive your analysis, decisions, and strategy development. For them to become intuitive features of your change repertoire, you first need to be introduced to their core concepts. Then, you need to try applying them and revisit them. Over time, they will become more and more a part of your intuitive responses and will help to make you a more successful change agent.

Theory is only usually applied consciously as it is being learned for the first time, then it becomes more automatic. Automated learning has been found to be critical for many professional fields, such as medicine and law, and occurs as people routinely apply key concepts or skills to new situations. Also, a particular theory described here might be interesting to readers, who can pursue additional information to guide them in the future. This chapter is not meant to introduce readers to every individual theory of change, but to the broader schools of thought of which they are a part and a sampling of related theories that can be researched further by readers.

I want to underscore that while theories can be used to identify strategies for creating change, they also need to be used to carefully analyze the situation at hand to understand which strategies are needed. These theories offer ideas for analyzing and determining an approach for change. In other words, when I speak about an approach to change, I mean the analysis component, as well as the action or strategy. Most books on change focus only on the actions to be taken, so this book is unique in prompting readers to think about the approach to change, which is why an understanding of the theories of change presented here becomes particularly important. The theories highlight ways to analyze key questions such as what type of change is needed or which aspects of an institution or state policy might shape a given change process? Some theories are better for analysis and provide less advice in terms of strategies for action. For example, cultural, evolutionary, and institutional theories are mostly descriptive, so they do not have as much to say about

TABLE 2.1. Characteristics of the six schools of thought related to change

	Scientific Management	Evolutionary	Political	Social Cognition	Cultural	Institutional and Neo-institutional
Why change occurs	Leaders; internal environment	External environment	Dialectical tension of values, norms, or patterns	Cognitive dissonance; appropriateness	Response to alterations in human environment	External pressures combined with internal norms
Process of change	Rational; linear; purposeful	Adaptation; Slow; gradual; Non-intentional	First-order, then occasional second-order; negotiation and power	Learning; altering paradigms or lens; interconnected and complex	Long-term; slow; symbolic process; non-linear; unpredictable	Exchange of adaptation and schemas, norms
Outcomes of change	New structures and organizing principles	New structures and processes; first-order	New organizational ideology	New frame of mind	New culture	New schema and norms
Key metaphor	Change master	Self-producing organism	Social movement	Brain	Social movement	Iron cage or soccer
Examples	Organizational development; strategic planning; reengineering; total quality management	Resource dependency; strategic choice; population ecology	Empowerment; bargaining; political change; Marxist theory	Single- and double-looped learning; organizational learning; paradigm shifting; sensemaking	Interpretive strategy; paradigm shifting; process change	Isomorphism; institutional entrepreneurship; academic capitalism
Type of change	Planned; organizational; first-order	Unplanned; external	First- and second-order; organizational and enterprise	Second-order and more individual in focus	Second-order; organizational; planned and unplanned	Unplanned; organizational changes tied to external environment

	Scientific Management	Evolutionary	Political	Social Cognition	Cultural	Institutional and Neo-institutional
Context of change	Largely ignored	Systems approach bringing in entire system with emphasis on external pressures and interaction with organizations	Different settings have different politics; but politics are transcendent of context to some degree	Context largely ignored	Historical, social, environmental, organizational—multiple levels and types of context explored	Internal environmental schema and their interaction with external environment are focus of context
Tactics	Create infrastructure to respond to changes; strong steering committee; have nimble and flexible structures	Create infrastructure to respond to changes; strong steering committee; have nimble and flexible structures	Create coalitions; identify allies; build agenda; create collective vision; negotiate	Create data teams; build data infrastructure; enhance system thinking through training; facilitate interaction	Appeal of values; examine history and context to understand underlying values; alter mission; create new rituals	Understand external forces; buffer institutions; analyze existing schemas and norms; align external interests in support
Criticisms	Lack of human emphasis; deterministic quality	Lack of human emphasis; deterministic	Deterministic; lack of environmental concerns; little guidance for leaders	Deemphasizes environment; overemphasizes ease of change; ignores values and emotions	Impractical to guide leaders; focus on universalistic culture; mostly untested	Hard to document external forces; does not account for agency; often overemphasizes lack of change or static nature
Benefits	Environmental emphasis; systems approach	Environmental emphasis; systems approach	Change not always progressive; irrationality; role of power	Emphasizes socially constructed nature; emphasis on individuals; habits and attitudes as barriers	Context; irrationality; values and beliefs; complexity; multiple levels of change	Attention to macro context; norms and their power; irrationality; fields and complexity of forces

strategies for creating change. By contrast, scientific management, social cognition, and political theories offer much more specific guidance for change agents with regard to strategies for change. Yet, all of them are important in the overall equation for creating an effective approach to change that includes analysis and strategy.

Scientific Management

The scientific management school of thought focuses on several related models and theories of change, including planned change, organizational development, strategic planning, adaptive learning, and rational approaches (Van de Ven and Poole 1995). Researchers within this school of thought assume that organizations are purposeful and adaptive (Cameron and Smart 1998; Carnall 1995; Peterson 1995; Van de Ven and Poole 1995). Change occurs because leaders, change agents, and others see the necessity of change (Eckel et al. 1999; Peterson 1995). According to scientific management theories, the change process is rational and linear and individual managers are instrumental to the process (Carnall 1995; Carr et al. 1996; Curry 1992; Nevis et al. 1996). Internal organizational features or decisions, rather than the external environment, motivate change. These models reflect intentionality among actors. Change is seen as positive and directed by goals. Key aspects of the change process include planning, assessment, incentives and rewards, stakeholder analysis and engagement, leadership, scanning, strategy, restructuring, and reengineering (Brill and Worth 1997; Carnall 1995; Huber and Glick 1993; Keller 1983, 1997; Peterson et al. 1997). At the center of the process is the leader who aligns goals, sets expectations, models, communicates, engages, and rewards. Strategic choices and human creativity are highlighted (Brill and Worth 1997). Goal formation, implementation, evaluation, and modification based on experience are an ongoing process.

The types of changes that are typically addressed with scientific management are planned changes at the organizational level. It is helpful during the implementation phase as leaders sort out which structures and processes are needed to build and maintain support for a change, including rewards or incentives. Context is largely ignored in these theories, as strategies are seen as transcending context, and planning is important in all organizations and settings. The metaphor for this model would be the *changemaster*, to use Rosabeth Kanter's (1983) image. The leader is the focus; this is a human model with the change agent at the center using rational, scientific management tools. This is, by far, the area with the most research and models (Kezar 2001).

Perhaps the best-known model or theory within the scientific management tradition is organizational development (Golembiewski 1989; Goodman 1982). Organizational development starts by diagnosing the problems within an organization and continuing to do this on an ongoing basis, so it is generative, and searching for solutions—in other words, change initiatives. Goals are set for addressing the change. Numerous group meetings are conducted to help the change initiative to develop momentum and overcome any resistance (Carr et al. 1996). Organizations proceed through distinct stages; it is the role of leaders to effectively manage the transition from one stable stage to another (Golembiewski 1989). Transition is a homogeneous, structured, and step-by-step process.

Reengineering, another popular scientific management approach, focuses on modifying aspects of the organizational structure as the key to creating change (Guskin 1996). The leader's role is to inventory and assess the organizational structures and to think about ways to structure things differently. Mapping organizational processes, which entails cross-functional teams meeting for extended periods of time to describe and chart a process from beginning to end, is a management technique helpful for reengineering. All divisions are involved, so participants hear and learn about the processes of other functional areas and identify the ways that processes can be altered, collectively. Technological advancements, new products, retrained employees, cost cutting, and other changes are facilitated by leaders who create a technology office, provide a new human resources office, or reduce the number of offices responsible for a particular function.

Scientific management theories offer up many strategies related to change because it assumes there is strong agency among change agents. The tactics offered range from strategic planning, providing incentives and rewards, restructuring efforts, implementing professional development and support, creating a collective vision, preparing ongoing communication and influence vehicles, and engaging in feedback and evaluation, as well as a variety of efforts that are often aligned with the specific work of individuals in positions of authority. Strategies that leaders use from scientific management will be reviewed in greater detail in Chapter 6, which examines the role of leaders in change processes.

The benefits of these models are significant, including the emphasis on the key role of leadership and change agents in the change process, the role of collaboration, staff development, the ability to forecast or identify the need for change, and helping organizations to survive and prosper in what could otherwise be difficult times. The limitations of these theories are that they tend to overestimate the role of leadership by those in positions of power/authority, ignore external context, downplay politics and the less rational side of human beings, and suggest change is more easily created by a strong planning process, downplaying the many barriers and obstacles that often emerge.

Evolutionary Theories

There are many evolutionary models and theories, including adaptation, resource dependence, self-organizing, contingency and systems theories, strategic choice, punctuated equilibrium, and population ecology. The main assumption underlying all these theories is that change is the result of, and dependent on, circumstances, situational variables, and the environment faced by each organization (Morgan 1986). Social systems are seen as being diversified, interdependent, and complex systems that evolve naturally over time (Morgan 1986). But, evolution is basically deterministic; people have only a minor impact on the nature and direction of the change process (Hrebiniak and Joyce 1985). These models focus on the inability of organizations to plan for and respond to change and on managing change as it occurs. Change happens because the environment demands that systems change in order to survive. However, some later models suggest adaptation can be proactive and anticipatory (Cameron 1991).

The main concepts of evolutionary theory reflect imagery from the study of biology such as systems, interactivity between the organization and environment, openness, homeostasis, and evolution (Birnbaum 1991; Morgan 1986). The concept of systems reflects how organizations are perceived as having interdependent and interrelated structures. So, impacting one part of the structure is believed to have implications for other parts. Openness refers to the relationship between the environment and internal transformation and tends to characterize change as highly dependent on the external environment. Open systems exhibit interdependence between internal and external environments (Berdahl 1991). The concept of homeostasis refers to self-regulation and the ability to maintain a steady state by constantly seeking equilibrium between the system and environment (Sporn 1999). Processes are inherently less important within the evolutionary models as change is mostly unplanned. Rather, change is an adaptive process (or one based on natural selection). Over time, it has become commonplace to assume the environment affects the structure and culture of an organization, but this was a contested issue until about 30 years ago, when these models began to be developed.

Resource dependence theory is a common evolutionary approach for understanding change. Leaders make choices to adapt to their environment; the organization and environment have an interdependent relationship, so the focus is on transactions that occur as part of this relationship (Gumport and Pusser 1999). This model differs from natural selection in its focus on leaders as active agents who are able to respond to and change the environment (Goodman 1982). Mergers are an example of organizational response to outside forces, for example. Resource dependence theory presupposes that organizations are not self-sustaining and need to rely on external resources; they are dependent on other organizations, leading to an inter-organizational and political view (Gumport and Sporn 1999; Sporn 1999). This approach has generated great interest since it stresses a more interactive evolutionary approach, whereby human agency can impact the change process.

In terms of type of change, these theories speak mostly to externally imposed changes and pressures, as well as unplanned change. This school of thought also emphasizes a more systems view of change and enterprise-level examinations of organizations as part of a much broader ecosystem. In terms of the context of change, these theories aimed to correct for the missing element of context in scientific management theories, helping leaders to understand the need to examine and manage their external environments. These theories focus mostly on economic forces and less so on political factors and, in very limited ways, social concerns. Nonetheless, context is a major feature within this school of thought.

While these theories downplay the role of leaders in change and often do not rec-ommend strategies or tactics that might be used to create change, which is viewed as a mostly organic and unplanned process. Still, some tactics for change have been offered. For example, being proactive and addressing external forces quickly has been identified as helping lead to stronger adaptation (Sporn 1999). These will be reviewed in more detail in Chapter 3, which is about the types of change. Organizations that have a flexible or nimble infrastructure are often better at gen-erating a quick response. In addition, studies have found that organizations that have strong and stable operations and do not allow parts of their organizations to become weak (e.g. finances, physical plant, talent) are better prepared to respond to external pressures and changes. Some have also suggested creating a body such as a strong steering committee that can be ready to address and make decisions quickly also enhances campuses adaptability (Clark 1998a). These are examples of the tactics that will be elaborated on in Chapter 3. Theories that downplay human agency in change provide much less direct guidance and advice for leaders.

The contribution of this school of thought is illustrating the impact of the con-text and environment on change, since organizations were formerly conceptual-ized as self-contained entities (El-Khawas 2000; Levy and Merry 1986; Morgan 1986). Assuming that organizations are systems advances different thinking about change, identifying new reasons or factors that shape decisions, and approaches to change. There are many empirical studies that illustrate the strength of evo-lutionary models for undergoing certain types of changes (Burnes 1996; March 1994; Phillips and Duran 1992; Sporn 1999). Also, examining how change is often unplanned and emerges from outside organizations was a novel insight when these theories emerged. The limitation of this school of thought is that by focus-ing on external forces it tends to overlook or ignore human agency and the role of leadership. Many studies have demonstrated that leadership can make a difference particularly in managing external forces.

Social Cognition Theories

Social cognition models and theories have gained popularity over the past 30 years. A variety of models emphasize cognition, from sensemaking to organiza-tional learning (Morgan 1986; Scott 1995; Weick 1995). A primary assumption of this school of thought is that change can be best understood and enacted through individuals and their thought processes (Harris 1996; Martin 1992). Cognitive models highlight the role of learning and development with regard to change (Kezar 2001). Studies of resistance to change illustrated that people were often not resisting a change because they disagreed with it, but because they did not truly understand its nature or how they might integrate it into their work and role. As a result, researchers examined more deeply the thought processes of indi-viduals involved in change and discovered that people often hold unconscious views that shape their worldview (i.e. paradigms and mental models); that peo-ple's views were complex and built on prior views (i.e. knowledge structures and schemata); that people are more likely to change their views if they receive feedback and ongoing information (i.e. cybernetics and feedback loops); that information that challenges prior beliefs can prompt change (i.e. cognitive dissonance); that people tend to make leaps in logic that make the root causes of problems elusive, so diagramming can help overcome this issue (i.e. cause maps); and that people are constantly trying to make sense of their world (i.e. sensemaking) through cues and retrospection (Albert and Whetten 1985; Bushe and Shani 1991; March 1991; Morgan 1986). These are all core concepts that are part of these theories.

These various concepts (e.g. cognitive dissonance) about the role of cognition in change were then further explored to learn how they could help facilitate change. For example, through research on knowledge structures or schemata, examining the way people build upon their prior knowledge, theorists showed how proposals for institutional change would be much more likely to succeed if initiatives could build on prior organizational knowledge (Hedberg 1981). Learning also occurs as two pieces of conflicting information are brought together, often labeled cognitive dissonance (Argyris 1994).

Part of the difficulty of creating change is realizing that people are interpreting their environment so differently from one another (Cameron and Quinn 1988). Also, facilitating change is sometimes explored as the process of allowing people to let go of the identities which are attached to past strategies and successes (Morgan 1986). Therefore, the focus of change strategies within social cognition models is how leaders can shape individuals' thinking within the change process—through framing and interpretation—and how individuals within an organization interpret and make sense of change (Chaffee 1983; Harris 1996; Kenny 2006). Because cognition is a major focus, language and discourse offer a way to access and understand these processes and are a significant part of analysis in studies using social cognition.

The reason for change in organizations is linked more to appropriateness and is a reaction to cognitive dissonance (Collins 1998). There is not necessarily an environmental necessity, developmental challenge, leader's vision, or ideological tension behind a change. Instead, people simply reach a point of cognitive dissonance, when values and actions clash or something seems out of fashion, and they decide to change. The outcome of change is a new frame of mind or worldview. The metaphor for this approach to change is usually the brain—complex, interrelated systems, mental models, and interpretation.

Good examples of social cognition theories are Argyris's (1982, 1994) and Schon's (1983) work on single- and double-loop learning theory. Single-loop learning refers to retaining existing norms, goals, and structures and doing better the things that are already done (Argyris 1982, 1994). Single-loop learning is often associated with first-order change and an internal standard of performance (e.g. employees' views of quality). Double-loop learning, by contrast, refers to the process in which existing norms, goals, and structures are reformulated to embark on innovative solutions. It is usually associated with second-order change and employs external standards of performance (e.g. state mandated regulations of quality). In double-loop learning, people (or organizations) come to terms with problems or mismatches in the governing variables (i.e. beliefs) that guide their action (Hedberg 1981). The common assumption that people are driven to fix inconsistencies between their thoughts and actions or between their actions and consequences was shown to be invalid in Argyris's and Schon's work. To acknowledge inconsistencies is seen as finding fault or mistakes in our actions, which people resist, particularly in hierarchical environments, where blame is often assigned and people are held accountable for mistakes. Argyris's and Schon's research identified how an environment of trust must be created in order for double-loop learning to occur, since people are reluctant to examine inconsistencies for fear of blame or reprisal (Argyris 1982). Organizational learning demonstrates why change is often uncommon, as it requires individuals to question existing knowledge, form wholly new perspectives, and to function in an environment that is supportive of such risk taking and experimentation in thought.

Other examples of the social cognition perspective include the work of Cohen and March (1974, 1991), Bolman and Deal (1991), Morgan (1986), and Weick (1995), which explores how individuals view organizations in very different ways, making change challenging. This research examines organizations through an interpretive perspective and demonstrated that individuals hold multiple views of organizational reality. These theorists suggest that leaders who view the organization through different lenses can better understand different interpretations and serve as translators and facilitators of change. Leaders create change by helping employees to view the organization through different lenses and by reframing issues so that different people can understand and enact the needed change.

Social cognition theories are focused on changes occurring within the minds of individual people—their thought processes—rather than organizationally or throughout the system. Yet, theorists also extend how thinking is collective and reflected in these broader parts of the system. But, the focus on the type of change is aimed at individuals and often second-order or transformational change. While these theories can be used for understanding smaller or first-order changes, they were created to explain changes that were more difficult to create. In terms of context, these theories do not have a strong emphasis on the impact of context as it relates to change processes.

Given the emphasis on organizational learning and sensemaking within cognitive theories, many of the strategies relate to vehicles that help to create these two outcomes. For example, organizational learning directs change agents toward creating data teams, building the data infrastructure, and enhancing systems thinking through training. Sensemaking suggests important tactics such as facilitating interaction among employees and engaging in professional development oriented at helping people to re-examine their current understanding of issues. Specific tactics will be described in Chapter 4, which focuses on organizational learning and sensemaking as approaches to deep change.

One of the major contributions of these theories is a more phenomenological approach to the study of change, vastly expanding the role of interpersonal and human aspects of change. Individual meaning construction was mostly left out of theories that focused on systems, organizational political tension, environment, or organizational structures (Magala 2000). These other schools of thought discount the human element of individuals that make up an organization or system; social cognition theories describe how change is about individual learning and sense-making. The realization that efforts often fail because individuals simply do not understand or comprehend the change at hand has been helpful.

The blind spot or limitation of this theory is that by focusing on the individual it misses other areas that can shape change processes that are emphasized in other theories such as external forces or organizational structures and culture. The theory also does not acknowledge the irrational or political nature of individuals, favoring a purely cognitive, rather than an emotion-based view of human behavior. Also, some research, particularly from the school of the learning organization, sees influencing people to change their views and underlying values as being easier than it may actually be. Some scholarship, including the work of Argyris and Schon, does demonstrate that learning is the exception, rather than the rule.

Cultural Theory

The cultural school of thought suggests that change occurs naturally as a response to alterations in the human environment; cultures are always changing (Morgan 1986; Peterson 1997). The change process tends to be long term and slow. Change within an organization entails the alteration of values, beliefs, myths, and rituals (Schein 1985; Shaw and Lee 1997). There is an emphasis on the symbolic nature of organizations, rather than the structural, human, or cognitive aspects empha-sized within earlier theories (Simsek 1997). History and traditions are important to understand, as they represent the collection of change processes over time. Cul-tural approaches share many assumptions with social cognition theories; change can be planned or unplanned, regressive or progressive, and can contain intended or unintended outcomes and actions (Smirich 1983). Change tends to be non-linear, irrational, unpredictable, ongoing, and dynamic (Simsek and Louis 1994; Smirich 1983). Some cultural models focus on leaders' ability to translate changes to individuals throughout their organizations through the use of symbolic actions, language, or metaphors as a key aspect of creating change (Feldman 1991; Gioia et al. 1996). If there is an external motivator, it tends to be legitimacy, which is the primary motivator within the cultural model, rather than profit and productivity, which exemplify the scientific management and evolutionary models.

Because the cultural system is implicit, change agents often overlook it. In fact, it was long overlooked by theorists who studied change. It was not until the 1980s that scholars of change examined and began to make sense of the way that under-lying values and assumptions deeply impacted change processes. Within higher education, recent studies have identified how successful change agents have matched the strategy or approach to change to be aligned with the institutional culture (Kezar and Eckel 2002a). Research demonstrates that change strategies are successful if they are culturally coherent or aligned with the culture. Institutions that violate their institutional culture during the change process have often experienced difficulty.

Cultural approaches tend to emphasize phenomenological and social constructivist approaches to the study of organizations, wherein scholars assume that there is not a single organizational reality and that meaning is constructed through experience. These approaches to research suggest that meaning in organizations is complex. Various groups often see or experience the same culture differently. Multiple and complex views of organizations also suggest the difficulty of deep change since there is unlikely to be consensus and a great deal of work is necessary to develop some common assumptions about the needed direction or approach for change. Also, major change involves core modifications that are unlikely to occur without alterations to fundamental beliefs. Anthropologists demonstrate how values become deeply instantiated in all human processes and structures. Thus, to change a method of teaching is not as simple as knowing the new mode of teaching one wants to put into practice; it also means unlearning the values associated with the existing mode of teaching.

In terms of type of change, cultural theories focus on deep or second-order changes, typically at the organizational level. Perhaps no other theory of change focuses as much on context as cultural theories do. Cultural theories bring to bear multiple levels and types of context ranging from professional norms to individual values, as well as history, environment, and organizational type. Schein (1985) is probably one of the best-known theorists of cultural change. Culture is a collective and shared phenomenon; it is reflected at different levels through the organizational mission, through individual beliefs, and at a subconscious level (Schein 1985). Change occurs as various aspects of the organizational culture are altered. For example, if the mission is realigned or new rituals or myths are developed, this can help to move a particular change initiative forward. Schein's (1985) perspective on culture is reflected in the symbolic action approach, in which managers create change by modifying organizational members' shared meaning—leaders recreate aspects of the symbolic system and culture. For example, leaders interpret events and history for people, creating ceremonies and events that alter culture, therefore creating change (Cameron 1991).

While theories of culture suggest that change is long term and that change agents can have only a minimal impact on significant or deep changes, this set of theories does offer some specific advice for change agents. Given the importance of history and context to cultural theories of change, change agents are better served when they are familiar with the history and context of the campus where they work, particularly as it relates to understanding the underlying values that are not always apparent through examining various artifacts and symbols. Also, because the symbolic infrastructure is significant to the success of change processes, leaders are encouraged to examine and alter the mission statement, appeal to current and aspired values, and utilize existing campus symbols and rituals, sometimes altering them slightly to relate to the new values that are to be integrated into the campus.

Chapter 5 examines context, particularly institutional context, and will further explain these concepts of culture.

The major contribution of cultural models to the change literature is its emphasis on context, values and beliefs, irrationality, the spirit or unconscious, and the fluidity and complexity of organizations (Collins 1998; Neumann 1993). This set of theories reemphasizes the temporal dimension of change, especially the extremely lengthy process associated with second-order change, which is not emphasized in the social cognition and scientific management models that gained popularity over evolutionary and political models in recent years (Collins 1998). Making the relationship between institutional culture and change apparent is also a major contribution. The limitation of cultural theories is that they usually leave practitioners with little practical or tangible advice for managing change. If change is long term, non-sequential, and possibly unmanageable, then it is hard for change agents to decide how they might facilitate the process (Chermak 1990).

Political Theory

Political theories of change evolved from the Hegelian–Marxian perspective in which a pattern, value, ideal, or norm in an organization is always present, along with its polar opposite (Morgan 1986; Van de Ven and Poole 1995). Organizations pass through long periods of evolutionary change, as the dialectical interaction between the polar opposites occurs, and short periods of second-order or revolutionary change, when there is an impasse between the two perspectives (Gersick 1991; Morgan 1986). Organizations' polar opposite, competing belief systems eventually clash, resulting in radical change and eventual synthesis or reconciliation of the belief systems. Conflict is seen as an inherent attribute of human interaction. The outcome of change is a modified organizational ideology or identity. For example, a campus that adopts a sustainability plan may begin to see itself as having a broad responsibility for future generations. This new ideology of working for future generations represents the outcome of the change process.

Political theories of change identify change as being a natural part of human interaction, occurring as different interests and agendas are negotiated. Political theories focus on bargaining, raising consciousness, persuasion, influence and power, and social movements as key elements of the change process (Bolman and Deal 1991; Childers 1981; Gumport 1993; Rhoades 1995). Leaders are important players within any social movement, so they are a central part of these models. Yet, collective action is usually the focus. Progress and rationality are not necessarily part of this set of theories of change; dialectical conflict does not necessarily produce a better organization. Organizations are perceived as political entities in which dominant coalitions utilize their power in order to preserve the status quo and maintain their privilege (Baldridge 1971; Hearn 1996).

Political models do not assume that everyone is involved. Instead, they emphasize that inactivity is quite prevalent (Baldridge et al. 1977; Conrad 1978). Similar to the fact that few people vote, few people participate in governance and are interested in change in organizations. People who create change can become involved in interest groups, flowing in and out of the process. When resources are plentiful, few people worry about changes or come into conflict. It is when resource constraints and pending changes might impact people (or when they encounter an inability to create changes because of a lack of resources) that people mobilize. These models focus on human motivation and needs; intuition is just as important to change as the facts and figures that are emphasized in other models (Bergquist 1992; Lindquist 1978). Social interaction is more critical than environmental scanning, planning, or assessing the life cycle of the organization. The metaphor for understanding the political school of thought is a social movement (Carlson-Dakes and Sanders 1998).

In terms of the type of change, political theories focus on a broad swath of changes—first order and second order, as well as change occurring at multiple levels within organizations and systems. In terms of context, political theories acknowledge that political issues differ by context, yet they see political concerns as transcendent and part of all human affairs. As a result, they do not emphasize context as strongly as cultural theories do.

Kotter (1985) provides an analysis of the skills needed to create political change. They are agenda setting, networking and forming coalitions, and bargaining and negotiation. Setting an agenda is different than establishing a vision, a process emphasized within scientific management models that is usually driven by organizational leaders. Instead, setting an agenda involves listening to people throughout the system and including their interests; agendas are responsive to stakeholder concerns (Bolman and Deal 1991). Networking is the next step for creating change. In order to build coalitions, change agents need to identify key people to facilitate change as well as individuals who will likely resist the change. One of the primary purposes of networking is developing relationships with key people who can overcome resistance so that they can be used to influence people when necessary (Hearn 1996).

Change agents must also develop a power base by succeeding at certain efforts and become aligned with other powerful individuals. Once the leader has an agenda, network, coalitions, and power base, the change agent is ready to bargain and negotiate in order to create change. Empowerment approaches to change represent an even more positive spin on the political approach to creating change. In these approaches, change agents are encouraged to examine whether a proposed change has mutually beneficial consequences for all parties involved, is moral, and whether it demonstrates caring for employees (Bolman and Deal 1991). A few studies have illustrated that empowerment models are instrumental in facilitating change (Astin and Leland 1991; Bensimon and Neumann 1993).

In terms of specific tactics, the review of models above highlights many of the key tactics that are also offered within political theories, including agenda setting, forming coalitions, creating networks, bargaining and negotiation, mapping power and influence structures, identifying allies, and creating a collective vision. Most of the tactics and strategies described within political theories can be seen in grassroots or social movements of change. These strategies and tactics will be given additional attention in Chapter 6, which discusses agency and leadership, in order to describe the ways bottom-up leaders need to operate differently. In addition, in Chapter 9 the literature about social movement theories is reviewed in order to understand the ways that changes might be scaled up across the academy.

A major benefit of these models is their departure from a focus on rationality and linearity (Gumport 1993; Gumport and Pusser 1995). Evolutionary and scientific management models emphasize that change is rational and progressive, leading toward something better. Many theorists could point to changes that were not for the good of organizations and often noted the erratic, political nature of organizational change (Morgan 1986). This school of thought also shows the value-laden nature of change and highlights interests that are at play. This model provides an explanation for regressive change and highlights irrationality. The more popular political models are those that emphasize social movements' and leaders' role because they provide a strong and hopeful analogy for change.

One limitation of this school of thought is that it may ignore the individual cognition process and mistake resistance for conflict or competing interests, rather than a lack of understanding or fear. Also, changes that result from a political model may or may not be pursued in the broader public interest. There is no way to evaluate the content or direction of these changes.

Institutional and Neo-institutional Theory

Institutional theory examines how higher education as a social institution might change in different ways from other types of organizations. The theory also examines the reasons change efforts might be difficult in long-standing institutions. Lastly, it examines unplanned change or drift. It draws on evolutionary and social cognition theories, yet creates its own school of thought. I will provide some additional detail for this theory, as it is often hard for people to easily understand. One of the ongoing debates in the literature is whether internal organizational features and conditions or external conditions such as state funding or accreditation standards have a greater impact on change. Institutional theory helps to examine the impact of both organizational and external conditions. In short, "institutional theory suggests that the regulation of organizational behaviors occurs through and as a consequence of taken for granted beliefs, schemas, and ideas that originate in larger institutional contexts," like the government (Leicht and Fennell 2008: 2).

Institutional theory has long questioned the independence and agency of individual institutions to change and suggests the role of external norms and influences from the broader field of which the organization is a part, yet also emphasizes the strong normative and mimetic pressure within organizations (Powell and DiMaggio 1991). An example of normative pressures would include faculty socialization into the profession through disciplinary societies. Institutional theory also suggests that college and universities—as institutions with long-standing missions tied to societal goals—will change more slowly and less often than other types of organizations with more flexible or shifting missions and that are less tied to broad societal goals. Institutional theory describes why change occurs as a complex interplay of institutional forces of inertia with varying external logics that push for new ways of doing things. Neo-institutional theories emphasize the role of human agency to a greater degree because earlier institutional theories were critiqued for being too deterministic and having no role for individuals to shape reality. Neo-institutional theory still suggests that agency is largely determined by organizational context, but allows for and explores the role of agency within change processes (Gumport 2012).

Institutional theory describes the impact of the broader societal field such as the nation-state, market factors, and the entire higher education sector (Powell and DiMaggio 1991). The societal field is external pressures that are farther afield than organizational fields and include economic change or political regulations. In addition to societal fields, institutional theorists also describe organizational fields, including disciplinary societies, accreditation, higher educational associations and the like. Organizational fields are entities which, in the aggregate, constitute a recognized area of institutional life: key suppliers, resources and product consumers, regulatory agencies, and other organizations that produce similar services or products (Powell and DiMaggio 1991). Colleges attempt to maintain legitimacy and support from these various constituents (Boyce 2003). All of these various fields impact the organization, but in varying degrees and depending on the power of the fields. The power of fields is dynamic and changes over time. Through this theory, a comprehensive perspective of change can be developed that integrates a variety of factors and conditions that have long been ignored because they seem so distant or removed from the particular college or university where a change is occurring. In addition, institutional theory helps to break change free from the organization and identifies the interplay with the external environment. Institutional theory also demonstrates how practices become embedded, or institutionalized, in the structures and processes of organizations, so it is difficult to change certain values or systems once they become embedded. While practices can become deinstitutionalized, the theory suggests that this does not happen often or easily. The process of change here is complex and it is hard to document interactions between processes of adaptation (described in evolutionary theories) and the internal schemas and norms (drawn from social cognition theories) that are being altered.

The outcome is a new schema and norms. Many have used the metaphor of the iron cage to describe the institutional forces that make change elusive. The external interplay of forces might be thought of as a sports field (e.g. a soccer field), where the players represent the external forces and the ball represents the shifted schema. Players may each have an impact, but a strong player is able to craft where the ball will go and may be more central to the outcome of the game.

In terms of the type of change addressed through institutional theory, the focus is on changes that are unplanned, mimicking, and institutional drift. The type of change is an organizational change but often is shaped by the enterprise or larger field of influence. Context is inherently tied to change in this process, as institutions are seen as leaning toward the status quo and institutional processes and structures as highly reinforcing of existing practices. Thus, changes are seen as mostly a result of powerful, outside forces that collectively shape institutions.

A core concept of institutional theory is a notion called isomorphism. Many researchers in higher education have used institutional theory to understand why colleges and universities with very distinctive missions have shifted over time to become more similar in character—in terms of their student bodies, mission statements, focus on research over teaching, curriculum, and other components that make up the organization. Morphew (2009) demonstrates how institutions from the 1970s through the present have become increasingly similar rather than maintaining their unique characteristics. Various forces across a variety of fields have been charted and demonstrated to alter the landscape of higher education. For example, disciplinary societies helped to emphasize the faculty role in research, rather than teaching (which is perceived as more prestigious than teaching), and it became adopted as a general norm. Presidents and trustees began to focus on prestige, such as being identified as having the best students through markers such as the number of national merit scholars, and began to press to enroll different students and infused money into recruitment. National associations, to offer another example, pushed for a more similar general education curriculum.

Another current idea from the higher education literature, academic capitalism, helps to illustrate this issue of "unintentional" drift being influenced by complex forces. Academic capitalism is an example of institutional theory as it can be seen as seen as sweeping, changes that emerged through the power of forces far from the campus. It differs in acknowledging direct agency among internal actors to seek out opportunities in their changing environment. As Sheila Slaughter and Gary Rhoades (2004) note, "The theory of academic capitalism sees groups of actors—faculty, students, administrators, and academic professionals—as using a variety of state resources to create new circuits of knowledge that link higher education to the new economy" (p. 1). Slaughter and Rhoades document how in the last 20 years most higher education institutions have become more corporate, with top-down and centralized authority, moved to market-based approaches to management and operations, and begun to encourage faculty, administration, and staff to generate revenue and operate more as a business than a strictly educational enterprise. For example, market-based business approaches can be seen in the move away from tenure-track faculty lines, which have been replaced by contingent, contract faculty positions that are more cost effective and offer greater budgetary flexibility.

Rhoades and Slaughter (1997; Slaughter and Rhoades 2004) describe how campuses changed their organizational processes dramatically, but that since it happened over time and as a result of different varying forces, the changes were less noticeable. These scholars document various pressures (and opportunities) from external fields that shaped these new approaches. For example, Slaughter and Rhoades (2004) demonstrate how government legislation such as the Bayh–Dole

Act, which allowed academics to capitalize on research findings through patents and licensing that had been considered open source, changed the value of research and the role of faculty. Groups such as the Higher Education Business Forum worked to develop research and development parks on campuses to support industry and corporate interests, which has continued to alter the nature of faculty work and increased the number of non-academic staff employed. Over time, it also became more prevalent for campuses to have board members and presidents who came from the corporate setting and emphasized a more business-oriented set of values and approaches to campus work. From far afield (e.g. legislation) to more intermediary groups (e.g. the Higher Education Business Forum), to those groups more directly involved (e.g. campus trustees and presidents), an assortment of activities from different fields or networks coalesced to change the nature of college campuses toward academic capitalism.

Slaughter and Rhoades (2004) demonstrate how the various fields or networks affected not only institutional policies, but became deeply embedded in institutional roles and practices. Faculty have become more entrepreneurial by seeking external funding for grants, having developed ways to generate revenue from educational endeavors such as development of professional masters and online degrees or creation of special programs to serve business and industry demands. Administrators have looked for new ways to generate revenues through auxiliary services, trademarking their institutions' brands for product licensing, signing exclusive agreements with vendors and service providers, marketing education as a product to students, and, as already noted, through patenting and licensing ideas and technologies produced through research. Their concept of academic capitalism demonstrates how an ideology can become embedded in networks (described as intermediary and interstitial organizations), flowing into the fabric of institutions and altering the underlying logic and practices. Slaughter and Rhoades (2004) use the theory of political economy to explain these changes, but institutional theory also fits well.

Institutional entrepreneurship is an example of neo-institutional theory, as it tends to emphasize the potential for institutions to be altered by individuals, rather than only acknowledging the impact of forces far afield (Seo and Creed 2002). Neo-institutional theory provides a place for institutional actors to move toward collective action against overriding schemas and ideologies through a variety of avenues. One is when the logic of an existing schema is found to be contradictory and creates cognitive dissonance. Institutional entrepreneurship also suggests that individuals move into collectives or coalitions that mobilize for change and help push people further along into cognitive dissonance (Dorado 2005).[2]

Like evolutionary theories, institutional theories provide limited advice or guidance for change agents about how to approach the change process. Instead, they help to make change agents aware of the broader forces that might be guiding behaviors and over which they may have little control. However, neo-institutional theories provide more credence to the role of individuals within change processes and identify greater opportunities for agency among individual actors. As I noted above, institutional entrepreneurship is an example of the way that neo-institutional theories have begun to describe the actions of individuals as being critical to creating changes in the face of formidable external forces. Many of the tactics described in the institutional entrepreneurship literature mirror those from political theories in terms of coalition building, agenda setting, and influence strategies. Change agents might also use the lessons from institutional theory to better understand external forces and buffer their institutions from unwanted or harmful changes. In addition, leaders can analyze existing schemas and norms in an effort to identify and understand the underlying values that prevent changes they are interested in making. Furthermore, change agents can carry out work to persuade or align external interests to be in support of a particular direction for change that may not have been amenable before.

The main benefits of institutional theory are that it combines internal and external analysis, looks at often implicit and hard-to-document changes, and focuses on unintentional changes or drift that can occur. It also positions individuals and change agents neither as rational nor as irrational actors, but more as being trapped in complex relationships, coping, and navigating. The main criticism of institutional theory is that it is extremely hard to document the various and often implicit, external interests and internal schemas. Any evidence to support assertions is itself hypothetical or based on second-hand patterns. Others suggest that it provides too limited a role for agency and focuses too much on macro-level forces, while ignoring how many individuals manage to negotiate or fall outside these broader patterns of behavior. The theory provides little explanation of the outliers or anomalies. Some suggest it overemphasizes a static view of institutions and misses the flux and institutional changes that also occur.

How to Think about Theories

The goal of this chapter is not only to introduce readers to the various theories about change and establish some foundational assumptions, but also to explain how change agents might use these theories. As the summary in Table 2.1 highlights, each theory traces why and how change occurs and the varying outcomes of change. Rather than seeing these simply as competing views of the same phenomenon, they can be understood as different layers of a complex process. Some change processes will involve institutional history (cultural theories) and current political interests (political theories), while others may not. Yet, knowing that these are important features that one might analyze helps to develop more complex strategies around change. These are merely different analytic categories that change agents should consider, which may or may not be relevant in all situations. First, these theories elucidate different *types of change* ranging from explicit, externally imposed changes (evolutionary theory), to implicitly shaped change (institutional theory), to intentionally created changes (scientific management and political theories), to changes that evolve through the course of history (cultural theories). Change agents can assess the type of change they are working with and utilize concepts from these various theories to help better respond and act in situations they encounter.

Second, these theories highlight *different contexts* that are relevant for analyzing and responding to change. Change initiatives might be encountered or unfold differently based on institutional culture (cultural theories), campus politics (political theories), campus members' schemas and mental models (cognitive theories), external pressures and circumstances (evolutionary theories), and institutional norms and fields (institutional theory).

Third, these theories also identify different levels of agency among leaders and different perspectives about who can play a leadership role in change. Scientific management theories focus on leaders in positions of authority, whereas political theories focus on bottom-up or grassroots leaders. In the remaining chapters, I will draw upon and explain how these theories are relevant to *concepts* change agents should consider as they embark on change. For example, scientific management suggests examining institutional structures, while political theories suggest an examination of interests and power. The key message is that all of these theories should be considered as providing insights to leaders, who are best served when they use all of these theories, rather than choosing a particular theory that they feel best suits their style or understanding. While each of these theories is not always intuitive or easy to understand, particularly institutional theory, leaders are best served when they work to use all of these analytic devices.

Summary

This chapter helps highlight how, depending on your assumptions about change, you will look to different foci, concepts, and aspects of the process. Most scholars of change identify how these theories, when considered together, add more insight, suggesting practitioners rely on several theories of change for analyzing a situation. But, such a process would not be easy if readers were only left with such a broad theoretical lens. The macro framework presented in Part II provides a helpful way to integrate these various theories meaningfully to create change. Several chapters will demonstrate how to take insights from differing theories and apply them to change through vignettes, cases, and examples.

Part 2

A Multi-faceted Framework for Understanding Change

This part of the book will review the elements of the change framework I have developed through research on how to successfully create change. Most change agents are focused on the content of the change initiative, whether it be integrating technology, setting up a multicultural center, or creating an access to college program. However, they spend little time focused on understanding the change process and the way the external and organizational context can shape their success and failure, the leadership available to create the change, or the characteristics of the change initiative as it relates to fit within the organizational culture and structures. This section provides rationale for why these various features (e.g. type of change, context, agency) are important to facilitate change, connecting them to the various theories reviewed in Chapter 2. This type of analysis is equally important to moving toward action and developing a strategy. Some theories are better for analysis and provide less advice in the way of strategies for action.

The macro framework for thinking about change encompasses the following aspects that will be detailed throughout the following chapters in Part II and is captured in Figure II.1.

The figure captures how change agents might first analyze the type of change and add this analysis to their understanding of the context of change as well as the amount of agency available. These three areas are then combined in order to determine an approach to change by reviewing and selecting from ideas within the six theories introduced in Chapter 2.

Chapter 3 will review how the type of change initiative needs to be analyzed to understand an appropriate approach to change. Following up on the type of

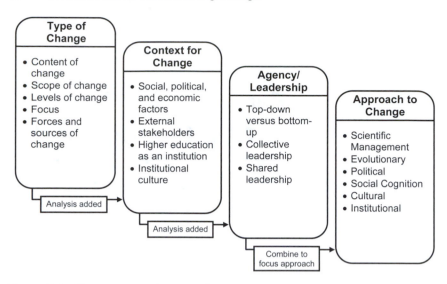

Figure II.1. Change macro framework.

change, Chapter 4 reviews approaches used for creating deep change using sense-making and organizational learning—both from social cognition theories of change. Chapter 5 will focus on the way various contexts (social, economic, and political forces, external stakeholders, institutional status, institutional culture) that shape change processes are important to analyze and consider before developing a strategy. Chapter 6 will examine the role of leadership in change processes and how different types of leaders have different forms of agency to exercise. The chapter also examines the potential of collective and shared forms of leadership. Chapter 7 draws together the lessons from the previous three chapters and analyzes five different cases of change through the macro framework and develops strategies for moving forward.

You may be wondering why there is no chapter on obstacles or resistance to change, as is often found within other change texts. Change agents find that resistance and obstacles are a reflection of poor diagnosis of the type, context, or the strategies for change. If these are more carefully understood, it is less likely that resistance or obstacles will emerge. In other words, obstacles and resistance are typically a byproduct of a poor approach. Yet, even with a well-designed approach, the change implementation needs to be constantly analyzed and evaluated for new issues that might emerge. In the final chapter in this part, Chapter 8, I review guidance on typical forms of resistance and obstacles encountered as change processes unfold, with advice from the theories in Chapter 2. This chapter also reviews how changes typically unfold in stages—mobilization, implementation, and institutionalization.

three
Type of Change

Sarah is a faculty member of sociology. Three years ago, she led a task force to integrate digital technologies into the scholarship and teaching of her department. She mapped the processes that needed to be changed, held professional development for faculty with the center for teaching and learning, and obtained an external grant to support a graduate student implementing the process and providing her some release time. She had a great deal of success and is now using those same techniques to integrate a multicultural initiative across the entire campus — with a goal of changing the campus culture. She obtained a grant, mapped the changes, and held professional development, but people have not showed up for the training and her graduate student cannot get responses from people. Literally, no one is responding. Unfortunately, she is not having the same success as before, so she is at a loss for what to do.

Not all changes are the same, although most research and advice for change agents treats all change initiatives the same. This is problematic. The type of change initiative shapes the approach and needs to be taken into account. As can be seen in this example, Sarah's attempts to create a more multicultural campus were met with different barriers and resistance than her attempts at integrating technology. Change agents who are unaware of differences based on the type of change are at a disadvantage. This chapter examines how the type of change, whether first or second order, or content of the change (e.g. diversity and technology) might shape the change process. The following issues will be addressed related to the type of change—content, scope, level, focus, forces/sources, and intentionality. The chapter draws on the theories presented in Chapter 2 to help explain why these differences are meaningful to change agents. In fact, these various theories often emerged because scholars were trying to explain and understand very different kinds of change processes. The chapter on sensemaking and organizational learning provides detailed advice for how to create deep or second-order change, which is referred to several times in this chapter. Before one can address second-order change, a leader needs to be able to diagnose whether it is needed. This chapter focuses on analyzing and diagnosing the type of change. The steps are highlighted in Figure 3.1.

The chapter also considers how change agents identify the type or direction of change. It is important to consider whether the reaction to change initiatives may be related to the degree to which people perceive the proposed change as being a fit for the campus or situation. We must also consider whether there is *a right* or *appropriate* change direction for any organization or campus or whether this always depends on one's interests and position. I summarize the contribution of each theory in Table 3.1, which will be elaborated on throughout the rest of the chapter.

Content of the Change

Sarah's experience highlights how different changes may be met with different reactions. *Political theories* of change often note how different change initiatives reflect different interests, so they will not be received the same way. Some changes

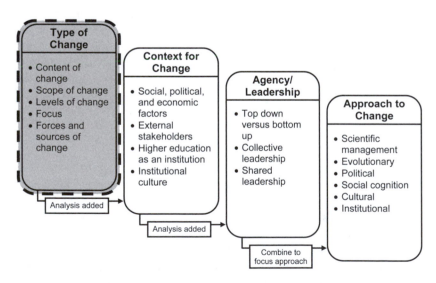

Figure 3.1. Change macro framework: type of change.

TABLE 3.1. Change as shaped by the type of change initiative: key concepts and insights

	Concepts	Insights
Scientific Management	Levels of change; focus of change	Helps support organizational level by providing structure and processes to support change
		Helps support structure and process changes by providing ways to restructure and revise processes
Evolutionary	Levels of change; forces and sources	Helps support sector or enterprise level by identifying stakeholders and groups that can be levered for change
		Helps identify forces shaping type of change as well as align strategies
Social Cognition	Content of change; scope of change; levels of change	Individuals will have greater resistance to changes that are outside their existing understandings or cognitive schema
		Second-order changes may require a change in schemas, to be facilitated through a learning process, cognitive dissonance, or sensemaking
		Helps support individual level
Cultural	Content of change; scope of change; levels of change; focus of change	Individuals will have greater resistance to changes that are outside their existing values
		Second-order changes may require a change in values, but may differ on the basis of the outcomes of a cultural assessment; leaders can reshape values through various cultural change strategies
		Helps support group level
		Helps support attitude changes
Political	Content of change; levels of change	Individuals will have greater resistance to changes that they do not perceive as serving their interests
		Helps support group level
Institutional and Neo-institutional	Levels of change; forces and sources	Helps support sector or enterprise level
		Helps identify forces, as well as align strategies, but provides only limited strategies

will be perceived as serving one's interests, although others will merely not be perceived as being opposed to them. Many people see technology as an inevitability that they must adjust to or align with their future career plans. This is not to say that everyone likes technology, but many people acknowledge it as part of the work environment of the future, making it an inevitable part of their interests. Multiculturalism, by contrast, is often viewed as being in the interest of faculty, staff, or students of color, but not always white faculty, staff, and students. This will surely vary by campus context and history, but some changes will be met with more resistance than others depending on whether groups or individuals see the change as pertaining to their interests. The faculty in Sarah's department knew that they could obtain a large grant they applied for if they upgraded their technology and innovated. However, the broader faculty on Sarah's campus did not see a driving interest as being served by becoming part of the multicultural initiative she was leading.

Cultural theories of change also speak to the issue of how the content of the change can impact the change process and resistance encountered. Every campus (or subunit within campuses) has a set of values that guides thinking and represents some shared set of operating principles. The values that are established within a unit suggest the potential degree of difficulty associated with a change initiative. Sarah had not thought about how her sociology department had revised its vision statement and policy documents in recent years to include technology as a key aspect of their operations and one of their core operating values. While these efforts had not been part of Sarah's plans, they clearly supported her efforts. The campus had not undergone any similar process of rethinking its mission, vision, or values to support multiculturalism.

Lastly, *cognitive theories* of change also speak to how the content of a change affects the process. Individuals will present greater resistance to changes that they do not understand that are not part of their cognitive schema. Technology has become commonplace, so people are forced to develop some understanding of it. A person can typically integrate technology without rethinking their underlying values and assumptions. Yet, for some individuals, changing technology may be a challenge that will prompt resistance. Multiculturalism often requires deep shifts in thinking and learning, requiring people to undergo double-loop learning[1] in order to fully appreciate the concepts. Double-loop learning is harder and less common, because it calls for people to question underlying principles. Multiculturalism involves understanding new cultures, recognizing privilege and power, and rethinking one's view of the world.

Through an analysis of Sarah's situation using *political, cultural,* and *cognitive theories* of change, we have a better sense of why she is encountering problems and what she can do to bring about change. First, she needs to work with campus administrators to provide more visible support to multiculturalism by rethinking the campus mission and vision (*cultural theories*). At present, the value system does not support multiculturalism and people within the organization will be looking for cues that this is valued to change their behavior. Next, she needs to provide some incentives, rewards or ways for people to consider multiculturalism to be in their interest as was part of the technology process (*political* and *scientific management theories*). Through political analysis she can see that there is no alignment of interests to multiculturalism. One way to accomplish this is the establishment of rewards. Sarah also needs to recognize that this change will be hard for many people to understand, so the campus will need to bring in speakers, hold dialogues, and find ways for people to think about and challenge their underlying assumptions about multiculturalism (*cognitive theories*). By learning more about multiculturalism, Sarah and others may be able to help people shift their identities and eventually their work roles. New strategies will help her address one aspect of how she failed to see how the type of change that she was working on might affect the change process.

Scope or Degree of Change

Sarah's efforts were also shaped by the scope or degree of change. The technology initiative was aimed at what researchers call first-order change, involving minor improvements or adjustments. The effort included creating a resource base of images that could be used in classes and for research. Sarah followed a pretty linear process, so there was minimal confusion or need to bring people along. By contrast, the multicultural initiative involves second-order change, where the underlying values, assumptions, structures, processes, and culture needed to be addressed in order for change to occur. The process is unlikely to be linear and will involve constantly helping others to understand the nature of the change and reinforcing why it is important for learning. The multicultural initiative is complex in that it needs be integrated at multiple levels (e.g. department, division, and cross campus) and is multidimensional (e.g. values, interest, schema). Second-order changes are likely to encounter resistance from within and outside the institution. When change is too radical or is vastly different from the existing system, the change threatens the environment, thus causing it to encounter stronger resistance.

The concepts of first-order and second-order change also relate back to concepts from Chapter 2 regarding the nature of change. Most theories predict first-order changes are easier and more typical, making it the type of change with which leaders have most experience. In fact, first-order changes are the focus of most *scientific management, evolutionary, political,* and *institutional* change theories. For example, *evolutionary theories* of change tend to emphasize the first-order changes (e.g. fluctuations in funding, new regulations) that are occasionally punctuated by second-order changes—such as the G.I. Bill or Morrill Act. In contrast, second-order change is less common and is experienced by leaders less often. Second-order change is often the focus of *cultural* and *cognitive theories* of change. *Political* and *cultural theories* also suggest that first-order changes are more likely integrated as they fit the existing systems. Also, cognitive theories, particularly sensemaking, articulate that second-order changes require greater time and processing.

Chapter 4 will focus exclusively on second-order changes and ways to approach it. In higher education, we are more likely to experience or be part of first-order change processes.

Yet, a common mistake is to not realize when second-order changes are needed or to plan for second-order change when first-order change would be appropriate for addressing a problem or issue. On many campuses, assessing student outcomes is addressed as a first-order change. Campuses establish a task force, develop a report outlining a process, and then offer faculty training. Yet, administrators typically do not realize that the notion of outcomes assessment often requires a fundamental shift in how faculty think about learning, their role, and their relationships with students. If faculty are not engaged in a process including a dialogue about how students learn, providing an opportunity to think about how assessment can be integrated meaningfully into their role, the implementation task force will likely have limited, if any, success. Change agents need to think about how student outcomes assessment may represent second-order change for faculty on many campuses.

There are other situations where change agents may believe a change should be made at a deeper level than is actually necessary. Some campuses may regularly engage in discussions about learning or the changing role of faculty, which would make initiatives relating to faculty work less likely to require second-order change. A campus leader might notice that few faculty are using few of the new technologies made available on campus and concludes that the issue is a lack of understanding about the value of such tools or instructors' lack of experience using them. If the leader spent time speaking with faculty about their concerns, she may realize that they have an appreciation of technology, but need some strategies for integrating tools and using them effectively. In cases like this one, some training and advice can help create the change without going through a long and protracted process.

Diagnosing problems or carefully evaluating where a campus is at in relationship to a particular type of change helps to determine the scope needed. The theories reviewed in Chapter 2 also help with diagnosing whether first- or second-order changes are needed. Using *cultural theories*, a cultural assessment (reviewed in Chapter 5) can be conducted to understand the underlying values of the organization; the *political theories* reviewed in Chapter 6 can be used to determine interests.

Levels of Change

Change happens at multiple levels (e.g. individual, group, organizational, and sectoral). Although we may aim to make change at the organizational or group level, to not consider what it takes to change individuals would leave out an important dynamic. While we may aim to scale up change across the entire enterprise, change agents need to consider what sorts of changes might be needed within particular campuses to support a sectoral-wide change. It may seem obvious that various levels of change need to be considered, but there are many examples of efforts where they were ignored.

Let's take, for example, the National Science Foundation's approach to funding and encouraging reform related to undergraduate Science, Technology, Engineering and Mathematics (STEM) education. The National Science Foundation has largely funded individual faculty members, assuming that if they developed new curricular and pedagogical approaches these would be disseminated across larger groups of faculty and become institutionalized on campuses. However, because their operating model or assumptions about change focused only the individual level, the change efforts largely stayed within the purview of the participating faculty members and were not expanded to the campus or the disciplinary level. At the organizational level, rewards, values, and structures remained in place that blocked change. At the disciplinary level there were no shifts in incentives or prestige. Unless there is an intentional examination or focus on the various levels, changes may not transcend or move beyond them.

The levels of change are important to understand when considering change in a systemic way. Change agents need to recognize the level of change that they are dealing with and match appropriate strategies. Furthermore, leaders need to think about how various levels of the system influence and help create change at another level. While Sarah's examples of change were both at the organizational level, she did not consider system-wide (enterprise level) levels of support that could have helped her efforts, nor did she consider the role of individual resistance. Her focus on the organizational level prevented her from accurately diagnosing the change and identifying all the levers of change at her disposal.

Social cognition theories of change provide a helpful resource for change agents to focus on the individual level, when necessary. Sarah would have benefited from understanding the ways that multiculturalism was not understandable to many of her colleagues on campus. Possessing that knowledge would have allowed her to focus on how people create meaning or sense around multiculturalism and to explore more of the research literature on this sort of change initiative. At the group level, she might have used *political* and *institutional theories* to map support and resistance across various disciplines and units. At the enterprise level, Sarah really missed out on opportunities to capitalize on support from national associations like the Association of American Colleges and Universities or the American Council on Education's Center for the Advancement of Racial and Ethnic Equity, events such as the National Conference on Race and Ethnicity in Higher Education, or resources like the *Diversity Digest* or *Diverse*. *Evolutionary theories* recommend reviewing the external landscape and identifying how it can help or hinder changes. At the enterprise systems level there are many supports for multiculturalism. Foundations such as Ford and Rockefeller could provide additional grants and legitimacy. Being aware of the larger fields from which a change agent can draw support is important.

Sarah recognized her change initiative was focused at the organizational level and matched strategies to shape overall campus processes and structures. This is often not the case, though. On many campuses, initiatives to improve the environment for women and minority faculty are often aimed at thinking about individual-level discrimination in search processes or evaluation. While individual-level discrimination plays a role, institutional racism and sexism can also play a significant role. There may be criteria in the evaluation procedures that systematically favor white and male faculty over women and underrepresented minorities. These criteria in institutional evaluation processes are often deemed neutral and may never be examined if change agents do not identify a problem at the organizational level. Another example is on campuses that are trying to create more collaboration. Leaders may see faculty autonomy as the key obstacle, so they focus on how to refashion faculty work and roles. However, on deeper consideration, many organizational structures and processes may emerge as shaping this issue, from rewards, departmental structures, and institutional values that were ignored when the issue was considered as a group-level problem, rather than organizational. Drawing on *scientific management theories*, change agents can see the change in relationship to organizational levers.

Most changes play out across multiple levels of the system, so the key for change agents is to understand and use several theories that help them see the ways that change operates at different levels. Knowing *cognitive* theories helps to articulate strategies for altering individual behavior, while *cultural* and *political theories* help shape knowledge of group actions, *scientific management* and *institutional theories* provide important information about organizations, and *evolutionary* and *institutional theories* provide insight into the system or enterprise level.

Focus

Focus refers to the phenomenon affected (e.g. structure). Three typical foci for change are structure, process, and attitude. Leaders often focus only on one aspect, either structural, process, or attitude, instead of matching their strategy to the various foci playing out within the change initiative. Structure refers to the organizational charts, the management information systems, or policies and procedures. Process relates to approaches to enacting certain operations like planning, admissions, or decision-making. Attitudes or values are the way people feel about their work within the existing structures and processes of the organization and are closely related to culture. Research suggests that changes focused on all three areas will be more difficult to achieve than changes in only one area (Kezar 2001). Furthermore, *cultural theories* of change suggest that structures and even processes can be changed relatively easily, but that attitudes and values can be much more difficult to change because they are tied to underlying assumptions (Schein 1985). *Cultural theories* can also be used to understand and tap into the values through a cultural assessment. *Scientific management theories* can be helpful in exploring and mapping structures and processes.

In Sarah's situation, the technology change affected the process aspect most. People did not need to rethink their attitudes or values about work, nor did the overall structure of the department change significantly. While change agents provide resources, there were not necessarily new rewards, policies, and procedures put in place to support the initiative. However, the multicultural initiative required preliminary changes in attitudes and values among a broad group of individuals and would likely also entail deep changes in process and structure. Various studies have identified how multicultural content raises issues of power, which requires faculty to be able to engage in controversial dialogues and emotions that need to be processed for learning to occur (Bensimon and Neumann 1993). To support multiculturalism, a variety of processes such as pedagogical approaches, curricula, admissions, and support all need to be re-examined. For example, students of color have some unique needs in terms of their level of awareness about college and the need for greater transition information. New structures may need to be put in place, such as a vice president for multiculturalism and new admissions or scholarship policies. The focus of change is much more wide reaching than Sarah's technology initiative. Readers may notice that there is some overlap in these concepts as scope—reviewed earlier in the chapter (pp. 49–50) —and focus both relate to the degree to which the change is more transformational (e.g. second order) or focused mostly on minor improvements (e.g. first order).

Forces and Sources of Change

In diagnosing which type of change is necessary, change agents need to examine where a change is coming from (e.g. the source). This evaluation also examines the why of change. What is the logic behind it? The literature typically speaks of the external environment versus the internal environment. Changes from the outside are often viewed with more suspicion from internal stakeholders. In Chapter 5, we will address in detail the various types of external groups that may be the source of a change—foundations, professional groups, accreditation, government agencies, or disciplinary societies. Scholars using *evolutionary theories*, described in Chapter 2, articulate how external forces will constantly be influencing higher education, making the role of change agents to determine how to best adapt to changes, be proactive, and, as noted in Chapter 1, manage change.

But, as a change agent, one needs to diagnose where changes are originating. The technology change Sarah was responding to was part of a larger dialogue in her disciplinary society about how to make sociology more relevant and legitimate within an environment that has become increasingly supportive of STEM disciplines, but more antagonistic to disciplines seen as not directly job related. There are jobs for students who come out of programs with these new technology skills; the economic imperatives make the technology change have more legitimacy. The multicultural initiative that she was heading on campus is part of a larger effort across the academy to create campuses more supportive to all populations, but Sarah is not directly connected with this larger movement. Instead, she is responding to an initiative of the provost on her campus. The source of change has power, but is a much more localized source or force for change. While sometimes a local champion can be a pivotal force for change, that may not always be the case. Sarah needs to consider how much legitimacy the provost has as a source of the change effort. The source of change also shapes its trajectory in important ways. Since the technology change was supported by multiple, credible sources, the disciplinary society and employers, it is likely to experience fewer barriers. The multicultural initiative is supported by many key sources—national organizations and policymakers, for example—but these outside sources may not operate to support change if they are not intentionally drawn upon. Both *institutional* and *evolutionary theories* predict that the convergence of several key influential individuals or organizations can ease progress. Thus, if Sarah drew upon the many sources of external support for multiculturalism, she could rationalize the initiative to internal campus members, as well as create a sense of urgency to move change forward. These theories also predict that without this support changes will be resisted and protracted.

Evolutionary Theories and Type of Change: Intentionality and Response

Both of Sarah's efforts represent intentional changes that she is trying to create. But as the concepts of source and forces are reviewed, we are reminded that not all types of change are intentionally created by change agents. *Evolutionary* and *institutional theories* suggest that many changes are happening in higher education institutions and that the role of change agents and leaders is more about responding to forces that are coming from outside the campus or one's unit. Sarah was involved with a planned, intentional change, but many examples already provided in this book do not fall into this realm (e.g. sudden declines in state funding or new regulations). While higher education does not usually have many mandated changes, the future may be different since stakeholders are calling for more accountability, which may result in new mandates. Also, many scholars have noted that there are always sources of unpredictable change, such as economic downturns, demographic shifts, reliance on multiple and shifting funding sources, macro politics, legal requirements, and political disaffection.

What do *evolutionary theories* tell us about how best to respond to these types of changes? Theories suggest the following are important for change agents to understand and utilize to best manage unplanned change:

- Being proactive;
- Broadly engaging organizational stakeholders;
- Responding strategically;
- Creating nimble structures;
- Having a clear understanding of strengths and weaknesses and creating priorities;
- Mapping and developing internal capacities;
- Becoming entrepreneurial; and,
- Organizational learning.

Most of these theories focus on those in positions of authority and what role they can play to mediate externally imposed changes. However, theories also suggest that institutions that involve campus stakeholders more broadly are more successful in navigating unplanned change. While studies have been aimed at leaders in positions of authority, bottom-up or grassroots leaders can also use these same concepts.

Being Proactive

Most of the evolutionary literature suggests that being proactive, rather than reactive, helps to best manage externally imposed changes. Change agents that do not respond quickly in a crisis are likely to experience negative outcomes such as declining funding, poor morale, or institutional instability (Argyris 1982; Senge 1990; Steeples 1990). Change agents are expected to be scanning the environment, protecting the institution from disruption from these external changes and helping steer the course of their organizations early on so that there is less chaos (Cameron 1991). Leslie and Fretwell (1996) examined institutions that were responding to significant budget declines to try to understand what helped make some institutions more successful than others in responding. Part of their success relies on strategic choices about the reallocation of funds. These strategic choices require preplanning, rather than a last minute response. Institutions that were successful had developed in advance plans to announce budget shortfalls because they were aware of external trends and the need to come up with contingency plans right away. Also, campuses that create a mindset that change is ongoing are better able to respond to unplanned changes that result from external pressures. External threats usually come quickly and require relatively swift action, so campuses that are unable to respond suffer worse consequences.

Engage Stakeholders Broadly

Evolutionary theory also suggests that organizations respond better to unplanned change by regularly engaging organizational participants (Cameron 1991). The fewer people that are involved, the more likely externally imposed changes will take a long time because key individuals needed to move change along will be unaware. Accreditation may be a time when campuses are engaged in implementing changes that are mandated, thus not the desire or intention of the campus. Student outcomes assessment is a change that many campuses are currently grappling with. Campuses that involve many people throughout the institution in setting up a system for student outcomes assessment are more likely to have success than those that create a small task force that appears to be working in isolation. Also, many campuses have been involved in implementing the Student and Exchange Visitor Information System (SEVIS) for tracking international students. SEVIS is the web-accessible database for monitoring information about exchange visitors, international students, and scholars subject to this program. It was established by the Department of Homeland and is administered by the Student and Exchange Visitor Program (SEVP). Broader input in implementation of SEVIS can ease problems as all the key stakeholders, from administrators, to student affairs staff, to faculty that may be approached if there is a problem with an international student, should be involved in its implementation.

Respond to Pressures

Evolutionary theory suggests that systems tend to return to homeostasis and incorporate changes into their processes and cultures as soon as possible. It is better for systems to incorporate a change, rather than to ignore it (e.g. address enrollment declines). If it is ignored, a change can become a larger crisis for the system. For example, Leslie and Fretwell's (1996) study of college campuses identified how environmental threats became a crisis because higher education institutions did not respond to pressures in their environment. Leslie and Fretwell describe how the decline of state funds is tied to decreasing public confidence in higher education and perceptions of a lack of accountability. As public higher education institutions continue to ignore public concerns, they create a situation of crisis for themselves. Clark (1998b) documented how universities are caught in an endless stream of pressures that creates demand overload—there are pressures to increase access, improve quality, increase accountability, create new areas of knowledge, lower costs, meet the needs of the knowledge economy, and meet the needs of an increasingly diverse group of students, as well as to do all these things with fewer funds. Yet, few institutions acknowledge or engage external trends. Thus, Clark predicted that increasing external pressures for unplanned change will continue to shape higher education in upcoming decades. Being proactive and understanding external pressures can alleviate crises and problems that might emerge, but higher education is not well positioned to respond in this way.

Examine Priorities

One of the key ways that campuses can respond to external threats is to examine their priorities and try to build on their strengths, rather than trying to be all things to all people. Too often, institutions, whether colleges or hospitals, try to provide all services and programs. In difficult times, this usually proves an unsuccessful strategy (Leslie and Fretwell 1996). So, when responding to unplanned changes, identifying campus strengths and weaknesses and utilizing them in planning and executing a response is a helpful strategy. Having a good sense of campus priorities based on an analysis of strengths and weaknesses also allows campuses to develop a thoughtful strategy to drive decision-making, rather than campus politics or shifting external priorities.

Create Structures that Facilitate Adaptation

Clark (1998a) documented that higher education institutions are not currently structured to respond to external threats and need to create new structures to be more responsive within an environment with increasing external demands. In addition to examining priorities in responding to external demands, Clark's case studies of five universities in Europe identify some core features that he believes are important for future adaptation within this new environment. While he studied European universities that were having challenges at adaptation, the insights have also been shown as critical to others countries facing the pressures of the neoliberal environment and globalization, described in Chapter 1. The first feature is a strengthened steering core (or decision-making body), a small group made up of trusted academics or faculty, as well as managers who serve on the Central Council or decision-making body. This steering core acts in the place of current faculty councils or campus committees. The steering core is a combination of centralized and decentralized governance, which maximizes managerial expertise, as well as academic/faculty values and goals. Without this, Clark predicts managerial interests would overwhelm institutions; many believe they have. Clark also suggests the creation of more interdisciplinary or transdisciplinary units and centers, which can help meet some external demands without significantly changing traditional departmental structures. He calls this an enhanced development periphery. To keep up with increasing demands, he also believes that institutions need to become more entrepreneurial and look for more diverse funding bases, rather than relying so much on government sources of funding. He stresses that entrepreneurialism has to be rooted in ideas and values that exist at the core of the institution, not the desires of a single person or small group. These recommendations suggest how most higher education institutions, as currently structured, are not well positioned to address external pressures.

Create Organizational Capacity

Leslie and Fretwell (1996) and Toma (2012) also point out that campuses encounter crises because external forces reflect and reinforce areas where there are internal problems (e.g. poor financial management) that are not being addressed, weakening their capacity to act when external pressures emerge. Thus, evolutionary theorists suggest that campuses need to watch certain internal problems that will shape the way that campuses are able to respond to unplanned changes and pressures. Deferred maintenance of the physical plant is an area that often gets campuses into trouble. Having a diversified and healthy financial base is also important in responding to external pressures. So is having a well-trained and functioning employee base with strong leadership. Campuses that have significant turnover and distrust among staff, faculty, and the administration are ripe for problems, especially when external crises and pressures arise.

Facilitate Organizational Learning

More recently, an important principle for responding to the external environment and successfully managing unplanned changes is organizational learning (Dill 1999; Gumport and Sporn 1999). Many other theories, such as strategic choice, open systems theory, and resource dependency, suggest that strategic planning and mapping the external environment are ways to manage unplanned change. Organizational learning theory builds on these others by suggesting that the data collected during strategic planning are important, but that this data and resultant learning through planning process are often not shared across the organization so that individuals can effectively respond to changes. For organizations, data collected through strategic planning and other processes can be distributed to facilitate problem solving at a more local level and help create strategic responses. This builds on another attribute of *evolutionary theories*, that the broader the involvement of organizational stakeholders, the more likely there will be success (Cameron 1991). Organizational learning typically involves creating teams of individuals to participate in examining an external threat or mandate and the organization itself in order to develop a more context-based response for a specific problem. It also emphasizes building upon the strengths of the organization that are identified. Chapter 4 will be devoted to organizational learning as a change strategy for both planned and unplanned change.

Context-based Adaptation

Reinforcing the findings later presented in Chapter 5 on the importance of context, studies of adaptation to external threats have found that institutions need to create their own unique strategies for responding to their specific circumstances (Chaffee 1983; Leslie and Fretwell 1996). Although studies suggest some general strategies, such as being proactive, having departments or programs that can track environmental demands, building on strengths, or being nimble by creating new governance structures (such as a central council), some suggests that these general approaches such as being proactive can vary from one campus to another (Chaffee, 1983; Clark, 1998a, and Leslie and Fretwell, 1996).

Evolutionary theories tend to focus more on functional responses to external pressures and ways to manage unplanned change, whereas *institutional theory* simply explains how institutions respond, whether functionally or dysfunctionally (e.g. through isomorphism). *Institutional theory* emphasizes that the way that many institutions respond to environmental demands is to mimic the response of other campuses. While research demonstrates that customized strategies tend to work better for campuses by drawing upon their strengths, by contrast *institutional theory* shows how campuses tend to look toward their peers and respond in kind (DiMaggio and Powell 1983). Through administrators' professional networks and associations, they tend to perceive which universities are successful and imitate their approaches to particular dilemmas, financial constraints, or issues such as the notion of a quality education. While mimicking another campus may work for some campuses, this has also resulted in many campuses adopting strategies that they cannot appropriately execute and creating additional challenges (Gumport and Sporn 1999). So, rather than suggesting effective techniques, *institutional theory* typically documents unsuccessful or unstrategic approaches to change.

An Example of Identifying the Type of Change Needed

Sometimes a leader thinks they have identified the "right type of change" for a campus, but have actually misread the situation and offer up a change initiative that is a poor fit. Let's consider an example of this situation (see website for the full case: http://www-personal.umich.edu/~marvp/facultynetwork/cases/olivet/olivet1.html). A case study of Olivet College documents the response of leaders when the campus erupted into a racial conflict, which attracted media attention and was elevated to national awareness. In this case, two successive presidents misdiagnose the problem and take the wrong approach. The president at the time the crisis began, who had been in office for many years, did little to resolve it. As a result, the board called for the president's resignation under pressure from external groups. The board hired a new president who appeared likely to be a strong change agent; she had been an advocate for diversity issues. The new president moved quickly to put measures in place to improve the racial climate on campus, including classroom inspections to ensure there was a safe environment for students—she was operating from a belief that first-order changes were needed. However, she had misdiagnosed the problem. While the racial crisis on campus was a visible symptom in the case, there were much deeper problems on campus for which the racial crisis was only a symptom. The challenges included poor morale, a loss of mission, a drift away from historical values and priorities, a fragmented and broken curriculum, a tradition of top-down autocratic leadership, fear and distrust among faculty, administration, staff, and students, an unhealthy and racist student culture, and declining enrollments and resources, to name only a few. For example, the racial crisis occurred because they had moved so far away from their historic mission as the first abolitionist campus. And the lack of relationship between faculty and administration led to limited communication and planning, which made the institution unable to address the slide in mission. It is not until a third president analyzes the situation in greater detail that the right type of change is identified and the campus is able to move forward.

When the third president was hired, rather than acting quickly, he spent time developing an understanding of the campus and examining the situation in order to identify the type of change that was needed. Through this time for analysis and reflection, the president identified the need for second-order or deep change. The president responded by addressing values, structures, and processes; he acknowledged that change is required at multiple levels and understood the internal and external sources of change. So, he began by mapping a strategy that will serve the appropriately identified second-order change, including sensemaking, organizational learning, facilitating dialogue, creating shared values and interests, and questioning existing assumptions.

While sometimes we are handed a change initiative to execute, other times we have a change we are passionate about, but yet in other circumstances we are trying to fix a problem or create improvements. In the Olivet example, a change agent sought to develop a plan for change to react to an unresolved problem. If we are asked to execute a change, we still need to examine whether the proposed initiative is the *right type* of change. Implementing a poorly conceived directive for the campus is a high stakes endeavor. We often feel that if we are asked to execute change we must do so as asked, without exercising agency. An impressive recent example is the San Jose State University faculty that refused to adopt MOOCs that were being mandated on their campus without proof of their value for their students. Instead, I encourage you to reflect on change initiatives put forward in your institutions and consider whether they reflect the *right type* of change, but also whether they are worth the time and energy required.

Other times, we might be passionate about an issue and want to move it forward, but our approach may not help to address problems or be an appropriate fit for the campus culture (in fact, it may be opposed to it). Our passions may blind us to whether the change is appropriate or indeed a priority given other challenges the campus faces. We may even decide to move an initiative forward when it is not strongly aligned with campus needs. In this situation, the assessment of type of change given the campus context helps to demonstrate the challenges that may be faced in implementing the change.

Summary

Having reflected on the type of change, Sarah can approach the multicultural initiative quite differently. First, now that she recognizes that this is a type of change that will elicit a political response and resistance she can consider slowing down and planning a strategy to address opposing views. She can discover who is resistant, why, and who supports her plans (*political theory*). Sarah can also engage a second-order change process, delving into people's underlying assumptions and values (*social cognition theory*). She can think through the learning and sensemaking that may need to occur because these changes are not well understood. Furthermore, in pursuing a broader organizational change she can now recognize the structures, rewards, and values that need to be examined and modified to support the change (*scientific management theory*). She also identifies and connects with resources across the higher education sector to support her initiative (*evolutionary theory*). Because the focus of change is comprehensive—being a second-order change—she works with allies to more broadly understand the attitudes, policies, procedures, and processes that need to be altered. In fact, she discovers that the belief held by many faculty that the curriculum is neutral and value free needs to be challenged and is a major issue that has slowed her efforts (and those of her supporters) (*cultural theory*). She also recognizes that some changes to the curriculum (*political theory*) committees are needed, as many of their members subscribe to antiquated belief systems. Sara discovers that the provost has little legitimacy regarding this issue as she explores the source of change, so she teams with the directors of the multicultural center, who many see as doing good work, but who have been blocked from influencing the curriculum (political theory). Through these efforts of recognizing the type of change at hand (e.g. content, scope, level, foci and source), Sarah creates a much more successful strategy.

four
Creating Deep Change

Ted, a dean for international education on a college campus, is finding it difficult to get people to appreciate the value of study abroad and exchange programs. Although Ted has provided research from the national survey of student engagement about the value of such programs, he continues to encounter apathy among most of the senior administration, as well as the faculty and staff, about rethinking their programs and requirements. He decides that the best way to influence or persuade people about the value is to take a set of administrators and faculty abroad to experience the program he envisions for students. While the administrators and faculty are hesitant to take the time, they agree to go. When Ted returns from the trip, he finds that the perceptions of the administrators and faculty have been transformed; they now strongly support the program. It was only by experiencing the program and seeing how it could foster learning in new ways that they could truly appreciate Ted's vision. Often, when we are making changes we have to help people to make sense of and understand the change to move forward.

One of the key challenges for change agents is how to create deep or transformational change, as described in this case with Ted. Campuses struggle the most with this particular issue, so this chapter offers insights and strategies to better understand how to overcome this challenge. This chapter addresses the challenges of second-order or deep change, which were noted as a vexing type of change within Chapter 3. First-order changes are more commonly pursued, often much easier to accomplish, and have been studied more than second-order change. It is particularly important for change agents to be aware of how to engage in second-order changes and the ways that sensemaking and organizational learning (both are concepts from *social cognition theory*) can be brought in as strategies to assist in this process. Ted was able to help people on his campus better understand the importance of study abroad and international efforts by having them undergo a sensemaking process through a trip abroad.

Many commentators have suggested that second-order changes are particularly difficult to make within higher education institutions. *Institutional theory*, which was reviewed in Chapter 2, provides some background on why second-order change is less common on campuses. Higher education institutions, as social institutions, are supposed to be long-standing and support an enduring mission. They are not expected or accustomed to undergo significant changes to their core purpose or values. Thus, at some level we would not expect much deep change within these institutions. However, some of the forces described in Chapter 1 suggest that some deep types of changes are needed to help colleges meet their missions. For example, recent research from cognitive science suggests people learn in different ways than was previously understood, suggesting that a new understanding about learning is needed to guide faculty members' and administrators' work. Dramatic changes to teaching and learning may need to be institutionalized.

In this chapter, I will define second-order change in greater detail. I will focus the rest of the chapter on two approaches for facilitating second-order change—sensemaking and organizational learning. It is important to note that second-order change is truly challenging. The research is not encouraging for change agents seeking to create this level of change. In part, this chapter serves as a cautionary tale about the difficulty of creating change at this level. Yet, this chapter also demonstrates the potential and some important lessons learned over the last few decades about mechanisms and processes that can propel second-order change. This chapter focuses on key concepts to help change agents create organizational learning, but for a more conceptual review of organization learning, please see Kezar (2005a).

Second-order Change

There are many names given to second-order change, such as deep, transformational, or punctuated change. It is sometimes also referred to as double-loop learning, wherein organizations challenge existing assumptions and beliefs in order to align with the environment—this often requires transformational change (Argyris 1994). No matter which term is used, the change process described is so substantial that it alters the operating systems, underlying values, and culture of an organization or system. Another commonality is that scholars have viewed process or structural alterations as unlikely to make a difference because the value systems and underlying thinking that need to change are so persistent. As noted in earlier chapters, the focus of *social cognition* and *cultural theories*, in particular, is on addressing second-order or deep change. *Cultural theories* are inherently tied to the issue of deep change because they emphasize understanding cultures through their underlying value and symbol systems. *Social cognition theories* describe how people make meaning in organizations, including how individuals' identities are connected to the way views are socially constructed. Scholars using *social cognition theories* also focus on resistance to change and the reasons people do not engage with particular types of initiatives. Through their examination of resistance, researchers identified how people's thinking patterns block their ability to engage with organizational change efforts. Both *cultural* and *cognitive theories* tap into and examine norms and the beliefs held by individuals within organizations to better understand how these factors shape change.

How does one know that second-order change has occurred? There are typically two indicators for identifying second-order change. The first is attitudinal or cultural evidence. This can include changes in the way groups or individuals interact with one another, the language used by the campus in referring to itself, or the types of conversations that occur, as well as the abandonment of old arguments or emergence of new relationships with stakeholders. A second indicator is the presence of structural elements. In higher education institutions, these might include substantial changes to the curriculum, new pedagogies, changes in student learning and assessment practices, new policies, the reallocation of funds, the creation of new departments or institutional structures, and new processes or structures for decision-making. Yet, the defining feature of second-order change is the attitudinal change that is simultaneously manifested in an organization's structures. A change in structures alone is usually not an indicator of second-order change.

How do change agents know when second-order change is necessary? In Chapter 3, I described how it is critical to try to understand what is the appropriate change needed. Trying to guide a campus through second-order change when it is not necessary creates a drain on human and financial resources. Not identifying second-order change when it's needed can result in making many smaller changes that only address symptoms rather than the heart of problems. Identifying whether the type of change needed is second-order requires reflection on the institutional context.

Several examples of second-order change will be provided in the book. I will refer here to an example from Chapter 7 in which a change agent assessed the need for second-order change to demonstrate this process. In Chapter 7, I will describe Jeff, who decides to create a more family-friendly environment on his campus. Jeff had learned about *cultural theories* and knows how to assess the type of change, so he was aware that his initiative required second-order changes to occur. First, he is aware of deeply embedded sexism and is able to assess the history of his sexism on his campus. Second, he can see how this value system is embedded in the many structures and aspects of campus culture (poor tenure and promotion policies, for example) that are unsupportive of and deeply resistant to family-friendly policies. Only through developing their knowledge of these histories are change agents able to be successful in crafting an effective strategy. As a result of Jeff diagnosing the need for second-order change, he sees the benefit of utilizing sensemaking approaches to create change. In this chapter, I highlight sensemaking mechanisms and will return to Jeff and his efforts at using sensemaking in Chapter 7.

Sensemaking: What It Is and How to Recognize It

Sensemaking is about changing mindsets, which in turn alters behaviors, priorities, values, and commitments (Eckel and Kezar 2003a). Second-order change really is about people making new sense of things. Making new sense means that individuals explore what change initiatives mean for their roles and responsibilities, their identity within an institution, and their overall perspective of the organization. Sensemaking is a recognition that perspectives are socially constructed with and through other people who are organizationally situated (Weick 1995).

Sensemaking can happen in one of two ways. The first is that individuals attach new meaning to familiar concepts and ideas (Eckel and Kezar 2003a, 2003b). For example, on many campuses the notion of the well-prepared professor might mean someone with well-organized lecture notes, clearly articulated outcomes for the course, and fair tests. A campus that has recently undergone a transformation might now think that a well-prepared professor is someone who uses technology in sophisticated ways to enhance teaching and learning, draws on relevant interdisciplinary knowledge, and utilizes a systematic process of mapping learning goals to student outcomes. These sorts of changes reflect deeper thinking around rather familiar concepts. A second way that people undergo sensemaking is that they develop new language and new concepts that describe a changed institution (Eckel and Kezar 2003b). For example, a campus that begins to speak regularly about the wellness of its employees, where the term and related concepts have not been used before, is undergoing a new way of making meaning. As sensemaking continues, the concept of wellness and related priorities become widespread not only in their use, but in changing the ways people think about their careers and lives on campus.

Second-order change only occurs if and when this understanding becomes collective, when it shapes institutional sensemaking (Weick 1995). If it only develops among a few individuals, sensemaking has occurred, but not in the way that is necessary for creating second-order change in the institution. However, in time it may transition into a more collective process. In order to become a collective or shared process among people within the institution, or at least within particular subunits or subcultures, certain practices need to be enacted that help create these new shared senses of meaning. Sensemaking does not entail a collective groupthink, though. Instead, sensemaking processes suggest that it is important for individuals to wrestle with what the new understanding or change is and what is means for them. Sensemaking is the opposite of collective or groupthink in that it does not simply involve the adoption of other people's points of view; it is not the mimicking of values.

Studies demonstrate that sensemaking is facilitated by change agents that can create vehicles for social interaction, help introduce new ideas into the organization, provide opportunities for social connection, and effectively use language and communication to help facilitate people's evolving thinking (Gioia and Thomas 1996; Thomas et al. 1993; Weick 1993). Sensemaking requires time because institutional change is accompanied by modifications in overall perceptions (Gioia and Thomas 1996; Thomas et al. 1993). It is most likely to take place when numerous avenues are provided, where information is detailed and transmitted consistently (Weick 1993), and when it involves a sizable number of people. Eckel and Kezar (2003a) identify how sensemaking processes happen in a somewhat unique fashion in higher education institutions because of characteristics such as their decentralized nature, the flow of participants in and out of key decision-making arenas, and because much of the institutional work is reliant upon autonomous individuals (Birnbaum 1991; Cohen and March 1974; Kennedy 1994). Opportunities for sensemaking to occur are best when the processes are repeated, ongoing, and inclusive. Efforts in higher education must be even more widespread, more frequently repeated, and continuous to be successful because of the sector's and institutions' decentralized character, fragmentation, and dual authority structures.

Organizational Learning

Sensemaking and organizational learning overlap in their emphasis on how people's mindsets can shift, but organizational learning follows a more rational and data-oriented approach. Organizational learning also has a much larger literature base than sensemaking, particularly as it relates to organizational change (Kezar 2005a). For close to 20 years, organizational learning has been one of the primary vehicles for creating changes within organizations.

The author most often associated with organizational learning is Chris Argyris (1994), who began his work in the 1970s. The underlying assumption of organizational learning is that once human beings detect errors they want to correct them and undergo change. Therefore, organizations need to create mechanisms so that people can detect errors, which often involves the collection and review of data. Organizational learning is itself a study of whether, how, and under what conditions organizations learn. While a variety of authors also examine conditions that help to promote organizational learning, this does not necessarily suggest that lots of organizations have these aspects in place or that learning is in any way inherent to organizations (Fiol and Lyles 1985). Two areas of literature are helpful for understanding the ways that organizational learning might be harnessed for change. The first is on process elements (e.g. the introduction of new ideas, creating doubt) that can that help facilitate learning within organizations, such as data or teams. The second area is on organizational factors or conditions (e.g. the lack of a hierarchy, climate of trust) that support these learning processes. Another promising area, but very limited area in the existing literature, includes scholars who combine organizational learning with other theories of change, for example *political* or *cultural theories*. As noted throughout this book, taking a narrow perspective on change can limit change agents' efficacy. Yet, most scholars of organizational learning tend to narrowly look at these mechanisms for change without considering other influential factors.

The concept of the learning organization evolved out of organizational learning research and became popular in the 1990s. Key writers on the learning organization are Peter Senge (1990) and David Garvin (1993). The learning organization is more an idealized model that provides techniques for individuals to identify and interpret problems differently. Scholars writing about the learning organization often promote the ease with which learning occurs. Proponents highlight the need to understand that individuals are operating on the basis of mental models, which are taken-for-granted beliefs and assumptions that prevent new learning. To learn we must become aware of our own and others' mental models, which can shape the possibilities for learning. The learning organization approach provides change agents with skills for reflection, introduces personal competencies such as how to create a shared vision or encourage team dialogue, and highlights the need for systematic problem solving.

While the concept of learning organization is drawn from studies of organizational learning and suggests key processes that can help individuals and organizations to learn, the key difference between the two is the degree to which each emphasizes the difficulty or ease of learning. Organizational learning theorists identify many individual and organizational defenses that emerge to prevent learning and emphasize that humans are more driven by politics and ego than rationality. Also, organizational learning suggests that learning is not always positive; it may go in undesirable directions. The learning organizations approach tends to suggest that all learning is positive.

The vast majority of the literature on organizational learning suggests that it is not a common phenomenon (Argyris 1991). In fact, a variety of researchers have spent their entire careers identifying and documenting what are called organizational defenses, or systems that get in the way of learning. Their research suggests that individuals and organizations are persistent in adhering to past patterns and practice, creating challenges for organizational learning. In order to explain why learning does not occur, organizational theorists have examined the features of organizations that prevent learning, as well as other particular challenges that emerge as barriers. Organizational defenses include policies, practices, or actions that prevent participants from experiencing embarrassment or threat, but also prevent them from discovering the causes of the embarrassment or threats (March 1991). For example, when data emerge that suggest a certain process is not working, managers or staff may deflect this data by having people focus on other data in order to hide what is potentially embarrassing. Organizational defense routines create a sense of helplessness, cynicism, and doubts about change processes and work against learning (March 1991). So, it is important to understand them in order to create organizational learning towards change. One of the key reasons that learning does not occur is that individuals are not aware of ways that they are moved off course and have difficulty bringing a group back to a learning mode. Thus, understanding anti-learning behavior is as important as knowing how to facilitate learning. By identifying anti-learning behaviors, leaders can help teams to move beyond them.

Sensemaking versus Organizational Learning

You might be wondering why these two approaches are separated and considered as distinctive processes, given that both are aimed at changing underlying assumptions? Fundamentally, each is built on different assumptions, although their core assumptions are not necessarily in conflict. Sensemaking emerged from studies of individuals and observations that people are constantly making sense of their own environments; these concepts are adapted and used as an entrée for understanding broader changes in human behavior. Sensemaking emphasizes the social interactions that humans engage in as a source of change and looks to conversations and language as key facilitators of new perspective. Vehicles for change involve facilitating human interaction, creating conversations, collaboration, and communication to help people to question their assumptions and increase their exposure to new ideas or values. Sensemaking scholars suggest that people are constantly making meaning, but also note that very strong norms often guide institutional processes in schooling, professions, and popular culture. So, while they certainly suggest that people's understanding of the world can be altered, sensemaking scholars also emphasize how norms make such change problematic and difficult. Theories of organizational sensemaking project a more malleable view of people than the evidence may support (Kezar 2001). This sort of view, an overemphasis of the ability for these processes to occur or their ease, has caused some tension in the sensemaking and organizational learning literatures. While studies suggest that a shift in people's underlying assumptions is possible, evidence suggests it's also not very likely to happen (March 1991).

Organizational learning also attempts to change underlying assumptions and beliefs through slightly different vehicles than sensemaking. Organizational learning is based on the assumption that by providing people with data, information, and inquiry methods they can detect inaccuracies or errors and work to solve problems by creating better approaches to organizational work. The rational bent of organizational learning often fits well with more managerial views of organizations. It has attracted far more adherents and interest than theories of sensemaking, which is framed by concepts related to human identity construction.

Another difference between sensemaking and organizational learning is that sensemaking tends to focus more on second-order changes. Organizational learning can often be used to understand first-order changes; not all learning involves double-loop learning in which underlying assumptions and values are challenged and need to change. Instead the majority of organizational learning is more single-loop learning where individuals detect errors in the environment and find ways to create changes within the existing assumptions and values.

Organizational learning and organizational sensemaking are similar in their emphasis on identifying characteristics of organizations (e.g. incentives, team structures, opportunities for facilitated interaction) and how they create conditions for learning or sensemaking. These characteristics (e.g. environment open to questioning) and these processes (e.g. teams and group work) are seen as indelibly tied to the organizational level. One of the challenges emerging from this assumption is that change agents that are not working at the organizational level (e.g. bottom-up change agents often work at group level) may find less direct application of this work. For example, grassroots leaders may not find the concepts and processes outlined in these theories to be particularly helpful, because these change agents do not always have access to the organization's hierarchy, are not equipped to build trust across major groups such as administrators and faculty, or cannot convene groups across the entire campus. However, although these theories have tended to emphasize the organizational level, there are still lessons and ideas that can be applied within subunits of an organization and networks. But, it is important to point out that the research has mostly been directed at the organizational level.

Given the decentralized nature of higher education and its fragmented infrastructure among departments and various subunits, leaders may be more apt to consider learning among organizational subunits than at the larger organizational level. Additionally, emerging conversations and research about inter-organizational learning, which happens between and among organizations through consortia, common projects, or various types of networks, may create opportunities to consider learning.

One of the major benefits of sensemaking theories, as compared to organizational learning, is that it can occur across large groups of people with much less depth of effort. For individuals to undergo sensemaking, they only need to appreciate how a change might shape their identity and adopt the perspectives that emerge through the change process. It is not necessary for individuals to undergo a deep learning process, where they think about particular problems facing the organization in new ways. In fact, the difficulty and complexity involved in creating organizational learning suggest that it may be challenging to implement, and sensemaking and organizational learning might be paired together in order to achieve desired deep changes rather than using one approach or the other exclusively. Others might suggest that using data to promote change through learning is an easier task than trying to guide people through a process where they re-examine their identities and values. Arguably, both are difficult endeavors and we actually have little if any research to understand which process is more difficult or time consuming to execute. There is far less research on sensemaking, which has been perceived as being a more elusive concept, including barriers to carrying it out in organizations. Over time it may be shown to be as challenging as organizational learning. With this background, I now move to strategies that are used to facilitate these deep change processes.

Vehicles for Creating Sensemaking: Sense Giving

Weick (1995) and other sensemaking scholars refer to the mechanisms that help people to make new meaning as sense giving vehicles, since they are a means used to help individuals in organizations to undergo a sensemaking process. Sometimes sense giving can be as simple as making a public speech, giving a presentation, or developing a vision statement. Some key sensemaking vehicles that are commonly used in higher education institutions are:

- Ongoing and widespread conversations;
- Collaborative leadership;
- Developing cross-departmental teams or working groups;
- Drawing on and discussing external ideas;
- Sponsoring faculty and staff development opportunities:
- Preparing and giving public presentations;
- Flexible vision; and,
- Creating documents and concept papers.

Weick describes several key concepts as connected with sensemaking; it is social, ongoing, helps people reflecting on identity, leads to rethinking assumptions, involves cues, and plausibility. It is social in that people make sense within social environments, not in isolation. Sensemaking occurs when new cues (described on pp. 70–74) are introduced and reinforced in repeated interactions. Interactions and activities need to help people reflect on identity as well as underlying assumptions related to the change, whether it be teaching, quality education, or student success. People need cues that can help them in rethinking assumptions and reflecting on their identity, such as new tenure and promotion guidelines or revised procedures. Cues help people to begin making new interpretations and rethinking their assumptions. Lastly, the change needs to seem plausible for the campus and individuals being asked to change. Plausibility is different from accuracy. Given the multitide of people, cues, interaction and interpretation, people do their best to create an interpretation that fits these various signals but may not be accurate. An interpretation that fits an institutional narrative, even if it is inaccurate, may be adopted. While Weick described other properties of sensemaking, I will focus on these while describing the vehicles below as they are most pertinent.

It is important to note that other sorts of activities may contribute to sensemaking, but that these were documented in a major study of transformational change in the academy called the Institutional Leadership and Transformation Project— see Eckel and Kezar 2003b. They provide examples for change agents to consider as sense giving vehicles for facilitating change processes on their own campuses.[1] I now review each of the sense giving vehicles listed above.

Ongoing and Widespread Campus Conversations

Ongoing, campus-wide conversations play important roles in helping institutions to adopt new mental models. Conversations allow people to recast key concepts (e.g. how to assess student learning or how the co-curriculum can support classroom learning) to fit new realities and explore how they fit into the emerging future. Through conversations held at retreats, seminars, roundtables, and symposia, faculty, staff and administrators can develop common language and consensus about ideas; they can work to reframe key concepts. In examples from studies, conversations occurred across a series of gatherings, with each new conversation building upon the preceding one; no single conversation stood alone. Conversations also need to be inclusive and widespread and involve open invitations to all different campus stakeholders. The conversations allow people to construct new identities collaboratively and openly (i.e. they are social). In many cases, these conversations are retrospective in that they discuss what was unfolding in light of events that had occurred or in comparison to past beliefs and activities. They frequently start from commentaries on the changing environment. They focus what is plausible for the institution given its history, norms, and social functions.

While those in positions of authority are often able to organize large-scale conversations such as retreats and town meetings, bottom-up leaders can organize brown bag lunches and other smaller gatherings that also allow for sensemaking.

Collaborative Leadership

Another way to create sensemaking is through collaborative leadership, wherein a broad base of stakeholders (e.g. faculty, staff, administrators, students) from across a campus work together toward a change initiative. Collaborative leadership is closely related to the next vehicle, using cross-departmental teams, which involves many people from different units in a particular change initiative or creating a robust and heterogeneous campus network. Collaborative leadership also builds on the notion of having ongoing conversations. As the number of change agents involved increases, individuals become more deeply engaged in questioning what the planned change means for them and for the campus as a whole. Collaborative leadership means involving people in more than a token way, providing them with authority, decision-making power, influence, or some other means of shaping the change process to enable them to exercise agency.

The notion of collaborative leadership helps people reconsider their identity as they are drawn into the change process in an active way. It is also social in that people engage other stakeholders on campus. It is ongoing as the leadership process unfolds over time and creates reference points as new participants bring in additional perspectives that become cues for considering new ideas or approaches.

Developing Cross-departmental Teams or Working Groups

Cross-departmental work teams bring together different combinations of faculty, administrators, and staff (and sometimes students) from across an institution, with each bringing unique perspectives and assumptions. Many institutions conduct most of their work through departmental "silos," with little interaction across units. The cross-fertilization of ideas has often helped to encourage the exchange of ideas and loosen tightly held assumptions. Teams are social; they bring people together to work through a set of concrete tasks. Clearly working teams are social and ongoing—teams typically meet many times to continue previous conversations—so further sensemaking in allowing interaction, particularly among people who may not typically interact. Change agents can use these forums to test the change initiatives fit with the institution and its goals, which enhances the connection to people's identity and plausibility of ideas. Working teams allow an opportunity to plant cues associated with the change agenda that provide the "seeds" of sensemaking. These cues also get distributed widely as the working teams bring together people from so many different units.

While it is easier for those in positions of authority to create cross-departmental teams, bottom-up leaders often form their own informal networks spanning various units to draw on the expertise of individuals with different roles. These networks can also serve as venues for creating sensemaking. In my research, I have documented how students, faculty, and staff have worked through informal campus networks to redefine how to serve underrepresented minorities, rethink what it means to be student centered, come to a new understanding about how to best teach a particular concept or subject, and reevaluate what it means for higher education to serve the public good.

Sponsoring Faculty and Staff Development Opportunities

Professional development is often a critical lever for making new institutional sense. Campuses that are successful at facilitating sensemaking offer a wide range of programs designed to meet the diverse needs of faculty and staff and aligned with the direction of the change agenda. Additionally, institutions often offer orientation programs for new faculty and staff, helping to influence their socialization into the institution or shaping their understanding of what it means to be a good teacher on a particular campus.

Faculty and staff development opportunities bring people together in social situations to learn skills and gain new knowledge related to the change unfolding on campus. Activities can be ongoing, including brown bag discussions, seminars, and faculty discussion groups. They sometimes focus on adapting ideas from elsewhere (e.g. portfolio assessment) and adapting them to make them a plausible fit for local contexts and challenges. Professional development often encourages rethinking of current roles and identity.

While many studies have focused on the ways that people in positions of authority can create professional development, bottom-up leaders also appreciate the opportunities to be involved in professional development. Bottom-up leaders might not have a center for teaching and learning to develop professional development but they can hold a brown bag or seminar series to help other grassroots leaders develop new sense.

Drawing on and Discussing External Ideas

Change processes can often benefit from ideas, comments, suggestions, and strategies originating from outsiders who have challenged key beliefs and assumptions in higher education. In many instances, these outsiders, such as invited speakers, outside change agents, or paid consultants, have been able to ask challenging questions that were difficult for campus change agents to raise on their own. Campuses can create sensemaking by sending faculty, staff, and administrators to activities off campus, including regional or national conferences. Change agents can also facilitate sensemaking by widely distributing thoughtfully selected readings and discussing them at retreats, during regularly scheduled meetings, or through organized reading groups or professional seminars.

Outsiders and the ideas they introduce can help individuals to reflect upon past ways of operating and thinking, challenge current ways of knowing and perceiving, and help an institution to consider which approaches to change are plausible. They provide cues by signaling visibly a new way to think about an issue and bring new perspectives on the changing environment. Outside ideas can be made ongoing by sending people to conferences annually, creating readings groups as part of continuing faculty development opportunities, or creating ongoing speaker series.

Flexible Vision

One of the ways that institutions can create greater opportunities for sensemaking is by creating a vision collectively with staff, faculty, and students for the change initiative. A vision for change created by a small number of people is difficult for others to fully understand. Having large groups of people work together to create a vision means more people will challenge their old views and invest in new views. Furthermore, once the vision is seen as completed or final, new people and stakeholders that may have been overlooked will feel that they were not part of the process. Successful change processes maintain a vision that is "flexible" and open to revision over time. Campus leaders commented how having a vision that is always draft and can be added to as new individuals join the initiative is a way to create ongoing sensemaking. Having a flexible vision allows different people to try out their identity on the new and emerging vision for the organization and to feel they can craft the vision to include a sense of identity that they feel is compatible with them. A flexible vision that is created with other people becomes a social process that is ongoing. And the vision itself provides a reference point providing cues for people to work through their new understandings. Vision also reflects a plausible sense of understanding—there is not one accurate or right vision for an organization to pursue, but one that leaders believe fits the particular social circumstances.

Creating Documents and Concept Papers

Closely related to the notion of a flexible vision is the creation of an evolving document that tries to capture the flexible vision. Change agents often organize processes to develop a guiding document (or a set of documents) or a concept paper to articulate the direction of their change agenda and connect it to important institutional values. Notice that the focus is on facilitating a *process* for creating a document, rather than just developing a document. Although these documents often make important contributions, the process of creating, drafting, circulating, discussing, rewriting, presenting, and polishing them sometimes makes a greater contribution to making new sense. Sensemaking only occurs if a large collective of people is involved in creating a document to guide the change—that the process becomes social. Writing down important ideas gets people to talk about their assumptions and encourages leaders to engage the campus continuously through faculty retreats, cabinet meetings, and campus forums. Creating documents also provides cues for campuses as people have visible places they can look to better understand and consider the proposed change. Even in bottom-up change processes where activities are less likely to be driven by formal documents, less formal concept papers are sometimes created and distributed to others in a network for feedback.

Preparing and Giving Public Presentations

Institutions can create numerous opportunities for a variety of people involved in a change effort to give public presentations. The process of putting together, delivering, and hearing presentations may help unfreeze mental frames and begin to foster the development of new models. First, organizing and creating a presentation demands that people think about their ideas and assumptions. Second, hearing their own presentations and speaking aloud creates another opportunity for an individual or group to catalyze thoughts. The audience also has an opportunity for sensemaking by engaging the ideas presented. Finally, the presenters have an opportunity to hear and respond to questions from the audience and both groups evolve their thinking.

The process of putting together public comments is rarely a solo activity. Public presentations often focus on what an institution or group has become or has accomplished and, thus, can be retrospective. It can also reinforce what is plausible within an institutional or group culture, building upon ongoing work, ideas, and accomplishments. Presentations proclaim what the institution is, what it is becoming, and why, touching on issues of identity. Institutions can bring together discrete elements of the change process and place them in a larger perspective, allowing people to take ideas they might have heard of but then helping connect people to the broader ideas that a change initiative is connected to. For example, calls for interdisciplinary research can be placed in the large dialogue among disciplinary societies and national research organizations and government agencies. The local economic and social needs that could be served through interdisciplinary research can also be explained. By connecting the initiative to many key areas important to the campus, greater connection to individuals' identities can occur.

National Projects Aimed at Sensemaking

ADVANCE Initiative

The ADVANCE Initiative, a National Science Foundation project, utilizes several vehicles that facilitate sense giving for creating change. ADVANCE aims to get more women and underrepresented minorities into STEM disciplines as faculty in higher education institutions. One of the underlying assumptions of the project is that key institutional agents such as department chairs need to develop a new sense about who can be a scientist and what it means to be successful as a scientist. ADVANCE also assumes that people are regularly unaware of the institutional sexism and racism. These underlying values and assumptions need to be surfaced and recognized so that people can make new institutional sense to overcome the barriers they create. One of the major vehicles used is department chair retreats, which allow these campus leaders to meet away from campus and escape the time pressures of their day-to-day work to reconsider their efforts to support faculty. Several campuses participating in ADVANCE have formed theater troupes that reenact meetings and events on campus such as those of hiring committees, promotion and tenure panels, mentoring meetings between a junior faculty member and department chair, or an interpersonal interaction between several faculty members with discriminatory overtones and actions. Department chairs are asked to watch the scenarios, reflect on what has happened, describe their emotions and feelings about the situation, and then some participants may be asked to take a try at role-playing the department chair in each scene.

Having conducted evaluations of several of these department chair retreats and the theater troupe activity myself, it is apparent that reenacting and reflecting upon the scenes helps to elicit a change in mindset among the department chairs participating in the retreat. These activities have been very influential in reshaping participants' thinking. Most department chairs note that they had read about bias before, but were more deeply impacted by witnessing or experiencing the reenactments of the various scenarios. Afterward, they often felt better able to respond in future situations on their campuses. But, most importantly, the reenacting of these common scenarios has allowed them to think about issues in light of their own identity and role, as well as in a retreat setting that gave them time to thoughtfully consider and integrate new ideas into their work. Department chairs experience these types of situations all the time, but usually do not have time to think deeply about them, learn from them, and reconsider their approaches.

The experience also permits opportunities for social interaction and exchange; participants are able to discuss each situation with the other department chairs. Typically, when these situations happen on campuses, they are isolated or do not occur in a setting or time when individuals can share their impressions with one another and rethink the situation. The theater troupe elicits particular cues (e.g. inappropriate language, undesirable body language) that help participants to examine each situation differently than if they experienced them in the day-today flow of their work life. By drawing out salient and important cues to focus the department chairs' attention, the troupes help in creating new sense. The process can also be retrospective; while the department chairs are watching a particular situation, it can elicit prior experiences they have had with a hiring committee or in a promotion and tenure meeting. This allows them to think retrospectively about their own experience and draw upon it as they begin to make new sense. In many ways, the theater troupe presents an interesting and highly beneficial way to create sensemaking that can lead to important changes on campuses.

Project Kaleidoscope

Another approach to creating sensemaking is used in Project Kaleidoscope, a national initiative that aims to promote more engaged and active forms of learning within undergraduate STEM disciplines. In a recent effort, Project Kaleidoscope asked different institutional teams to create symbols, slogans, diagrams, or representations to convey their views of interdisciplinarity and how they could make it a priority on campuses. The campus teams met and created powerful slogans such as "broad is beautiful" or symbols such as interlocking hands working together. These ideas became emblematic and were brought up regularly over the next several years in project meetings as guiding symbols and slogans that expressed what interdisciplinarity meant to them. So, these symbols and slogans became points of reference for them over time and helped in their sensemaking. Each symbol, slogan, or representation was grounded in each individual's identity, but was also created through social interaction with others. Each group was not aiming to come up with an actual definition of interdisciplinarity, but their own unique interpretation, based on their understanding and experience over time.

Another example from Project Kaleidoscope is a vision exercise where campuses are given a set of Lego and asked to build their vision for undergraduate STEM reform. The activity is social in that participants work with other individuals from their campus to create the physical embodiment of their vision. It also builds upon these change agents' identities because the participants are asked to reflect on their creation in the context of how they are rethinking their own work and roles. And, the activity is ongoing because participants can revisit their Lego creation over the course of the three-year project to see how their understanding and sense about STEM reform has changed or stayed the same. In this way, the physical embodiment of the change initiative in the Lego also becomes retrospective, as well; individuals can look back at their sensemaking at one point in time and use it as a reference as they move forward, seeing and understanding advances and changes in their perspectives. The physical embodiment also makes participants' interpretations of the environment more real for them.

Now, I will transition to organizational learning and some ways that change agents can draw upon vehicles to move changes forward.

Vehicles for Creating Organizational Learning

The literature on organizational learning describes certain facilitators that can create learning, such as new ideas, acquisition and distribution of information, professional development, interpretation of data and systems thinking, teams and groups, leadership, promoting doubt, and valuing mistakes. These mechanisms are taken from the literature on both organizational learning and the learning organization.

Introduce New Ideas

Learning is more likely to take place when new ideas are presented, which helps to give a fresh look at current modes of operation. These new ideas can be acquired from experience (e.g. working on another campus), example practices from other individuals and organizations (often identified through benchmarking), or reviewing routine data differently by asking new questions with fresh eyes. Many campus projects I have worked with have used these practices to initiate organizational learning. A common practice is to send individuals to other campuses to see how they approach diversity or technology and then bring those ideas back to their campus. For example, increasingly, campuses are examining what their peers are doing with regard to assessment to see if others' ideas and approaches would work well on their own campus. In addition, campuses are beginning to conduct pilot experiments. An interdisciplinary course might be offered simultaneously with a disciplinary course on the same subject to determine how interdisciplinarity impacts student learning. These types of experiments help to provide evidence of approaches that work.

Acquisition and Distribution of Information

In addition to bringing new ideas or information in to prompt learning, data and information about the system itself can help prompt opportunities for identifying problems and learning. Organizations need to create robust information gathering and distribution systems in order to facilitate learning in this way. On college campuses, institutional research offices often play a key role in acquiring, disseminating, and packaging data for campus teams and decision-making. Campuses that create organizational learning support data collection on important issues for the campus such as student success, learning outcomes, productivity, cost analysis, and the like. While institutional researchers, offices are present on many campuses, many challenges exist to them being part of a learning process. First, many institutional research offices on campuses are not set up to create learning and merely collect data to address regulatory mandates; they are not focused on campus improvement. Second, higher education's siloed organizational structure often makes data acquisition difficult since different units do not always share information. Data cannot just be collected, but must be presented to decision-makers in ways that mean they can easily review and make sense of it. Data presentation is just as important as data collection because it aids interpretation, but IR offices are not versed in data presentation.

Professional Development toward the Use of Data

An organization can have a strong institutional research office and knowledge management system in place, but lack the professional development to help people across the campus to use data toward meaningful inquiry that can lead to change. Many early studies of organizational learning suggested that organizations focused too much on the development of data and reports and too little on their digestion and use by individuals who needed to turn data into knowledge. Currently, very few campuses have the infrastructure in place to help campus stakeholders to use data effectively in decision-making processes and change initiatives. Recent literature on institutional research has been promoting the importance of including institutional researchers on the campus team so they can help to teach individuals on these teams to make better use of data (Borden and Kezar 2012). Few campuses actually have any training in place for faculty and staff, typically because they do not think individuals would take advantage of such opportunities.

Interpretation of Data and Systems Thinking

The interpretation of data is not a straightforward process. A variety of issues can emerge that prevent knowledge generation and systems thinking from occurring. Many scholars refer to data and information as distinct from knowledge (Brown and Duguid 2000). Knowledge is created by thinking about or interpreting data and information, sometimes in ways that can aid in addressing complex problems. People tend to look at data and think about short-term fixes rather than longer-term solutions. The same set of data can lead people to arrive at very different conclusions or solutions, depending on the perspective and interpretation brought to the data. When interpreting data, people tend to look for simple cause-and-effect relationships, focusing on local causation and often leading to a misdiagnosis of issues. Systems thinking, by contrast, is based on the notion that there is a set of causal relationships, which are often nonlocal and complex, that can be described and can lead to greater awareness and learning.

People also have a tendency to break things into pieces, which prevents them from seeing problems more holistically. Silos of information impede the systematic analysis of data. As noted earlier, offices and divisions across campus often do not share data. Without adequate data across multiple units, systems thinking is not likely to occur. So, data teams need professional development and strong leaders who can help with data interpretation; merely having data will not lead to the best learning.

Creating Groups or Teams

Interpretation of data tends to be richer when multiple perspectives are brought to bear on the data. Organizational learning scholars typically describe the importance of creating a team, committee, or task force to review, interpret, question, and turn data into knowledge (Kezar 2005a). Yet all of the studies also show that the creation of a group alone will not yield learning because groups are susceptible to dysfunctional operation without savvy facilitation. Group members need to be carefully selected, orientated, and socialized. An environment needs to be created in which members get to know each other, trust is developed, leadership is provided to help move the group along toward review of the data, and openness and strong interpersonal interactions allow people to question and share openly. Also, research demonstrates that information garnered in groups and teams needs to be translated out to the broader organization and communicated in ways that are capable of convincing other stakeholders who have not been a part of the learning process.

Critical Leadership to Enable Dissonance and Prompting Doubt

Organizational members all hold assumptions about various processes, for example whether hiring practices are fair, admission processes are selective, or enough support is in place for students. If individuals interact with any of these processes or functions in their work, they are likely to hold views about how they operate that are potentially more favorable than reality. Learning is more likely to be prompted when data that challenge existing beliefs are provided and people are open to questioning their beliefs, leading organizational stakeholders to suggest new directions. If people believe that they are already successful in educating students and providing enough support, they will only be dissuaded from their positions if data about high dropout rates or poor learning outcomes demonstrate that they are not correct. Campuses that want to create opportunities for doubt to be considered will tend to put an outsider or critic who will force uncomfortable discussions on a committee or team working on a task.

Valuing Mistakes

Similarly to promoting doubt, organizational learning theorists describe the importance of valuing mistakes in the learning process. On most campuses, to admit that a particular service or program is a failure would be political suicide, perhaps bringing an end to one's career. Colleges and universities are not unique in their lack of tolerance for mistakes. As a result, the ability to learn from them is frequently lost. Often, our fear of sharing data stems from a concern that it will point out mistakes or low performance. So, instead leaders do not make information available to other campus stakeholders or the public. This also results in very controlled data being released by institutional research officers, which can withhold information needed by campus teams to identify problems. Yet, until it is acceptable to acknowledge mistakes and learn from them, organizations will not undergo the important learning needed.

Examples of these vehicles for organizational learning have been documented in Bauman (2005), Dill (1999), Leiberman (2005), and Ramaley and Holland (2005). While they are not always common, these vehicles are beginning to emerge on some campuses and within particular change projects. In fact, the Equity Scorecard, Achieving the Dream, and the Campus Diversity Initiative, profiled next, demonstrate these practices in use.

National Projects focused on Organizational Learning

Equity Scorecard

The *Equity Scorecard* is a national project that uses principles of organizational learning to create changes specifically related to increasing the success of under-represented students on college campuses. Using the best principles from organizational learning, the Equity Scorecard first calls for assembling a cross-campus team including expertise from institutional research, faculty, and other staff who work with and contribute to the success of students of color. Next, campus teams audit their current success with students of color on a variety of measures to help understand the specific nature of the problem on campus. Then, campuses use a benchmarking tool in order to identify the necessary campus interventions. The review of data in teams takes place with a trained facilitator who helps campuses to take an inquiry-based approach and doubt-oriented mindset to sidestep many of the organizational defenses and barriers to learning. As a result, the teams are more likely to undergo a learning process. The ultimate goal of reviewing the data and working together as a team is to create interventions and an action plan for helping to promote the success of students of color.

As noted on the Equity Scorecard website:

> Evidence team members learn to shift the focus away from commonly held beliefs in which responsibility for academic success and failure rests entirely with students. Instead, they begin to ask what their institution, and they themselves, can do to improve results. This change in emphasis allows them to approach the problem of inequity as a solvable problem of professional practice.
>
> (Center for Urban Education n.d.)

In the past decade, the Equity Scorecard has worked with nearly 100 campuses across the country, helping them to think differently and creating significant organizational change.

Achieving the Dream

Achieving the Dream is another national project that uses the principles of organizational learning to drive change. The project began in 2004 and currently works with nearly 200 colleges, 100 coaches and advisors, and 15 state policy teams work-ing in 32 states and the District of Columbia. The aim of the project is to help more community college students, particularly low-income students and students of color, stay in school and earn a college certificate or degree. The components of the project that focus on organizational learning are using evidence and data to sup-port institutional improvements that help students be more successful. The project also helps to generate knowledge by creating action-based inquiry studies on cam-puses to support action. Much like the Equity Scorecard, Achieving the Dream creates campus teams that work with data to better understand why students are succeeding and failing, then use data to create interventions and new approaches for working with students. Institutional teams are supported by data coaches who help them to run institutional reports, interpret data, and learn how to use data for decision-making and change. The project is organized around a five-step process for increasing student success through institutional improvement:

1.   Obtaining a commitment to the process from each participating college;
2.   Using data to prioritize actions;
3.   Engaging stakeholders in supporting interventions that the data suggest are appropriate;
4.   Implementing the necessary changes and using data to evaluate and refine the process on an ongoing basis; and
5.   Establishing a culture of continuous improvement, supported through the earlier steps, that sustains the change beyond the initial project and creates the infrastructure of a learning organization on campus.

Recognizing that creating a culture of evidence-based decision-making, some-times called an organizational learning environment, is difficult in higher educa-tion. The process involves a network of support, including the data coaches, the Achieving the Dream support organization, and state policy advisers who provide professional development, help with data interpretation and presentation, and ask questions to create doubt. Achieving the Dream also recognizes the importance of leadership committing to the process and providing the needed support so that a learning culture can be created. The project has created many resources that can be used by other campuses to support their own move towards organizational learning:

-   Monthly data notes that present data on important topics relating to stu-dent achievement such as gateway courses, remedial education, differences in student outcomes, and disaggregated data about retention;
-   A series of publications, titled *Cutting Edge*, that provides guidance on topics such as building institutional capacity for data-informed decision-making; and
-   The Knowledge Center, which includes publications on a wide variety of topics from engaging faculty in review of data, to interventions derived

from data analysis, to how to conduct particular forms of data analysis such as cohort analysis, to ways to build the institutional research function within the organization, as well as a variety of change readiness tools.

Campus Diversity Initiative

Another major project that uses an organizational learning approach is the *Campus Diversity Initiative*. The Campus Diversity Initiative partnered with 28 independent colleges and universities in California from 2000–5, working strategically to improve campus diversity. The information provided here has been drawn directly from the project's final report, *Building Capacity: A Study of the Impact of the James Irvine Foundation Campus Diversity Initiative*.[2] Campuses that participated in the project increased their capacity for diversity work by making it a priority and building leadership. Organizational learning was created through initial campus audits, priority setting, creating frameworks to direct their work, and in an evaluation process, where they followed the progress of their implementation. The organizational learning approach was mostly embedded in the evaluation model, which helped each campus to use data to monitor its achievements and outcomes on an ongoing basis. The campuses that actively utilized the evaluation process to guide and assess their actions had the strongest motivation to achieve their goals, pointing to the efficacy of organizational learning. Those institutions that continually engaged in a cross-institutional analysis of progress understood how and where the process needed to be corrected to ensure the successful attainment of goals. This process helped those campuses that were successful to actually understand why they were successful. Furthermore, by providing a systematic means for monitoring and interpreting efforts the Campus Diversity Initiative brought together key participants on each campus and adopted a more collective approach, which contrasted sharply with other evaluation models that rely on a single person or small group to evaluate outcomes and create reports.

The study found that an organizational learning model of evaluation did not come naturally to many of the campuses. They needed to be trained repeatedly to engage this approach. The Campus Diversity Initiative reports documented many common challenges that emerge when trying to create organizational learning to inform future efforts in higher education:

- Team formation is critical to success. Campuses that did not set up truly representative cross-campus teams did not make as much progress.
- Campuses with strong institutional research functions are more likely to make progress.
- Institutional research offices that provide weak data or reports are less likely to support progress.
- Fear that the results of data analysis will expose poor progress and affect an institution's reputation prevents learning.
- Including institutional research staff on teams helps to facilitate learning.

- Campuses generally do not like to set specific benchmarks to be met, which prevents effective data use and accountability.
- Data silos on campuses lead to a lack of communication, which impairs their capacity to learn.
- Open forums for presenting data beyond the teams helps to secure buy-in from stakeholders for the ideas and interventions that are proposed. Efforts for change are helped when ideas move from the team to the broader campus.

The important recommendations for future projects utilizing organizational learning include building institutional research capacity, utilizing institutional frameworks, helping campuses to establish and use benchmarks, having broad-based campus groups review data, being honest and open about problems and mistakes that are discovered, and maintaining effective communication and information flow throughout the process. The Campus Diversity Initiative project points to both the promise and some of the challenges of an organizational learning approach to change, which often does not fit well within higher education's current structure or the culture and values of many institutions.

Summary

The primary aim of this chapter was to help readers develop a better understanding of what second-order change entails and when it is necessary in change processes. The second goal of this chapter was to describe approaches for creating second-order change through sensemaking or organizational learning—key strategies in *social cognition theories* of change. Both approaches emerged out of studies that sought to discover why second-order change is often so difficult and why resistance often emerges.

There are two main reasons that change agents should remain committed to considering and creating sensemaking and organizational learning, even though each has had many challenges. First, many of the important changes that are proposed within higher education will not occur unless sensemaking or organizational learning occurs. Second, government agencies and foundations believe in the efficacy of organizational learning, in particular, and will continue to fund initiatives in this area. Accreditation agencies are also investing a great deal of energy, effort, and resources to help campuses to use data for learning and creating change. As more and more external organizations see the potential of organizational learning and provide support for creating additional infrastructure for learning on campuses, it may become less of a challenge to get higher education institutions to use this approach, making it more a part of everyday operations.

While today's campuses may not feel prepared to be learning organizations, they have already come a long way from 20 years ago. Institutional research offices are becoming commonplace and more support is being provided to build their capacity. Information and data are increasingly shared on campuses among stakeholders who sometimes never received data before. Faculty are being required to consider student outcomes assessments and think through the use of data to changing their practice through accreditation processes. In the next decade or so, campuses will increasingly become organizations where organizational learning is not only facilitated, but perhaps expected. The decision for change agents is whether sensemaking, which might be easier, or organizational learning is needed.

five
Context of
Change

Albert is a staff member at a liberal arts college that is creating a new student leadership development program. He conducts research and investigates benchmarks for leadership development programs from various sectors—business, policy, and non-profit organizations. He has discovered many strong models. He develops a proposal for the new program and brings it to the student affairs division meeting. Several people object to the proposal because it has adopted models from outside higher education and they feel the somewhat hierarchical models do not fit into the culture of the academy. Another group makes reference to a previous proposal for a leadership development program that seems to have had many of the same elements, which failed. Yet, others ask why the proposal does not include the Council of the Advancement of Standards' guidelines for leadership development. A high-level administrator notes that she likes the emphasis on entrepreneurialism in the model. The division head asks Albert to refashion the proposal and bring it to the next meeting, taking into account all of the feedback provided.

What was Albert missing in his preliminary attempt to promote the change and how can he be more successful at the next meeting?

In addition to being cognizant of the type of change being implemented, to be successful change agents also need to map and understand the various contexts that shape change initiatives, whether historical, external, or organizational. This short vignette about Albert illustrates some of the elements of context that are often missed and can affect a change process. This chapter looks at research on how the external and organizational contexts affect change processes and how learning about various contextual conditions can help change agents to be more successful. This chapter encourages change agents to look at the process of change as inherently embedded within larger contexts. It draws upon *evolutionary, institutional* and *cultural theories,* as well as practices that help change agents to examine and understand the broader environment and how it might shape change processes. It focuses on the second part of the change macro framework summarized in Figure 5.1.

The context for higher education continues to evolve and leaders need to be aware of how to create change within an increasingly academic-capitalist environment. In the past decade, the academy has moved to a largely non-tenure-track faculty, funding is extremely limited, and revenue generation has become the focus of institutional operations. These changes fundamentally alter the possibilities for change and the approach. In this chapter, I remind the reader that this changed context needs to be considered when developing initiatives. The aspects of the changed environment were already detailed in Chapter 1.

Early research conceptualizing change tended to ignore context and sought to identify universal principles that could be used regardless of the situation or organizational setting. These notions are embedded in the step or stage models of change, which was noted in the Preface, that were the hallmark of *scientific management* approaches to change. Recent research from *evolutionary, cultural* and *institutional theories* demonstrated the impact of all sorts of different contexts. So, let's look more closely at the different contexts that meaningfully affect change. While Albert's change did not relate to all of these contexts, it did reflect some important ones to consider, including the impact of professional societies, trends

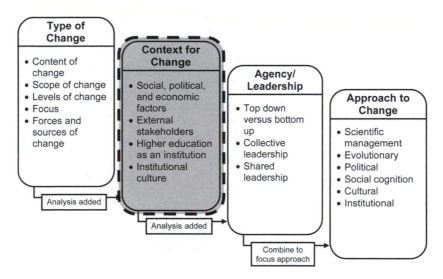

Figure 5.1. Change macro framework: context of change.

toward academic capitalism, and the unique traditions of higher education such as shared governance and egalitarianism.

Evolutionary and *institutional theories* describe two key sources of influence within various contexts. First, there are social, political, and economic factors to be considered. Second, stakeholders within the environment have an important role and cannot be overlooked (see Figure 5.2). The chapter begins by describing these two sources of influence. Next, it will highlight two main contexts described in *institutional* and *cultural theories.* They are the institutional context of higher education as a unique sector and the institutional culture that exists on particular campuses, which varies by institutional type and other conditions. The chapter will end with a review of the concept of organizational capacity for change, which can be better understood once these various contexts are analyzed.

Social, Political, and Economic Factors

At the very broadest level, change agents might need to consider the social, political, and economic factors that shape or relate to a particular change initiative. While many campus leaders are likely to be aware of declining state budgets, change agents often stop there. Yet, there are so many other external trends that are important to understand. For example, campuses that are working to provide healthcare benefits for the partners of gay and lesbian university employees should be attentive to the string of recent legislative and initiative victories favoring same-sex marriage rights in several states. The success of these recent bills and ballot

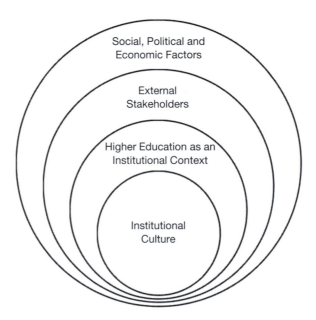

Figure 5.2. Layers of context that shape change.

initiatives suggests an increasingly hospitable climate within particular states. Campuses can leverage this positive momentum in pursuing a change in policy.

Another example is to follow public policy polling about views of higher education and affordability. If a community college is about to propose a bond measure for increased funding, it will do better if it understands local public views on affordability. Understanding the views that stakeholders have of the campus, as well, will have a significant impact on the bond initiative and its success. Because such initiatives are incredibly costly and require intense amounts of time, having an informed understanding of the probability of winning and concerns that need to be addressed is important.

While social views are powerful, political factors also loom large in higher education. Perhaps the most profound example of the impact of government policies on higher education is financial aid, which has enabled substantial enrollment growth in higher education. Financial aid has helped low-income students afford a college education, as well as to believe higher education is an opportunity that is available to them. Another example is the G.I. Bill (formally known as the Servicemen's Readjustment Act), which resulted in a surge of veteran enrollments. The G.I. Bill prompted higher education institutions to begin to change services and programs to better serve older or non-traditional students who often had different work and life experience, as well as families. The Morrill Act of 1862, also known as the Land Grant College Act, created new institutional types (e.g. land grant institutions) and additional purposes for higher education, opening extension and outreach offices. The list of federal legislation relating to higher education is long. Some other examples include Title IX that ensures gender equity in athletics programs, the Federal Educational Rights and Privacy Act (FERPA) that protects students' right to privacy, and the Americans with Disabilities Act (ADA) that ensures that campuses are accessible to physically challenged individuals. Campuses are also subject to affirmative action laws ensuring that historically underrepresented groups are provided an advantage in hiring if they have equal qualifications, civil rights laws that protect individuals from discrimination, hazing regulations, and alcohol enforcement laws to ensure a safe environment for students to live and study.

State laws, regulations, and policies vary and usually relate to financial aid policies such as the Georgia Hope scholarships, bond measures, and performance funding plans. There are also college completion initiatives, tuition policies, the recently introduced common core standards which relate to college readiness, and state-level immigration policies that are impacting access for certain populations. Additionally, each state has commissions and coordinating boards that regulate and shape education policy for state institutions.

A more detailed description of an example of federal legislation and its impact on campuses may be helpful. The Bayh–Dole Act of 1982 made it possible for colleges and universities to make money from patents and licenses they created, which encouraged universities to profit from inventions and to become more entrepreneurial. Since the Bayh–Dole Act was implemented, patents and licenses for higher education institutions have gone up exponentially. Campuses have been able to use this additional revenue stream to offset shrinking state appropriations, but the law has also led to concerns about the availability of research findings that are often funded by the federal government, as well as the non-disclosure of research that might impact a profitable patent or license. At the state level, the California Civil Rights Initiative, or Proposition 209, meant that colleges and universities could no longer consider race and ethnicity in the admissions process, which changed the demographics on many campuses.

The government typically focuses on setting policy relating to public policy issues that are of more general concern—finances, tuition, access, accountability, and equity, for example. Government policies can be levers or barriers to change, but need to be acknowledged. They can be substantial barriers if unacknowledged. Yet, in recent years, the list of new legislation has been staggering, so it is harder for change agents to meaningfully follow all of the new laws and regulations.

Clearly, economic trends have also shaped change efforts in higher education. In recent years, the recession has caused many campuses to restructure, reduce staff and faculty, and rethink their priorities and missions. Economic growth after World War II fueled growth in higher education, resulting in a much larger system, the development of community colleges, and enrollment growth and increasing research funding. Economic trends have been inextricably linked to the growth and retrenchment of higher education for decades.

These broader trends are more likely to be overlooked than internal factors by change agents working at the grassroots level. Individuals at this level often do not have the same infrastructure that administrators have to map these forces, such as vice presidents of external affairs, directors of outreach, or directors of legislative affairs. Even administrators who have resources to follow trends tend to narrowly focus only on state and federal policies or trends that shape campus budgets and policies. While *evolutionary theories* often illustrate the impact of external forces, *institutional theory* is helpful for charting how these farther afield forces shape and impact campuses.

Campuses often enjoy a great degree of autonomy and can forget to map these broader social, political, and economic conditions, which can impact change initiatives on campuses either positively or negatively. Change agents should be aware of trends and think strategically to mitigate or leverage these forces in order to succeed in creating change. Often, these social, political, and economic factors involve external stakeholder groups such as foundations, government agencies, and disciplinary societies that also shape and impact change in a variety of ways.

External Stakeholders

When Albert presented his leadership development program, he discovered that there are many external groups and stakeholders that need to be considered when developing a change initiative. In Albert's particular situation, the standards developed by the Council for Advancement of Standards in Higher Education, a professional organization, were brought up as a key document that should have been considered when preparing the proposal. *Evolutionary* and *institutional theories* stress the importance of tracking, anticipating, and leveraging external factors, trends, and stakeholders for managing and creating changes. In Chapter 2, under institutional theory, I described the societal versus organizational fields that shape higher education. Societal fields refer to policymakers who through government regulations shape the higher education environment, pressures that often come from outside the sector. However, the organizational field is made up of entities external to campus, but that are more closely related, such as disciplinary societies or professional organizations. Both are considered external stakeholders, but they have different relationships to campuses. Change agents are often more likely to be aware of influences in the organizational field.

Higher education is a very interdependent sector that operates in conjunction with disciplinary societies, professional societies, the federal and state governments, government agencies such as the National Science Foundation (NSF), unions, private foundations, and accreditation agencies. There is an extended ecology that shapes higher education and needs to be considered when planning for any change proposal. In fact, many of these external stakeholders have a role in helping to improve higher education, so they become primary players in our efforts. Take, for example, accreditation agencies, which now consider their primary objective to be the improvement of higher education—essentially, their role involves creating ongoing change. Private foundations and government agencies typically provide funding to support higher education and may stipulate that institutions alter their policies, practices, or processes to become more interdisciplinary, improve access, or become more internationalized. These external groups can be used as levers for change, but can also serve as impediments. This vast web of actors and groups—foundations, government agencies—represents another set of factors that successful change agents need to map. This means being aware of their activities, understanding their priorities, and recognizing their interests. As discussed earlier in sections on *institutional theory*, the influence of these various organizations and groups is not always explicitly noticed and has been referred to by some as "the invisible hand" (Altbach et al. 2011). Below, I discuss a few groups and their influence on higher education change processes. As campus change agents begin to consider an initiative, they need to be aware of how these external stakeholders might impact their efforts negatively or provide leverage for advancing them. Additionally, these stakeholders often pressure higher education for changes that shape campus contexts and often need to be managed by leaders. For example, there are calls for eliminating remediation courses from college by policymakers. If remediation were eliminated without examining the consequences, hundreds of thousands of students might be negatively affected.

Foundations

Various scholars have examined how the funding initiatives of foundations have shaped the direction of higher education (Altbach et al. 2011). Foundations have long been a source of innovation shaping new efforts in higher education. In the past, foundations created new fields of study, introduced or fueled new pedagogies such as service learning, supported multicultural efforts, developed campus and community partnerships, created international initiatives, and the like (Rojas 2012). Currently, the Bill and Melinda Gates Foundation is funding efforts to use technology to provide access to higher education to more and new students. The Lumina Foundation has also funded efforts to increase productivity in higher education and improve access and completion. The Teagle Foundation is supporting campuses' efforts to conduct student outcomes assessments, as well as to think about the quality of liberal arts education in a new era. Being aware of these and other external funders may help to provide leverage and support for change agents' work. Even if an initiative does not receive funding, the status associated with working in a manner that is aligned or coordinated with a major foundation's programs can advance efforts to create change.

Accreditation Agencies

Accreditation agencies are the entities tasked with ensuring the quality of higher education. In recent years, their efforts have focused on promoting changes for ongoing quality improvement. There are six regional accreditation bodies, as well as many different field-based or disciplinary accreditors that evaluate and credential colleges and universities. The Council for Higher Education Accreditation (CHEA) is a non-profit organization of colleges and universities that serves as the national advocate for voluntary, self-regulation through accreditation. The major power that these entities have for promoting or creating change is that institutions that are not certified by regional accreditors cannot receive federal financial aid (disciplinary accreditation is not tied to financial aid). The accreditation system is complex, so I recommend that individuals who are not familiar with these entities and their work visit the websites of the appropriate regional accreditors (e.g. Middle States, New England, North Central, Northwest, Western, and Southern) and CHEA for more information.

Accreditation is often criticized for not creating enough innovation in higher education or setting low standards and minimal qualifications. But, regional accreditors have pushed for some significant changes in higher education. For example, in recent years they have supported efforts to induce campuses to assess student learning outcomes and address the benefits and challenges of educational technology and online learning. Some disciplinary accreditation bodies, such as those in the fields of Business or Engineering, have also been major forces for change in shifting the curriculum, developing outcomes assessments, and mandating new approaches to teaching and learning. Many campuses have made changes as a result of an accreditation visit; change agents have sometimes used the accreditation process as a lever for change. While foundations are clearly focused more on introducing innovations and governments seek to influence policies around funding, access, and equity, accreditation is a lever for creating changes around more basic campus infrastructure and operations like governance (in addition to shaping the teaching and learning environment). Accreditation has been used to improve communication and governance structures, clarify faculty, staff, and administrative responsibilities, and redirect resources. Accreditation focuses on campus processes, so it is often best used to push for changes in processes like governance, budgeting, and planning. However, it increasingly emphasizes the importance of improving student learning outcomes and may be leveraged for changes in this area, as well.

Disciplinary Societies

Disciplinary societies shape the ways that scholars within and among fields think about knowledge construction—what are the ethical obligations of scholars, should knowledge be interdisciplinary, or should work occur in collaborative teams? Should scholarship be oriented more toward practical purposes or remain more abstract? How can research benefit from international scholars working together? How can technology facilitate scholarship? Disciplinary societies also influence the way that faculty think about teaching. For example, is teaching problem-based, collaborative, or organized around service learning? They also inform faculty members' understanding of their roles and responsibilities, such as their priorities for research and teaching, participation in governance, and attitude toward service. Disciplinary societies occasionally release statements about their positions on these and many other issues. They also establish professional guidelines that shape the behavior and values of their members. As change agents consider initiatives that will result in changes relating to research, teaching, student life, or faculty roles, they should be aware of disciplinary societies' policies, documents, and views. *Cultural theories* of change can be invoked to better understand how disciplinary societies influence change through their socialization of professionals by shaping or perpetuating values and incentives in each field, which can be strong and hard to shift.

Government Agencies

While government, in a broader sense, has shaped higher education through legislation and policy (described earlier in the chapter, on pp. 86–88), a number of specific government agencies often have a very direct role in influencing higher education. For example, the National Institutes of Health, National Endowment for the Humanities, and National Science Foundation have been instrumental in affecting policies and practice in the different fields of study in higher education. They have also supplied funding for the creation and advancement of research, new program areas, or professional development to improve teaching. These agencies also shape the fields that students will be employed in after they graduate. For example, the Securities and Exchange Commission might advise or inform proposed changes for business student education. Over the years, many of these agencies have provided funding to persuade higher education to experiment with new forms of teaching or more collaborative and interdisciplinary research.

There are many other external groups, but this helps to demonstrate how various groups shape higher education, but in quite different ways and with varying emphases. These groups are often present, but may be ignored or overlooked by change agents who are not taking a systemic view. Albert would have been better prepared if he thought about these external contexts and stakeholders, which are reviewed in *evolutionary* and *institutional theories* of change.

Higher Education Sector as an Institutional Context

Albert did not consider higher education as a particular context in which change happens. He found that his colleagues were concerned about the imposition of values from business into his proposal for a leadership development program. Values relating to leadership in business are often considered to be quite different from those associated with the historic principles of shared governance long embedded in the academy. Thus, one of the first factors that should be considered and analyzed for any change initiative is its fit within the higher education context, specifically, which is itself in transition. Change initiatives and processes that violate the values of the academy are more likely to encounter difficulty.

Institutional theory suggests that higher education is a social institution. Like other social institutions (e.g. healthcare), there is the belief that higher education should not be swayed as much by external forces or market conditions and should maintain long-standing missions that are important to society. Studies of non-profit institutions demonstrate that resisting change and maintaining stable operations is important for survival; it leads to growth and renewal (Salipante and Golden-Biddle 1996). Change processes within institutions often involve extensive debate among many different stakeholders because campuses serve so many distinct societal needs. The alteration of any aspect of the campus may mean jeopardizing a particular, long-standing mission. *Institutional theory* suggests that institutions need to respond slowly and with great care, as their underlying character can be dramatically altered with a change to mission.

Higher education's status as a social institution suggests a unique change process is needed. It is a less open system, environmental influences are frequently met with suspicion, and deeply held organizational habits, norms, and logics will likely need to be examined to effectively create change. It is often difficult for people to recognize the unique characteristics of higher education institutions, particularly since many professionals in higher education have only worked within the sector and do not recognize how other institutions or sectors like businesses, the government, or medical institutions might operate differently. In this section, I summarize some of the meaningful ways that higher education has a distinctive context in which changes will occur, and that taking these factors into account when formulating a strategy for change will help facilitate the implementation of change. Yet, as I will emphasize toward the end of this section, some of these elements of the traditional higher education institutional context are eroding and some of these unique factors are no longer as prevalent on many campuses.

Professional Bureaucracy

Higher education is a professional bureaucracy, a unique type of institution with a distinctive structure and culture that is different than what is found in businesses or government. Professional bureaucracies are characterized by dual power and authority systems. Professionals (e.g. faculty and sometimes staff) are considered to be autonomous workers who are involved in their own evaluation, develop policies governing their working conditions, and plan and coordinate much of their work on their own. They are given a high degree of authority and autonomy with the understanding that they will be accountable to one another and will engage in self-policing and peer review. In order to ensure this accountability, faculty undergo lengthy training and socialization that begins in graduate school and continues with the observation of professional standards and going through tenure and promotion processes. Also, because they possess specialized knowledge, higher education professionals are considered to be different from traditional workers or employees in other organizations. For example, administrators serve as managers of institutions, but historically have not had a direct role in overseeing the work of faculty. Instead, they oversee other sorts of campus operations such as facilities, budgeting, and planning. When it comes to the academic mission, administrators share authority and responsibility for decision-making with faculty such as determining the curriculum, pedagogies that will be utilized, and aspects of student life. The administrative or bureaucratic structure operates differently from the academic realm of the campus; it is characterized by more hierarchical or top-down relationships between individuals and operates more like a traditional business organization wherein managers direct and coordinate the work of employees.

Shared Governance

The professional bureaucracy structure also resulted in shared governance, an agreement between governing boards, presidents, administrators, faculty, and students about the appropriate role of each part of the campus community in decision-making. Faculty are granted primary decision-making authority in areas such as curriculum, pedagogies, and student life (e.g. advising, co-curriculum), while administrators are granted primary responsibility for finances, alignment of strategy and policy, and creation of overarching institutional goals. As professionals, they have a right to participate in decision-making and emphasize their collective responsibility for governing the institution. This structure is not without its difficulties and tensions. Administrators are often pulled toward standardizing and centralizing processes, whereas faculty often favor decentralization and collaboration on processes. Also, bureaucracies tend to focus on goals of efficiency, while professionals tend to focus more on effectiveness and downplay efficiency.

Dual Power and Authority Structures

The tradition of the professional bureaucracy has created a unique power and authority structure within colleges and universities that differs from most organizations. Authority is the right of a person or office to demand actions of others and expect those demands to be met (Birnbaum 1991). Power is generally described as the ability of a person to influence or exercise control over others. Within the bureaucratic part of the campus, power and authority are clearer and are established through a chain of command. However, within the academic part of the organization, power and authority are not so clearly defined by position or hierarchy. There are faculty members who hold positions of authority, such as department chair or head of the academic senate, which seem to parallel more traditional authority structures in organizations. However, the literature about department chairs suggests they are conflicted when it comes to their authority and status in relation to other faculty and do not see themselves as having bureaucratic power and authority, favoring working through more collegial, expert, or referent forms of power. Collegiality is a deferential form of power where long-time colleagues garner power. But in general power differences are minimized. Expert power is exercised when individuals allow themselves to be influenced by others because they possess some special knowledge. Referent power represents the willingness to be influenced by another person because he or she is identified as a colleague or as being someone who is trustworthy. Various studies have identified how faculty are more likely to be influenced by expert or reference power of others whom they perceive as holding specialized academic knowledge, who share similar values, and whom they trust as colleagues.

Governing Boards

Scholars have also identified how internal authority and power systems are impacted by the external authority vested in trustees. College and university governing boards or boards of trustees have the legal right to act on behalf of systems or institutions, deriving their authority from the government, political organizations, and statewide governing boards. Governing boards can attempt to use bureaucratic or position-based forms derived from their legal standing. Birnbaum (1991) speaks to the unique tradition of boards of trustees in the United States, which ultimately have complete authority over decision-making for institutions, but have decided to delegate decision-making to administrators that can be revoked at any time. The power that boards of trustees possess is quite unusual for institutions but has not been utilized by most boards, yet this could be an area that is key to change processes as they have so much formal authority. For example, a board could dictate a new general education curriculum. While boards have not exerted this power, they have the authority to dictate such a change.

Collegium

The professional bureaucratic structure and shared governance model contribute to a collegial environment on many campuses. Collegiality is embodied in a focus on consensus, consultation, and deliberation, which is perceived as more important than efficiency. Many campuses strive for common commitments, shared values, aspirations, and try to equalize power as they see professionals as generally holding equal status. Collegiality also suggests mutual respect and equality among members of the community. For many years, administrators were individuals who moved up through the ranks of faculty and were seen as first among equals. This tradition is fading as administrators increasingly come from outside higher education.

Loose Coupling

The professional bureaucratic structure also results in what is described as being a loosely coupled system. Tightly coupled organizations are centralized and highly controlled, with a strict division of labor. By contrast, loosely coupled systems are uncoordinated, have greater differentiation among component units, and are characterized by high degrees of specialization among workers, with low predictability of future actions. The academic part of the campus has resulted in many decentralized processes wherein decisions are made at the level where the expertise resides, such as at the department or unit level. Because of decentralization, many campus processes are uncoordinated and draw upon the specialization of different workers. Change processes within loosely coupled systems tend to favor local, bottom-up changes. Many researchers have suggested that loose coupling also results in a more political environment for change where power dynamics are unclear (Cohen and March 1974).

Organized Anarchy

Some people suggest that the loosely coupled nature of the system and multiple power and authority structures have resulted in an organized anarchical process and system of decision-making (Cohen and March 1974). Loose coupling feels like anarchy because the formal authority structures do not accurately represent where power resides and influence processes are very ambiguous and hard to understand. The fact that many decisions are decentralized and are not always communicated through the few central decision-making structures, like academic senates, makes these local processes somewhat invisible. Further, Cohen and March (1974) suggested that higher education's inherently ambiguous goals, unclear technologies, and uneven participation in decision-making contribute to higher education being an organized anarchy. Different groups on campus (students, faculty, and staff) often identify distinctive goals for the campus. Even decided-upon goals such as quality education might vary in terms of interpretation or understanding across groups. The technology infrastructure is teaching and learning that are offered in many different ways and there is no clear agreement on this process. Because of the dual authority structures, faculty participate in only some decisions. Different faculty are called for different types of decisions. Therefore, different faculty are revolving in and out of decision processes, which leads to uneven and fluid participation.

Institutional theory suggests that change processes will be more successful if change agents acknowledge loose coupling, dual authority, or organized anarchy because adopting a less linear change process will be more likely to be responsive to multiple, often hidden forces and influences.

Values driven

Researchers have also identified how higher education institutions are values-driven institutions, but with a competing and complex values structure (Birnbaum 1991; Clark 1983). All organizations are guided by values and beliefs, but what differentiates colleges and universities is that operations are often driven by a more diverse set of values or belief systems that are sometimes conflicting or contrasting. Clark (1983) documented some of the shared and deeply held values of members of the academy, including the importance of research, integrity in the research process, freedom to teach what is considered appropriate, the importance of shared governance and academic freedom, specialization of knowledge, and broad access and inclusion. Yet, scholars have also emphasized that beyond some of these shared value systems there is a great contrast between values among different disciplines with different priorities and perspectives. For example, mathematicians may stress logic and consistency, whereas art historians might stress perspective and interpretation. Faculty in general, as professionals, value deliberation, autonomy, collegiality, shared power, and effectiveness. However, administrators tend to value efficiency, hierarchy, bureaucratic norms and structures, rationality, action, and direct control.

Varying roles (e.g. faculty, administration, and staff), vastly different disciplines (e.g. humanities, science), and stakeholder groups (e.g. alumni, community agencies, local political figures) with different perspectives and priorities also bring their own unique value systems, making for a complex set of interacting values. These very conflicting sets of values are only continuing to get more complex as campuses are hiring more diverse individuals from different racial, ethnic, international, and socio-economic backgrounds that bring another layer of difference to the value systems held on campus. Research demonstrates that individuals from a different race, gender and social class often have different experiences that shape unique views of education and campus operations (Kezar 2001). The marked ideological differences make *political theories* of change more salient and come to the forefront of change processes. These different values also reiterate and further confirm the necessity of examining and understanding people's individual meaning making processes through *cultural theories*.

Long-term Employee Commitment

Historically, a common facet of higher education institutions that has made them unique has been the long-term commitment of employees, both faculty and staff. In the past, faculty tended to work for the same institution for their entire careers. Staff often mirrored this tradition and were also long-term employees. Few organizations have this type of stability in the workforce. Some campuses may still experience this degree of stability, which will shape change processes. Increasingly, though, higher education is becoming an enterprise that relies largely on temporary or contingent employees. Seventy percent of faculty are now on semester-to-semester or annual contracts, enjoying far less stability than in the past. The academy is moving from an enterprise comprised of long-term, stable employees to having an unstable employee base. These characteristics of employees will have significant implications for change processes in higher education. On the one hand, having lots of long-term employees often makes propositions for change difficult because people are used to their old habits and particular norms. On the other hand, having a less stable group of faculty members on campus affects the efficacy of change since there are fewer individuals who can engage change initiatives, there is little ability to get anyone's time and attention, and no institutional memory for continuing a change initiative. Both the long-term and short-term employee phenomena suggest the importance of employing *social cognition theories*, understanding how to change highly instantiated schemas, attract the attention of short-term employees, and the limitations of short-term employment for change processes.

These unique characteristics (e.g. shared governance, loose coupling, dual authority structures) of higher education vary by institution type. Many people suggest that anarchical structures are more prevalent within research universities, whereas shared governance is more prominent in liberal arts institutions. Contingent employment is more prevalent within community colleges and low-resourced institutions. Strong shared governance is likely a facet of elite liberal arts colleges and research universities more so than other sectors. Thus, while these characteristics still shape the academy, they vary significantly from one institution to another.

Fading of the Historic Features

While the last section spoke to the historic view of higher education as a sector and characteristics that have long shaped higher education institutions, many of these features are currently changing in today's context, which needs to be considered as change agents frame their efforts. Higher education, as a system, has become more open to external influence in recent years. As *evolutionary theory* would suggest, higher education has become embroiled in negotiating among many more external pressures and messages that have the potential to reshape the character of the enterprise. And, evidence suggests that it has done just that. The enterprise is undergoing fairly significant alterations. The historic characteristics are now being actively contested as a result of the rising influence of the neoliberal and corporate logics (outlined in Chapter 1) that are reshaping higher education (Slaughter and Rhoades 2004).

First, the professional nature of faculty roles is deteriorating as administrators centralize power and authority, delegating less and moving away from a shared governance structure. New values of efficiency, revenue generation, entrepreneurialism, and accountability are now as prevalent in the nomenclature on campuses as the traditional values of inquiry, academic freedom, and social mobility. New values are driving campus operations and structures. As professionals are no longer seen as central to institutions' operations, non-tenure-track faculty have become the vast majority of faculty and the long-term employment that has long been a hallmark of higher education is beginning to break down.

Because this shift was already described in earlier chapters, I just refer to it here to note how it stands in contrast to the long-standing higher education context that has shaped the nature of change initiatives in the past. What this means for change agents is that strategies organized around decentralized efforts, working through shared governance, or appealing to certain values such as equity, which were once key to success, may no longer be adequate on some campuses. Change agents may need to adjust to the new operating principles of an increasingly hierarchical and corporate system of power and authority. Yet, it also means there may be certain new opportunities for change as there are not people who have been on campus for a long time with set views. Still, the turnover of faculty and staff is relevant for change as there is not leadership or personnel to fuel change. So, the logic of change processes must also adapt to these new "institutional" contexts and realities that are emerging.

Savvy change agents will understand higher educations' historical status as an "institution" and track current changes such as academic capitalism, using knowledge of both to navigate change. For example, Albert should have been more aware of shared governance, collegial traditions, and the values-driven aspect of his institution. Also, he could have leveraged the interest of administrators operating more from a logic of academic capitalism to advance his proposal and override some of the resistance from others.

Institutional Culture

While the overall enterprise has some distinctive features (e.g. professional bureaucracy, shared governance, academic freedom), each campus is also characterized by unique cultures that change agents need to understand if they want to be successful. Understanding the institutional culture is critical to avoid barriers, navigate progress forward, as well as to use as a lever for creating changes. *Cultural theories* of change emphasized the need to analyze and be cognizant of underlying systems of meaning, assumptions, and values that are often not directly articulated, but shape institutional operations and can prevent or facilitate change.

Culture also includes the history of the campus. As Albert discovered, an earlier effort to develop a leadership program was affecting the way people viewed his proposal for change. There is a history behind almost any initiative, and it is best to investigate and understand these issues first. Then, a change agent can come into a situation with the rationale for why the previous concerns are no longer relevant or have been addressed in the current proposal. Being blindsided by history is all too common, but can easily be avoided with a little research—or simply by speaking to long-time members of campus community. There are several other key aspects of culture that change agents can focus on to be more successful in developing the right strategy.

A key finding from research on institutional culture is that change agents are more successful when they align their strategies with the institutional culture (Kezar and Eckel 2002a). For example, on a very decentralized campus, trying to develop a universal policy for all divisions and units might be met with great resistance. However, change agents can work from the bottom up within their different units to advance policies that are supportive of change initiatives campus-wide. By working within the institutional culture, which is decentralized, the change agents will experience more success and support than is likely to come from pushing for universal policy at the campus level alone. That approach would likely face persistent barriers and result in little or no change occurring. Kezar and Eckel (2002a) demonstrated how savvy change agents conduct a cultural assessment and align strategies with the institutional culture.

Cultural Assessment

One of the most important mindsets for a change agent to acquire is that of an anthropologist. Being able to see one's campus context "anew" and to not be blind to the underlying values and assumptions that drive actions across the campus are particularly important. So, a cultural assessment is critical to determining which strategy to use, based on the culture. Many of these areas for assessing culture are derived from Schein's (1985) work on institutional culture. Areas of emphasis include assessments of the institutional history, values, symbols, language and metaphors, artifacts, and rituals and ceremonies.

Institutional History

Albert's example points to the importance of understanding the history of an issue before trying to move a change initiative forward. On most campuses, there have been many prior efforts at changing the curriculum, adopting new technologies, implementing new business practices, and the like. Understanding how individuals and groups reacted to earlier efforts, as well as the barriers that emerged and values that surfaced, is critical to a change agent's success. By speaking with people across the campus, you can better understand the history and potential impact of your issue or change initiative. Institutional history and traditions have been found to strongly influence change processes and the way people make sense. So, change agents must carefully analyze the history of an issue they are embarking on changing.

Values

Values can be elusive because they are often more aspirational or espoused rather than actual. Actual values guide behavior, but often in a way that happens unconsciously. Actual values are often not clearly expressed and are difficult for people to articulate. Behaviors of people on campus reflect a system of values, as do the artifacts and symbols that exist—sometimes these are a better reflection of values. It is important to recognize that espoused values are not always the actual values of an organization. In fact, espoused values, examples of which are found in campus mission and values statements, are often aspirational—they reflect what a campus would like to be. So, espoused and aspirational values can be potentially significant levers for change because they represent specific areas where stakeholders across the campus might be willing to invest resources and effort to achieve goals.

You may recall that in Sarah's situation in Chapter 3 the provost held an aspirational value that the campus should embrace multiculturalism and diversity. If she does some work to prepare, Sarah is likely to find these same aspirational values reflected in various documents on campus or locate individuals who share her interest in making multiculturalism a priority. However, only through speaking with many individuals and monitoring their reactions can she determine that actual values on the campus do not include support for multiculturalism. It is very important that change agents are not fooled by the manifestations of espoused values, which often lead individuals to believe that changes are going to encounter greater success and less resistance. Conversations with multiple individuals across a variety of departments and units on a campus are likely necessary to help determine the "actual" value system. Also needed are observation of behaviors and analysis of campus artifacts.

Symbols

As an anthropologist of the organization, you can interpret and analyze symbols that hint at or convey the underlying value system. When you are analyzing symbols on your campus, look for specific ones that might support your cause, represent resistance, or whether there seem to be few, if any, symbols that could be used, which might suggest a lack of values that are supportive of change. Campuses are full of symbols (e.g. mascots, logos, art) that suggest the potential or difficulty of change. Faculty on a campus may be trying to discover if there is support for service learning programs and more engaged forms of scholarship. They may observe that the campus's communications documents include images of bridges, which appear a symbol of community engagement. For example, newsletters that are distributed to community groups, alumni, and local non-profit organizations all utilize this symbol. They might also find that, in recent years, campus leaders have hosted several community days, where people across the state and community were invited to campus to discuss partnerships. These efforts were described as being symbolic of the institution's desire to create relationships with groups beyond the campus walls. However, those walls—the ones that literally encircle the campus—are high. Although they are intended to create a safe environment for students, for people outside they represent an historic gap between the community and the campus. They may remind many external stakeholders of a long history of disengagement, which is an obstacle to future efforts at working together. Thus, a mixed message emerges from the historic and current available symbols on campus.

Language and Metaphors

Institutional culture can also be captured in the language people use on campus. People may use metaphors to describe and articulate meaning within settings and that capture views about change or particular issues. For example, a change agent might be aware of how women faculty describe the tenure and promotion process as "hazing," or entering a tenure-track faculty career as "the childless zone," suggesting they have to forsake any hope for a family. This language and these metaphors used to refer to tenure and promotion suggest there is a lack of value for family, but also convey a sense of the discrimination that women sometimes experience when engaging these processes. This language can be purposefully used to uncover or help articulate the lack of value around family, while new language might be invoked to support family-friendly policies. Repeating key metaphors or language that helps capture the existing value system assists in making the need for change resonate with people.

Artifacts

Artifacts are tangible representations of the value system of the organization. They can include policies, particular programs, or practice, such as a way a campus goes about hiring employees. Symbols are images that communicate an idea, while artifacts are physical embodiments. Artifacts that might help a change agent understand whether family-friendly policies would be welcome on the campus are institutional or departmental policies speaking to issues around creating or sustaining family-friendly environments. If change agents examined all the documents around tenure and promotion, they might notice that there are artifacts in place explaining affordances for children, family care, or other family-friendly policies. Another example might be the existence of professional development programming that is intended to help faculty and staff achieve a more balanced lifestyle or the presence of an office on campuses specifically established to promote family-friendly policies. An example of a practice is having the affirmative action officer speak to the value of being inclusive when looking for candidates to fill vacant positions and being considerate of their interests when describing the work environment. If a change agent examined a campus, and found there are no supportive artifacts present, this may suggest that second-order change is necessary. While structures and processes do not always reflect underlying values, because they are dynamic, they often are an indicator of underlying assumptions and values. In other words, they are not always "pure" reflections, but artifacts might hint at some aspects, but not represent others.

Rituals and Ceremonies

Campus events can also reflect the institutional culture, typically described in *cultural theory* as rituals and ceremonies. Colleges hold ceremonies such as convocations or graduations. Rituals might include sorority and fraternity formals, regular campus speeches, or football games. A very basic example of ritual might also be committees' routine use of *Roberts Rules of Order*. All of the various rituals and ceremonies that occur can offer insight for planning a change process. Community events hosted by a campus to enrich its external partnerships are an example of an emerging ritual to foster a commitment to community outreach. Sponsored events such as "bring your child to work day" or including families in events celebrating faculty or staff accomplishments could similarly convey increasing priority or value for family and family-friendly policies. The way rituals and ceremonies are organized can indicate when a value does not exist (e.g. family are not invited) or that a value is being developed (e.g. family are now invited to events, but were not before). So, rituals can be assessed to understand potential barriers to change, as well as a lever for advancing it.

How Culture Affects Change

Different cultures can result in different types of changes playing out on campuses. A STEM reform initiative at an open access community college is not likely to look the same as one at an elite research university. At an open access community college, the core, driving values usually relate to student support, diversity, and egalitarianism. So, a STEM reform initiative on such a campus will embrace supplemental instruction to support student success out of the classroom, examination of gateway courses that might be preventing students from succeeding, exploration of data about how different types of students are performing, and development of strategies such as learning communities to increase retention among STEM majors. However, an elite research university is more likely to be driven by values of competition, excellence, and individuality. A STEM reform initiative there might focus on creating undergraduate research opportunities to socialize students to become future scientists. Initiatives might also examine the level of critical thinking required in courses using National Survey of Student Engagement data to move away from memorization toward more higher-level thinking. Faculty might be engaged in professional development around cutting-edge content and learning which pedagogies are best for teaching science.

Tierney (1991) developed a framework for considering institutional culture in higher education that explores six key aspects of a campus: environment, mission, socialization, information, strategy, and leadership. Environment includes the physical layout of the campus, the space, buildings, and sometimes artifacts as they relate to campus structures. Mission is the overarching purpose of the institution, which is often described in the form of a mission statement. Yet, it can often be best understood by observing what people focus their time on as they work. Socialization is the process by which individuals learn about the values and practices of the campus. Orientation is an example of a socialization process. Information is the type of data or stories that are transmitted that describe values and meanings on campus. Strategy is the overall plan designed to achieve long-term goals and ultimately the mission, as well. Strategy includes processes like decision-making and long-term planning. Strategy may be visible in planning documents, but may also be found in policies, procedure guides, and other key documents. Leadership is the group of individuals who make things happen on campus, those who create changes. It is also the group with the greatest influence over campus activities.

Analysis consists of examining each category in depth, asking questions such as: How is the mission defined and articulated? Is the mission used as a basis for decision-making? What constitutes information and who has access to it? Or, how are decisions arrived at and who makes them? How do people respond to external groups like accreditors? How is strategy developed and by whom? How do people learn about norms when they arrive on campus? This approach assumes that the values, beliefs, and assumptions of an institution are reflected in its processes and artifacts, like the *cultural theories* noted above. This approach has change agents look into processes occurring on a campus that are sometimes easier to understand than broader areas such as values, symbols, or history. Some change agents find the tangible quality of looking at processes to be easier for identifying and exploring a cultural setting. The key is to develop a technique that helps you explore and discover the culture.

Let's consider an example of how one might conduct a cultural assessment using Tierney's (1991) framework. We can use Albert from the case at the beginning of the chapter, but will place him in another setting—a small Jesuit institution. First, in examining the environment, Albert might realize that the Jesuits' teachings and values are strongly connected to most programs and practices on campus. So, he should consider whether they are represented in his leadership development proposal. There are also many religiously based leadership development frameworks he might want to consider or at least be knowledgeable about, such as servant leadership. Next, the mission of the institution also integrates Jesuit values of service and justice, which might be included when developing a leadership program. For example, the proposal will likely be a better fit to the institution and mission if it incorporates service learning. Individuals at the college are socialized through lots of interpersonal contact; there are no formal mentoring or training programs. For example, new people tend to go out to lunch with many people to learn about the campus. *Information* is also communicated rather informally; people do not send official memos or create reports. *Strategy* emerges through conversations among stakeholders, not through conducting formal strategy sessions. And *leadership* tends to be conferred rather than assumed. Thus, in terms of a change strategy, Albert likely needs to meet with many different people to discuss the change proposal and frame it more as an emerging idea, not a proposal set in stone. He will also want people to confer on him the status of change agent and not be considered as assuming control on his own. Through his conversations, people may come to identify him as the right person to lead. So, taking too much initiative too soon could be detrimental. Through analyzing how things operate—the processes on campus—change agents can better craft their strategy to fit the unique characteristics of the campus culture.

Institutional Cultural Archetypes

While we each need to assess conditions on our own campuses, Bergquist (2007) identified a set of six cultural archetypes that largely reflect most college campuses.[1] These archetypes can serve as a way to begin thinking about the culture on your campus if you find the exploration of values, artifacts, rituals, and symbols to be too challenging. Bergquist hypothesized that different strategies would be needed or appropriate within the six different academic culture archetypes—collegial, managerial, developmental, negotiating, virtual, and tangible cultures. The *collegial* culture arises primarily from the disciplines of the faculty. It values scholarly engagement, shared governance and decision-making, and rationality. It focuses on values such as consensus, egalitarianism, respect, quality, and mutuality. This culture is most associated with traditional and historic higher education culture.

The *managerial* culture focuses on goals, roles, and rules. This culture values efficiency, effective supervisory skills, and fiscal responsibility. Many of the more recent types of postsecondary institutions to emerge such as for-profits, online institutions, and community colleges have these managerial qualities. This contrasts with the *developmental* culture, which is based on the personal and professional growth of all members of the collegiate environment. This culture is often found at liberal arts colleges and masters institutions with a strong student-centered focus. The developmental culture is often epitomized in the student affairs divisions with a focus on development, mentoring, and support for students.

The *negotiating* culture values the establishment of equitable and egalitarian policies and procedures and also values confrontation, interest groups, mediation, and power. Campuses with unions often epitomize the negotiating culture, which is more prevalent on community college campuses. However, this culture exists wherever politics is an overriding focus of the institution. The *virtual* culture emerged more recently, prompted by the technological and social forces that have emerged over the past 20 years. It is most prevalent on campuses that have moved the most to integrate technology, online education, and globalization. These campuses find meaning by being closely linked to knowledge generation and dissemination; they view technology in an open, shared, and responsive way. Campuses with a strong virtual culture do not fear fragmentation resulting from global and technological connections. Instead, they see these as resources for a much broader sense of community that goes far beyond the campus walls.

Lastly, institutions with a *tangible* culture value their roots, community, and physical location. The tangible culture is typical of land grant and community colleges, which have a strong local mission. Due to the virtual culture there has been a resurgence of values related to local place and personal contact, which are embodied in the tangible culture. The tangible culture values the predictability of a value-based, face-to-face education in a physical location. This culture focuses on the importance of community, emphasizing engagement. Learning is seen as inherently social and community based; these institutions focus on the reintegration of learning from a local perspective.

Bergquist's (2007) set of archetypes can serve as cultural barometers to begin your exploration to better understand your campus. Bergquist also describes how each culture reacts differently to change. For example, he illustrates how the managerial culture might hinder an institution's ability to change structures, while a collegial culture is better equipped to modify them, since there is greater trust among stakeholders. Top-down changes might be more characteristic of managerial culture, whereas bottom-up changes are more prevalent in collegial or developmental cultures. Student-focused changes are likely easier to pursue in the developmental culture than in a negotiating culture.

Kezar and Eckel (2002a) provide examples of how campus change agents have aligned their change strategies to Bergquist's archetypes.[2] For example, if change agents determine that they are on a campus with a more developmental culture, they typically focus more on strategies that involve professional development. They appeal to campus stakeholders' concerns about how to best support students to provide rationale for changes; they also work with various stakeholders in a more participatory way. By contrast, in campuses with a negotiating culture which are more political, change agents assess power relationships, build coalitions, and examine the multiple interests the change agenda might serve to incorporate different perspectives. Being unaware of the culture affects how change happens on a particular campus and only serves to undo the change agent.

Organizational Capacity and Readiness for Change

A last element of context is organizational capacity and readiness for change. A variety of institutional structures and resources have been identified as helping to build capacity, such as having nimble structures, healthy decision-making processes, training and professional development, strong communication systems, stable employee base, or incentives and rewards that can be aligned with efforts to create change. Campuses without strong capacity will struggle to integrate any changes.

More recent literature emphasizes that campuses are better prepared to engage in change if they build their organizational capacity (Toma 2010). While change agents may feel the change is a priority and have identified champions who are willing to take the lead, there may be significant organizational issues that prevent the institution from being able to engage in the change initiative. Research suggests that institutions can enhance their capacity for engaging change and be better prepared by examining core operational areas for their health and functionality. Within the higher education environment, Toma (2010) outlined the following as necessary for more smoothly engaging in change processes:

- A clear and meaningful mission;
- Structures that support the mission and vision;
- Healthy governance processes;
- Policies that support institutional mission and vision;
- Streamlined and clear processes;
- Healthy information resources that are well shared;
- Facilities;
- Technology;
- Human infrastructure;
- Capital assets that are continually maintained and updated; and,
- An institutional culture that promotes the predominant values of the mission and vision.

One of the main reasons for focusing on campus capacity is that change initiatives often start off successfully, but then fail during the implementation phase, when they need to draw on campus infrastructure, structures, or policies. These areas can become barriers to change if they are not addressed. Therefore scholars who are interested in sustaining change and making sure it is fully institutionalized have begun to think more about organizational capacity and its relationship to and role in the change process.[3]

In addition to the organizational capacity for change, campuses may also have different levels of readiness. Readiness for change is influenced by and related to many of the other factors and conditions detailed above (e.g. support for the mission, infrastructure, existence of policies). But, it also takes into account elements from institutional culture, history, and values. If there is a history of a particular type of change, it might prepare members of the campus for altering norms, potentially making them more open to or ready for new change initiatives. The undergirding value system also plays a significant role in the campus's readiness for change.

Change agents need to consider the alignment between their change initiative and the existing value system. Organizational readiness may depend on the type of change being initiated (as noted in Chapter 3). In working with campuses on many different national projects, I have observed that campuses have varying levels of experience with a proposed change initiative. For example, one campus may have had significant experience with STEM reform, while another may just be considering it for the first time. Lacking experience may not automatically mean that an organization is not ready for change, but it may require some additional work.

Instruments have even been developed to explore organizational readiness within different organizational contexts, among different types of change initiatives, and customized to suit particular institutional contexts. These surveys ask about organizational capacity issues, external forces and factors, as well as history and values. While no such instruments exist in higher education, change agents may adopt surveys and tools from other sectors if they are interested in investigating and better understanding the context in which they are operating. An assessment is, of course, much more likely to happen in more formal, top-down change processes, rather than in more organic change processes from the bottom up. But, even without formally surveying a campus, change agents can conduct their own internal assessments and form an opinion of conditions. *Just acknowledging that all campuses are not in the same place when beginning a change initiative is a good start.* Knowing to look at readiness complexly in relationship to these many context factors (e.g. human capital, technology, governance) is the key message of this chapter.

Almost every theory speaks to the importance of context, but in different ways. *Evolutionary theories* speak to broad social, political, and economic factors and key stakeholders; *cultural theories* speak to the impact of values, history, and institutional culture; *institutional theory* speaks to the ways that institutions become invested in deeply engrained norms that make change challenging and suggest the importance of readiness, but also how fields like disciplinary societies or foundations (often from afar) shape change.

Summary

Let's now return to Albert. He returned to his next staff meeting with a whole new plan. First, using strategies from *cultural theory*, he interviewed several staff members about the earlier initiative. He found out about their reservations and concerns that the new program would end up taking away funding from a long-supported leadership program (*cultural theories*). He met with his supervisor to try to work out the budget and included information about how the program will be paid for in the next proposal. Next, using advice from *evolutionary theories*, he went back and examined the Council for Advancement of Standards (CAS) standards. He actually found that they supported many aspects of his proposal. He made sure to develop a document that outlined the similarity of his proposal to the CAS standards. Albert also showed how the business aspects he borrowed were not so different from the CAS standards and the way they complement them.

Using *institutional theory*, he highlighted the many ways his proposal fits into historic values around shared governance and collegiality, but also demonstrated how it integrates qualities students need in the changing environment, such as entrepreneurialism. Drawing on *evolutionary theory*'s advice to leverage stakeholders, he also illustrated how two foundations have supported leadership programs similar to the one he has developed. At this next meeting, the proposal was approved—with no lingering doubts.

six
Leadership and Agency of Change

Melissa is director for the Multicultural Center at a research university with a troubled history of racism and sexism. She has been working for years to help support students of color. When she first came to campus, she was a strong advocate for students and knew she wanted to be an agent of change. However, quite early she recognized that her strong advocacy was causing her to lose credibility and to be perceived as always complaining. She was frustrated at how people frequently misinterpreted her actions and were taken aback. She was unsure how she could move forward in trying to do the work she knew was important—helping students of color on campus to be successful. Melissa has been asking her colleagues how she can be a more successful change agent.

Within all of my research on change, leadership emerges as perhaps the most important facilitator. Without change agents' energy and enthusiasm, there would be little change. While I do not want to suggest that leadership is a panacea for change, it is important not to underestimate its role in responding to unplanned changes and crisis, as well as in creating intentional changes.

Theories of change speak to who is viewed as being a change agent, the different levels of agency among different actors, and the degree to which change agents can impact or shape change processes. They also speak to different approaches to increase or enhance agency. The approach taken in this book is not to rely on any one school of thought to address this issue but to draw on all theories to help shape a robust theory of action around agency. Chapter 5, on context, helped change agents consider ways change may be shaped by differences in context. This chapter will highlight how change agents can act within these sometimes-constraining contexts, but still create change. The concepts presented in this chapter are captured in Figure 6.1

Three major ideas are presented in this chapter. First, change theories (predominantly those from *scientific management*) have overemphasized the roles of individuals in positions of authority, ignoring other change agents within institutions. This means that strategies and approaches for others to create change are less well documented. I will emphasize and focus more on bottom-up and grassroots leaders, so that their roles can be made clearer. Also, I demonstrate how leaders with different agency have to use different approaches to change. This chapter will draw on *political theories* that have long demonstrated the role of bottom-up leaders.

Second, leadership is typically described as an individual, rather than a group or collective process. In this chapter, again drawing on *political theories*, the role of collective or group forms of agency is explored. Leadership teams are often much more successful than having leadership efforts rest with a single individual (Bensimon and Neumann 1993; Kezar 2011). Also, the complex strategies and approaches to leadership (embedded in the various change theories) will be difficult to implement since most individual leaders will not posses all of the capabilities necessary. In order to have the human capital required for advancing the change effort, additional stakeholders with a broader set of change capabilities across all skill areas—politics, cultural, planning, and relationship building—should be assembled to enhance the process.

Melissa, in the vignette opening this chapter, epitomizes the struggle of the lone leader trying to create changes. The vignette also typifies the many pitfalls that leaders often face when they do not work in concert with others or think about change as a joint or shared process. One of the main suggestions that Melissa will receive from her colleagues is the importance of connecting her efforts to others

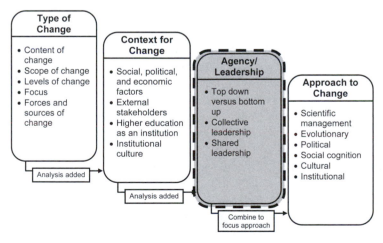

Figure 6.1. Change macro framework: leadership and agency.

throughout the organization. They will also recommend that she allow others to play a leadership role, rather than always being out front on issues, particularly when her credibility is being threatened. This way, her opportunity to provide leadership will not be lost for good.

Third, shared approaches to leadership that include top-down and bottom-up leaders may have the most robust capacity to bring long-term changes to campuses. The difference between collective and shared leadership is that collective leadership involves a group of people, but does not necessarily include those in positions of authority and those without. Shared leadership intentionally brings together and includes both of these groups in a change effort. This chapter examines the opportunities and pitfalls for shared agency and leadership. *Social cognition theories* of change examine schemas and what thinking is needed to create shared leadership. Also, *cultural theories* of change suggest concepts for enhancing the potential of shared leadership.

Being a successful change agent requires a broad and expansive view of leadership, beyond individuals in positions of power to collectives or networks of individuals—to include all members of the campus. Successfully exercising change agency also demands an understanding that different types of leaders operate under different conditions. This chapter suggests that it is important to reflect on your own agency, considers collective processes to develop a strong core of leadership skills, and provides strategies for creating shared leadership that can result in more sustained change. The chapter will be organized by three main areas: top-down versus grassroots leadership, collective leadership, shared leadership.[1] I will use the terms grassroots and bottom-up leaders interchangeably to discuss those change agents who are not in positions of power. I will also use the terms top-down leaders and those in positions of authority to refer to those who are in formal leadership positions.

Top-down versus Grassroots Leadership

Traditionally, leadership has been synonymous with individuals in positions of power, such as presidents and chief executive officers (Kezar et al. 2006). When people think about who creates changes they typically think of those with higher rank or appointments within institutions. But in the last 20 years, a variety of scholars have proposed that leadership is not synonymous with authority. These scholars have examined the role of other individuals within the organization and their contributions to change (Astin and Leland 1991; Kanter 1983; Meyerson 2003; Pearce and Conger 2003). Scholars began to question definitions of leadership that focused on the activities and roles of those in positions of authority, such as budgeting or planning. Instead, they define leadership as the creation of change (Astin and Leland 1992; Kezar et al. 2006). As it has become more conventional to define leadership as facilitating or creating change, leaders have been found to exist at all levels of organizations. Thus, when thinking about creating a leadership process, change agents might consider all sorts of leaders who can be allies—students, staff at all levels, including support and secretarial staff, and all sorts of faculty, not just the administrators that have often been the focus. I describe these individuals outside formal positions of authority as grassroots or bottom-up leaders.

Before describing distinctions in the strategies used by leaders with different agency, it is important to note some of the similar strategies they can use. Most theories (e.g. *evolutionary* or *cultural theories*) can be used by those in positions of authority, as well as bottom-up or grassroots leaders. *Evolutionary theories* that suggest the importance of tracking external forces for support or resistance can be used by both of these groups of leaders. Also, *social cognition theories* that describe the importance of helping people to learn are important for top-down leaders to overcome resistance to change, but might also be important to grassroots leaders as they try to sensitize those in positions of authority to the changes they are advocating. *Cultural theories* of change that demonstrate the impact of history, values, and contexts of change are important regardless of one's placement in the organizational hierarchy.

Leadership Strategies of Those in Positions of Power

There are some important differences in terms of how leaders at different levels can operate. We are most familiar with leaders in positions of authority and the approaches and strategies they often use, which have been studied extensively and documented as part of *scientific management theories* of change. For example, these leaders often have the ability to mandate change, alter rewards structures, use devices such as strategic plans, refine mission and vision statements, and have other mechanisms to support changes. Their roles are embedded within formal structures that they can draw upon to create changes. The various mechanisms that they have are also potent for creating institutionalization because they can affect key levers like rewards or underlying assumptions such as the values embedded in the mission statement. As strategies and approaches relating to organizational elites are likely to be more familiar to readers, I will only review these briefly. I will instead concentrate more on strategies for bottom-up leaders, which remain largely unknown since these individuals have not been the focus of much of the literature.

Establishing Core Values, Vision or Mission

Those in positions of authority have the ability to articulate the organizational mission, vision, and values. Perhaps the most frequently described strategy in the *scientific management* literature related to change is the importance of articulating a vision for change, so people can see and understand the direction in which they are moving (Kotter 1985). Change often invites risk and an uncertain future, so having a compelling reason for change and a clear direction is crucial. A motivating vision or mission can become the blueprint and compass for many employees. This metaphorical compass directs people to move toward something new and beneficial, not just into the unknown. Only those in authority can change the official mission of the institution or formally establish its vision, but bottom-up leaders can still develop a vision for their change initiatives.

Using Planning Mechanisms

One of the most common recommendations from the *scientific management* literature is using strategy and planning as vehicles to advance change. While a vision or revised mission gives direction, the planning process provides an implementation plan and assigns roles and responsibilities to various individuals within the organization. It also serves as an accountability tool by determining who is responsible for bringing various changes forward. Again, only individuals in positions of authority can create a formal plan and provide the financial and human resources to support it. Certainly, grassroots groups can develop implementation plans, but they often do not have the same access to institutional resources to develop, influence, and execute the plans.

Using Resources and Funding

Only those in positions of authority can reallocate funds within institutional budgets in order to support change—whether to create a new structure or process, hiring new people, or developing incentives and rewards. The allocation and reallocation of funding is one of the fundamental levers that those in positions of authority possess.

Motivating People through Incentives or Rewards

Another key difference is that those in positions of authority have the ability to develop or modify incentives and rewards structures to motivate changes in behavior. These might include allocating additional resources, offering course releases to faculty, or giving punishments such as a poor performance appraisal. Those in positions of authority can also modify tenure and promotion processes to garner greater support for a change initiative. Rewards have consistently been identified in studies as ways to encourage employees to channel their efforts from existing activities to new or additional ones. The range of incentives can vary from computer upgrades, to summer salaries, to merit increases, to conference travel money, to public recognition and awards (Eckel et al. 1999; Roberts et al. 1993; Tierney and Rhoads 1993). Although a motivating vision or mission provides people with a compelling reason to engage the change process, incentives can be strong vehicles for continuing or enabling change, as well. Enabling faculty and staff to attend a conference on assessment, for example, might be the necessary incentive to have them be able to facilitate change (McMahon and Caret 1997). By attending the conference, faculty and staff develop the inspiration, skills, and motivation to move the change initiative forward.

Restructuring or Creating Support Structures

Campus organizational structures are a representation of the values individuals hold and the way that budgets have been allocated over time to support those values. Departments emerged as disciplinary expertise came to be valued more highly. New programs and departments such as student affairs, alumni affairs, multicultural affairs all emerged as each of these became priorities on college campuses. Creating new centers or positions, realigning roles, and reallocating resources are all central to sustaining and achieving change (Curry 1992; Guskin 1996; St. John 1991). Developing structures allows for the necessary focus, effort, and resources to be committed (McMahon and Caret 1997). Those in positions of authority can, at any time, decide to withhold funding for programmatic or service areas, combine areas, or undertake other forms of restructuring to represent different priorities and values.

Hiring and Training of Employees

Individuals in positions of authority typically create staffing plans, hiring priorities, allocate funds, and have final authority on hiring. Certainly there are exceptions, with entry-level staff or faculty hired more locally at departments or units without obtaining approval at higher levels, although even these decisions are increasingly moving from faculty or staff to deans and vice presidents. Campus leaders that want to create change can execute strategic hires related to the areas they are interested in making changes in. Those in positions of authority can also mandate or recommend that people attend training. While this would typically be directed at staff, there are some campuses that mandate that faculty attend certain types of faculty development, as well.

Those in positions of authority clearly have different levers available to them because of their position of power within the hierarchy. While there are many strategies that are only available to those in positions of authority, others are not exclusive to them, as noted earlier such as understanding institutional history. An example of an exclusive strategy is organizational vision; bottom-up leaders cannot define an organizational vision, but they can create a vision and a plan for their specific initiative (Eckel et al. 1999; Lindquist 1978). Next, I review research on specific strategies that are important for bottom-up leaders to be effective in creating change. Bottom-up leaders cannot hire or create rewards, but they can get appointments to hiring committees, for example, where they can try to influence who is hired or provide informal recognition of change agents by talking about their work and having others recognize their efforts.

Strategies of Bottom-up Leaders

While *scientific management theories* can be used to better understand the strategies that are often successful among those in positions of authority, *political theories* have developed important insights into how bottom-up leaders can create change.

Political theories suggest the importance of allies, coalition building, agenda setting, and negotiation of interests. Studies of grassroots leaders in higher education describe the strategies and approaches that work well from the bottom up on campuses and that complement the more generic findings from *political theories* of change. Bottom-up leaders on campus can leverage student relationships and curriculum, areas not available within other types of institutions. Studies of grassroots leaders also identify different conditions of power (e.g. being fired) that grassroots change agents face, as compared to those that are more prevalent among those in positions of authority (e.g. lack of buy in). Kezar and Lester (2011) found that grassroots leaders could leverage nine strategies for creating change and exerting agency:

1. Intellectual opportunities;
2. Professional development;
3. Leveraging curricula and using classrooms as forums;
4. Joining and utilizing existing networks;
5. Working with students;
6. Hiring like-minded people;
7. Gathering data;
8. Garnering resources; and,
9. Partnering with influential external stakeholders.

These strategies all share a connection to reinforcing the academic values, student learning, and the education mission of the institution. This common thread relating to the education mission is critical for deflecting resistance from others, who might try to portray the change as peripheral or oppositional to the campus. Because it is easy to squelch bottom-up changes, they need to be very carefully framed and crafted. These strategies have been used by successful grassroots change agents and have worked across a variety of higher education contexts.

Intellectual Opportunities

The first strategy is to host or create intellectual forums where issues of interest can be intelligently discussed and debated. Examples include ongoing lecture series, periodic forums, or luncheon groups; these are ways grassroots leaders on campuses continue to foster dialogue on important issues around which they are planning to create change. These intellectual forums serve many purposes. They provide a way for people to become informed of research that they can use to make a compelling argument for their change, as well as to craft a vision. In addition, these forums allow people to come together and form loose networks and meet allies.

Professional Development

Another means for creating change is faculty and staff development opportunities. Professional development plays a similar role to intellectual opportunities by raising consciousness and helping to create or nurture a vision. Faculty and staff describe a preference for professional development that they have created within their own units or opportunities to go off campus. Administratively sponsored professional development was noted as typically not reflecting grassroots leaders interests. Faculty and staff development helps to bring in new ideas and generate awareness. It is particularly important for employees who tend to stay in the same position for much of their career, as is the case for many faculty members. It can facilitate vision development, as well as help with implementation by creating opportunities for faculty and staff to meet people who have already made changes and learn about successful approaches. Professional development can also link change agents to people with similar interests, who can act as a support system.

Hiring Like-minded People

Hiring is a prevalent tactic used by grassroots change agents to create change, because faculty and staff involvement in various hiring and socialization processes is fairly common. While they may not make the final hiring decision, on most campuses grassroots leaders are included in the process in ways that allow them to exert influence. They can also work to recruit applicants to affect the hiring pool. Through the hiring process, grassroots leaders have the opportunity to build a critical mass or network of individuals with a commitment and passion for the issues around which grassroots leaders hope to make change. So, many faculty and staff grassroots leaders dedicate themselves to participating on hiring committees or lobbying their members.

Garnering Resources

Unlike businesses, colleges and universities have very little research and development money available to test ideas, particularly among actors outside the administration. Grassroots leaders need to find ways to obtain seed funding to support their change initiatives, often through grants and other external sources. On many campuses, a diversity initiative, campus and community partnership, or service learning project gets off the ground because of its success securing external funding. Grants can be used to mobilize people—providing a way to bring people together, fund meetings and conferences, and helping to create collective action. Grants are also critical for gaining influence because obtaining a grant often helps legitimize an idea. Unlike those in positions of authority who have ready access to resources, grassroots leaders need to think more creatively about outside resources they can tap into to seed their idea.

Working with Students

Faculty and staff use different approaches to working with students, such as creating a coalition with students, mentoring them to take direct action on campus, or working with student clubs. Working with students is an important tactic because faculty and staff know that the core mission of academic institutions is education and shaping students. Nothing is more compelling to other campus stakeholders than knowing that a major constituent group like students has given its support to an initiative. Working with students is also a form of coalition building, wherein change agents align their efforts and partner with a group that has substantial power on many campuses.

Leveraging Curricula and Using Classrooms as Forums

Another way to work with students is through the curriculum or engaging them in the classroom. Faculty and staff can use courses and the curriculum more broadly to raise consciousness and generate awareness about their initiatives among students. For instance, faculty concerned with environmentalism on campus might improve students' and their colleagues' awareness by making changes to the curriculum and translating growing awareness into a sustainability plan for the campus over time. Staff members can also partner with faculty to get their initiatives (e.g. diversity, environmentalism, social media) included in classes. Staff can also use co-curricular experiences to highlight issues in the residence halls and within student life programming. Curricular and co-curricular tactics can also further efforts to partner with student allies.

Gathering Data

Grassroots leaders on college and university campuses can collect and use data on campus to tell the story of an initiative, raise consciousness, mobilize action, and garner support. Like grants, collecting and presenting data is a way to obtain additional funding or support for bottom-up initiatives, particularly from internal sources. Since the importance of research-based evidence is so engrained in higher education institutions, data becomes extremely important when trying to garner resources and support for an initiative. For example, if a faculty member has obtained support to create a tutoring center, she should evaluate the project on an ongoing basis to ensure it is generating positive results. These data can be used to secure additional support and maybe even new funding for the project. Change agents need to understand that obtaining data alone is not the endpoint, but that telling a good story with the data is also important.

Joining and Utilizing Existing Networks

Grassroots leaders have described using existing networks such as those based on common interests (e.g. problem-based learning), a cause (e.g. environmentalism), or concern (e.g. dropout rates among underrepresented students) to further their changes. All sorts of informal networks exist on campuses. Successful change agents become familiar with and leverage them. Some grassroots leaders have even drawn support from more formal institutional bodies such as the academic senate or campus committees. Committees and campus groups are often considered part of shared governance. It is culturally normative for faculty and staff (and students) to participate in committees that make decisions, solve problems, and facilitate organizational change. Committees can be used to gain support for collective action as more people become connected to the change initiative.

Partnering with Influential External Stakeholders

A final tactic, particularly well suited to community college and liberal arts contexts, is partnering with key external stakeholders. Partnering with alumni and local business, political leaders, and community groups can help to garner support and enhance the validity of the initiative. The support of influential stakeholders can help change agents to overcome internal resistance and inertia by mobilizing support through partnerships with influential groups and individuals. Local politicians and community organizations are able to influence community college operations because of the unique missions of these institutions. Similarly, alumni are able to influence the affairs of a liberal arts college because alumni often provide support and resources for institutions.

Change agents can be much more successful in creating change if they understand that different tools are accessible to them and that these resources vary based on their position within the institutional hierarchy (e.g. department chair, entry-level staff member) (see Table 6.1). Some individuals will fall somewhere in the

TABLE 6.1. Comparing bottom-up and top-down leaders

Underlying change concept	Top-down strategy: scientific management theory	Bottom-up strategy: political theory
Mobilizing, aligning, and energizing people for action	Using planning mechanisms	Gathering data; joining in and utilizing existing networks
Creating infrastructure for change	Using resources and funding	Garnering resources
Motivation garnering support; creating networks	Incentives and rewards; restructuring and creating support	Holding intellectual forums; leveraging curriculum; working with students; partnering with external stakeholders
Raising consciousness, mobilizing people	Hiring and training of employees	Hiring like-minded people; creating professional development

middle of the hierarchy, so they may have access to some of the same levers as those in positions of authority (e.g. director of center for teaching and learning), but also can and often do utilize more bottom-up strategies. The most important point is that you must identify what level of agency you have and match strategies to your available resources. Your level of agency will also expose you to different power conditions, which you need to navigate in order to create change.[2] But, as I describe next, change agents do not need to work in isolation. By working with others, change agents can build their agency for change.

Leadership as a Collective Process

While it has been hard for many to imagine how agency and leadership function in change processes beyond those in positions of authority, it has also been challenging for people to think about collective agency. This is particularly true in higher education, which is a fragmented and autonomous enterprise. Melissa, the change agent introduced in the opening vignette for this chapter, is like many faculty and staff on campus who have attempted to promote change on their own, rather than working in concert with others. A lone ranger view of leadership, which prevents people from seeing the value and perhaps the necessity of a shared or collective leadership process, is all too prevalent within our society.[3]

Increasingly, though, leadership is considered to be a process involving groups, rather than only being exercised by individuals. Over time, departing from traditional, hierarchical, and authority-based approaches, new models of leadership have emerged such as team-based, shared, and distributed leadership (Astin and Leland 1991; Bensimon and Neumann 1993; Komives and Wagner 2009; Pearce and Conger 2003). *Political* and *cultural theories* of change, which emerged in the last 20 years, focus more on the ways that people are interconnected and how change processes are inherently part of human systems and not isolated (Pearce and Conger 2003). The advantage of utilizing collective leadership in change processes is that it encourages more individuals to be a part of the process, which in most studies has been shown to facilitate change (Pearce and Conger 2003). Collective leadership is not necessarily the same thing as shared leadership, though. Shared leadership involves agents at the top and bottom of the campus hierarchy working together to create change. Collective leadership, however, may be confined to a group of leaders holding positions of authority or a network of bottom-up leaders exclusively.

Advantages of Collective Leadership

A number of research studies support the need to expand leadership from the hands of only a few leaders to a broader group of stakeholders in organizations (Bensimon and Neumann 1993; Pearce and Conger 2003). In fact, Pearce and Conger (2003) demonstrate how studies over the past 100 years have pointed in this direction, but that the overwhelming bias toward heroic, individual, or hierarchical leaders has prevented scholars and practitioners from conceptualizing and adopting the lessons of these studies. In other words, the efficacy of involving multiple individuals, outside positions of authority, and working collectively has repeatedly been confirmed in studies as being important to supporting leadership outcomes such as problem solving, change, innovation, and strategic decision-making. Outcomes supported by collective leadership include increased problem solving capabilities, greater creativity and organizational effectiveness, increased motivation and dedication by members of leadership groups, greater satisfaction with decision-making, increased social integration, more positive relationships within organizations, more cognitively complex decision-making, greater buy-in for change and accountability for decisions, and improved collective efficacy (Bensimon and Neumann 1993; Pearce and Conger 2003).

The research on grassroots networks and groups also identifies the benefits of working in a collective fashion (Pearce and Conger 2003). Grassroots leaders operating alone are subject to significant power conditions and often face a lot of resistance to their efforts. Working in groups helps them to have a network of support and source of comfort in difficult times. Also, by working collectively, an individual is less of a lightning rod for any backlash, since no one individual can be seen as driving the effort. Another advantage of working collectively is that when resistance does emerge those change agents who are encountering the brunt of the resistance can move into the background, while others take a more visible leadership role for a while.

One of the major advantages of working through a collective leadership approach is that you will have a support network that can help you to maintain resiliency in the face of difficulties. Another advantage is that this approach draws upon ideas and information from across a lot of different groups or networks on campus, and can develop more complex and complete solutions. Also, networks have many more nodes (e.g. connections among people) than isolated individuals working in pockets, so they can have a broader impact across the entire culture of the campus. Rather than only impacting a particular subculture or group on campus, a network can attempt to work broadly and create changes across various departments and units.

An example of the benefits of collective leadership, specifically among grassroots leaders is described in the research of Astin and Leland (1991). Astin and Leland studied women faculty and staff on campuses who participated in the women's movement and created a variety of changes on campuses to support women and people of color. These efforts included curricular change, development and support services, and recruiting and admitting more women and students of color. This study demonstrated that collectives of faculty and staff working together could make significant changes in the face of significant barriers and in a culture that is not open to the types of changes proposed. The advantage of bottom-up grassroots leadership is that it draws on the expertise of people close to the women students and students of color, leaders who often have the needed expertise to resolve and create solutions. In a collective leadership process, the effort can capitalize on the commitment and interest of faculty and staff to generate the energy and buy-in needed to sustain the change.

To work effectively in a collective leadership role and obtain increased agency requires skills in working in groups. Yet, change agents are often not adept at working in leadership groups. Strategies for leaders are usually designed for individuals, not groups or group processes. The literature on teams is often used to extrapolate key processes to enhance the use of collective leadership. The following is not an inclusive list, but highlights skills with which change agents should be familiar to follow collective leadership.[4]

Relationship Skills

Collective approaches to change do not work when intra- or intergroup conflict overwhelms the process. In order for these processes to work effectively, change agents need to develop interpersonal skills such as conflict resolution, empathy, communication, and emotional competence. Research demonstrates that communication and conversation patterns often reflect a bias toward politeness rather than dialogue, which reflects mutuality, listening to the other's point of view, and a true sense of inquiry (Komives et al. 1998). Change agents often do not know how to read others' body language for clues to how they are feeling and receiving messages. Also, few leaders know how to effectively manage conflict that emerges within the group. These are key skills that need to be developed for strong collective change agency.

Group Process and Development Skills

Many times, groups promoting change start informally, but eventually begin to become more organized. As they do, more attention to group processes is needed because the individuals in the group may not all know each other as it grows. One of the main dimensions to consider as a group grows is how to create shared values and goals to support and undergird the group. Helping new people feel included is also important. Change agents should not assume everyone has the same level of knowledge and awareness, so creating some form of orientation to the group becomes essential. Also, as groups develop, they need to sort out who will play which roles and hold particular responsibilities (Bensimon and Neumann 1993). Growth also increases the likelihood that different perspectives will emerge, so change agents need to find a way to create openness and respect new voices (Bensimon and Neumann 1993).

Shared Sense of Purpose and Goals

While I identified many different group development skills necessary for operating in a collective fashion, a particular skill that many scholars describe as being very important is the creation of a shared sense of purpose, values, and goals (Komives et al. 1998). While most change processes will not have a homogenous group with identical values or goals at their core, having some similar sense of purpose or general direction is needed for functionally working together and communicating effectively. Most often, scholars describe change agents as being capable of creating meaningful dialogue and helping to translate, synthesize, and connect perspectives that may seem divergent, but that have similar underlying values.

Shared Cognition

Building on the notion of having a shared direction, scholars have also examined shared cognition. Shared cognition refers to the extent to which team members have similar mental maps regarding their internal work, as well as the nature of the external environment. Shared cognition is an important aspect of team dynamics and has been identified as important to team effectiveness (Knight et al. 1999). If the mental models of various stakeholders that come together are too different, then efforts at collective leadership will be continually fraught with problems. Burke et al. (2006) have developed a model identifying the key constructs that enable shared cognition within collective leadership—meta-cognition, mental models, situation assessment, and attitudes. In the first element, meta-cognition, team members are aware of their own cognitive processes and are able to understand and manipulate their own cognitive process. In other words, they need to be aware of their own biases and perspectives, be open to others, and be able to shift their view as they encounter new information.

The second element, mental models, describes the importance of creating shared mental models around two key factors, the team and the situation. Members of a leadership team might differ substantially on a variety of mental models. However, as long as members believe that the group has the same goals and roles and can agree about the situation that exists (say, for example, they can agree on what the problem in the campus community is), then other differences are likely to be worked out. However, if they cannot agree on these two fundamental issues, it is unlikely that they will be able to move on to more complex cognitive thinking. This agreement about the situation refers to the third area of situation assessment. The fourth area is attitudes that allow shared cognition. Scholars also suggest that shared cognition is more likely to happen when there are some general shared attitudes or beliefs, such as collective efficacy (e.g. that through working together they can improve the problem at hand), that it is acceptable to have fluid leadership (e.g. emerging within different members of the group), and a collective orientation to problem solving. If these attitudes are missing among members of the group, then shared cognition is also difficult to create.

Acknowledging and Working with Diverse Perspectives

Shared cognition does not mean groupthink. Successful collectives understand how to support diverse perspectives. Bensimon and Neumann (1993) describe the importance of creating a team culture through building relationships and trust over time. Teams do not have to think alike to work effectively, but need to feel that there is a safe and productive culture in which to conduct their work, where divergent viewpoints can be shared. Bensimon and Neumann's work suggests the importance of group processes that can make collective leadership more success-ful, from carefully choosing people to participate in leadership teams, to orienta-tion sessions, to group development, to spending time developing relationships and thinking prior to making decisions. Diverse leadership groups come undone by the pressure to make decisions quickly before people understand each other's and their own perspectives. Therefore, skills in group development also ensure that diverse perspectives can flourish.

Group Maintenance Skills

As we have seen, group formation is critical to the development of trust, shared vision, and cognition, as well as for making people feel they have a safe space to work and voice concerns or opposing views (Komives et al. 1998). If the group has formed successfully, its next step is to consider ways to maintain itself through ongoing communication, different types of interaction that are salient for group members, how to create a sense of accomplishment toward shared goals through the celebration of key milestones, and ways to keep members accountable for work (Bensimon and Neumann 1993). Ongoing communication might involve emails, tweets, blogs, and other forms of interaction that are virtual or in person, as well as episodic or more regular.

Influence and Motivation Skills

Change agents working in groups cannot mandate action, so they need to influ-ence each other to act (Pearce and Conger 2003). There are often no incentives, rewards, or institutional means to influence others. Instead, change agents need to develop skills for motivating and inspiring others to act. This can range from an attitude of optimism, to celebrating people's successes, to providing a place to vent concerns, to understanding people's driving interests and trying to appeal to their interests or concerns.

Working through Status

Research suggests that status and power differentials make collective leader-ship difficult, causing more traditional, individual leadership to emerge, instead (Pearce and Conger 2003). Bensimon and Neumann (1993) suggest that a key part of any collective leadership model is addressing power and status differ-entials. Part of the group development process should be an acknowledgment of the fact that certain individuals hold privileged positions by virtue of their power, authority, expertise, or membership in a dominant group (e.g. race, gender). As a result, those in dominant groups may not understand how less powerful members are alienated and are often blind to their own privilege, as well as how it makes them see the world differently. If more privileged group members are alienating others, the team leader needs to pull these individuals aside and point out some of these issues to ensure that the team continues to move forward together by maintaining positive relationships. If the team leader is the dominant actor, then someone else in the group with the greatest power needs to communicate the status issues.

Shared Leadership

Both top-down and bottom-up leaders can benefit from shared leadership. It can enhance the efficacy of their change efforts, but the jury is still out about how it shapes the agency of each group. Some evidence suggests that it may actually mute the agency of bottom-up leaders (Kezar and Lester 2011). As noted earlier, shared leadership includes change agents working together who span those in positions of authority and those who are not. Shared leadership has clear value for those in positions of authority. Many research studies report a very high failure rate for top-down change efforts, approximately 70 percent (Burnes 2011). Often, a lack of buy-in and support from individuals throughout the organization is a major factor in this high failure rate. For those in positions of authority, working with a shared leadership approach creates growing support or buy-in for the proposed change as more people are brought into the process. Shared governance processes on campus emerged out of an understanding that, by having multiple stakeholders involved in the process, support across groups can build and implementation of the changes can be made easier. The many benefits of working in a shared leadership fashion surfaced as scholars examined the challenges that lone leaders (typically people in positions of authority) faced as they attempted to create changes in an organization's culture.

The value of shared leadership for those in positions of authority is that there is greater legitimacy and credibility for their change efforts than when they operate in a unilateral, top-down manner. The value of shared leadership for grassroots leaders is that they improve their chances of institutionalizing important changes they are interested in implementing because they can gradually gain access to the levers available to top-down leaders such as reward structures and budgets. Too often, change initiatives are led from either the top or the bottom exclusively, resulting in higher rates of failure and feelings of frustration. So, we need to recognize leadership as a collective process. If we can operate in a shared fashion across those in positions of authority and grassroots leaders, there is a greater opportunity for success in creating sustained change.

Shared leadership requires quite different skills than hierarchical or top-down leadership, but also additional skills beyond those described in the earlier section on collective leadership. A few of these skills are reviewed below.[5] Most of the research that surfaced these skills was based on cases wherein those in positions of authority chose to share power with others who did not have as much formal power. Shared leadership also can draw on the research on skills needed for collective leadership, but there are some specific areas that are distinctive to fostering shared leadership. These three areas are drawn from studies focused on top-down leaders delegating power to bottom-up leaders: empowerment, learning/development, and accountability.

Empowerment

Shared leadership processes require that those in positions of authority delegate and provide responsibility to other individuals so that they can play a leadership role when it makes sense (Spillane 2006). But empowerment also means making sure that people have adequate training, support, resources (financial, material, and human), and information to enact additional responsibilities and authority appropriately. Shared leadership models can be supported when change agents make sure to think through what infrastructure is needed to empower individuals throughout the process. For example, those who are delegated authority may need to ensure that information that was not always shared in the past is disseminated among everyone participating in the process and that they are invited to meetings.

Learning and Development of Others

Cognitive theories of change note the importance of learning as a key process to promote change; this is also critical for shared forms of leadership (Pearce and Conger 2003; Spillane 2006). If those in authority positions are not going to be the only ones responsible for creating change, then other leaders need to be engaged in the processes to learn, grow, adapt, and develop the knowledge needed to make sound decisions and with fidelity. This means there is a need for much broader distribution of data and information, as well as more conversations and sense-making among the larger group. See chapter 4 for more details on how to create learning.

Accountability

If authority to enact change is delegated to others, then there needs to be some system in place to establish accountability for the work that is executed. For instance, if a president decides that several faculty members will be given decision-making power and a budget to create a new environmental center, then the president would be well served by establishing a process for ensuring the work is done. She will need to know a reasonable plan is put in place and some reporting of progress over time should be called for, including an accounting for how funds are being used to accomplish the goal.

Shared Leadership Strategies: Approaches to Working from the Bottom up

While some studies document the strategies that top-down leaders can use to create the conditions for shared leadership, other studies examine the approach that bottom-up leaders can use to create shared leadership. A study by Kezar and Lester (2011) examined and documented strategies for bottom-up leaders who want to team with those in positions of authority. This study demonstrates that bottom-up leaders' efforts to merge with top-down leaders only worked about one-third of the time.[6] Often, their efforts were co-opted and changed once they became conjoined with those of top-down leadership and lost their original purpose or orientation. But, a set of strategies emerged for more successfully converging with top-down leaders to create shared leadership. These are showcased below.

Assess timing

Bottom-up leaders should assess whether the timing is right for converging with top-down leadership. Creating a vision, network, and support seems important for ensuring the campus is ready for greater institutional support from the top. Grassroots leaders who successfully converged with others in positions of authority typically had long-standing histories and had already been working at the grassroots level for 5, but sometimes 10–15 years. When several groups have attempted to move from a set of enthusiastic faculty, with some formal leadership support, to the larger campus, they quickly hit a wall when other faculty resisted fiercely. They went back to the drawing board, realizing they needed more champions from across the campus and greater awareness of the benefits of their reforms. Trying to move a bottom-up initiative forward too quickly can jeopardize its success because there is not enough support. Campuses that were successful with convergence took their time and built relationships within the grassroots group, tried to connect with allies, create and connect to champions across campus, and were generally patient with the process—they only went forward when the timing was right. Acting prematurely before the timing is right can lead to tremendous backlash.

Capitalize on Opportunities

Closely related to timing is capitalizing on and being open to opportunities. For example, a group of faculty who are part of an environmental initiative might test the waters from time to time to determine if there are any opportunities to work with senior administrators for expansion. If the president hires several new administrators who share an interest in promoting environmentalism, change agents could seize the moment to broaden their efforts. Missing opportunities can prolong expansion or ultimately lead to the end of a change effort. Thus, carefully watching for opportunities is very important.

Translators

Another important tactic for bottom-up leaders is relying on translators (e.g. a director of a diversity office or faculty who are former administrators) to help them frame their change initiative, identify the right data for packaging their ideas, and use appropriate language to garner attention and support. Translators can play a key role in helping bottom-up leaders to understand how to present ideas to leaders in positions of authority. Bottom-up leaders are often so involved with the language of a movement (e.g. campus engagement, process-based guided inquiry guided learning—needs to be replace throughout—guided inquiry left out often. learning) that they do not recognize that outsiders will not understand certain terminology or philosophical arguments. Translators also play a secondary role. They are liaisons that communicate information up from the bottom and down from the top, creating a channel for communication that typically would not exist. In my research on one campus, for example, the director of the multicultural center worked with bottom-up faculty change agents who did not know how to frame their interest in multiculturalism in ways that the administrators could understand or appreciate. The director of the multicultural center helped them to reframe the words they used, which were often drawn from ethnic studies, as well as to align their goals to institutional goals for retention and student success. Successful grassroots leaders learned to understand the importance of translators, to identify the right individuals to serve this role, and to maintain a close relationship with them.

Sensitizing Those in Power

A critical tactic is sensitizing those in power to the change initiative. Through concept papers, speaker series, letter writing campaigns, posting signs, holding informal meetings, working through translators, using data, sending information to administrators, and having students present information, grassroots leaders can help top-down leaders to understand the importance of their change initiative. Grassroots leaders can use multiple approaches to appeal to different top-down leaders. For example, on one campus where a group sought to create an environmentalism major, they focused on producing a concept paper to make people aware of the challenges of global warming. A joint faculty and student group then presented the paper to the administration, having developed a more focused message. In addition, they held a series of debates on campus, inviting key people and groups and making sure that senior administrators were aware of the events. Later, they also sent research papers, newspaper articles, and resource materials about environmentalism and global warming to administrators who had expressed some openness to these concepts.

Securing Membership on Key Committees

Another tactic many grassroots leaders have used is securing membership on key committees to encourage the merging of their efforts with top-down initiatives.

Committees or task forces on campus provide an arena where grassroots and top-down leadership can come together because there are already representatives of different groups throughout campus within the membership. Because they typically involve administrators, faculty, staff, and students, committees provide an avenue for influencing and impacting those in positions of authority, as well as influencing their planning efforts. If bottom-up leaders can get several representatives on a committee, they can work toward securing greater influence on campus.

Negotiation Skills

An important tool for ensuring the core grassroots interests are maintained when working with top-down leaders, preventing efforts from being subsumed, is negotiation skills. Negotiation skills help to demonstrate compromise on the part of bottom-up leaders. One example of negotiation skills taken from my research occurred when faculty and staff on a campus who led a campus sustainability initiative presented a more ambitious goal up front than they actually expected to achieve. In other words, they asked for more sustainability initiatives and goals than they expected to achieve. The administration may not agree to all of the issues or initiatives raised, so it is important to be ambitious in goals to be closer to the desired outcomes. They asked for an 80 percent reduction in the carbon footprint and the administration agreed to a 65 percent, but they had only really hoped to obtain a 50 percent reduction. Had they started at 50 percent it was unlikely they would have obtained that goal. Often grassroots leaders start with an ambitious plan so by the time the administration scales back their efforts, they will obtain close to what they hoped for. Also, being flexible is important as well. On another initiative, the faculty asked for ten new faculty hires but the administration felt that number was too high. The faculty were unwilling to negotiate the number, so ultimately the administration decided not to hire any faculty. Grassroots leaders who have shown no willingness to negotiate have often found themselves being shunned, or at least their initiatives had not been embraced by top-down leaders.

Creating Coalitions

Aligning one's interest with other grassroots initiatives or top-down initiatives with a similar goal often proves effective in the process of converging with top-down efforts. Grassroots leaders can use their coalition to create a base of support so that top-down leaders see that there is even greater support for the initiative. Grassroots leaders who look at their initiative narrowly and do not align with similar change efforts lose out on allies and support that they could garner by reaching out and identifying these common interests. Leaders in positions of authority often hesitate to support change initiatives if they do not believe that people across campus broadly embrace the effort. Diversity and environmentalism advocates often create broader coalitions to move their efforts forward, incorporating many parallel or like-minded groups in a wide-ranging bloc. Grassroots leaders who connect their initiative to other groups can generate more support.

Skepticism and Suspicion

Those in positions of power often do not share similar interests with grassroots leaders. So, grassroots leaders who have maintained skepticism about whether the interests of top-down leaders were genuinely aligned with their own ended up coming closer to meeting their original goals. An example might help illustrate this point. On one campus, top-down leaders held different views of diversity than faculty and staff. For administrators, diversity meant addressing community needs and improving retention rates. It had more to do with public relations than improving the campus. For bottom-up faculty and staff leaders, the goal of diversity efforts was to try to develop a broader understanding of social justice and equity on campus, as well as making white and class privilege more visible. Faculty and staff leaders were interested in fundamentally changing the curriculum and learning experiences by integrating materials and lessons that better resembled their understanding of diversity. It is important to identify when the commitments of top-down leaders are genuine and to not be fooled by empty rhetoric. Many in power are now embracing issues like globalization, interdisciplinarity, diversity, sustainability, or environmentalism because they see how these issues can be commodified and marketed. Thus, a skeptical approach is generally encouraged.

Summary

This chapter suggests that as change agents consider the strategies they will adopt, they are best served by working collectively with others to analyze the situation and create a course of action. This chapter also suggests the value of searching among many different stakeholder groups and different levels of the organization for possible allies. A common mistake of grassroots leaders is they often do not consider those in positions of authority as part of their leadership process. They distrust their motives or commitment, jeopardizing opportunities for institutionalizing change or making it more permanent. Similarly, in their haste to make quick changes, those in positions of authority often do not involve other leaders on campus who could provide support and legitimacy for their efforts. Shared leadership toward change is less common on campuses than it should be. This chapter offered advice for working in groups and collectives toward creating the leadership necessary for change. Lastly, it examined how leaders form strategies that take into account their level of agency and the amount of formal power they possess, as well as matching strategies to conditions.

Let's return briefly to Melissa, who had a great meeting with her colleagues where they offered several recommendations for moving forward. Using advice found in *political theories*, Melissa realizes she has become a lightning rod for criticism and can no longer effectively lead efforts for the changes she cares about. So, she has decided she will now work with faculty in ethnic studies and staff in student affairs to achieve her goals. In fact, several of her ideas, including a new scholarship program, are being adopted by other change agents on campus who are now helping to advance her ideas, but who are seen as being more legitimate leaders who are less confrontational. These faculty and staff also sit on 17 different campus committees and have agreed to bring her ideas to all these groups.

Melissa directs her efforts toward developing a strong coalition across these various groups and committees. But, she realizes there are other less threatening strategies she can use right now, so she is holding a brown bag series and bringing in speakers to talk about college completion among students of color. Her efforts are aligned to the president's interest in college completion. Through this approach, she is sensitizing those in power and others to her change ideas and aligning joint interests. Melissa also decided to create smaller goals. Her earlier, more ambitious goals were creating difficulty and frustration for her and could end up impeding her efforts because the timing is just not right for a bold plan. She is also working with student groups on campus who may be able to take a more radical approach, having them promote ideas, such as a cluster hiring program, that are just too controversial for her colleagues in ethnic studies to raise. Through this new approach to leadership and rethinking her role as a change agent, Melissa is making amazing strides.

seven
A Multi-theory Approach to Change

Case 1a: Developing an International Branch Campus

Ken is an associate dean of faculty working to establish a branch campus for his university's business school in Saudi Arabia. He recognizes that this is the culmination of much earlier work by the university to be a pioneer in international education. Because of the significant work of other change agents, the formation of the branch campus is a first-order change for this campus. However, it will still require work at multiple levels (among individuals, groups, and the overall institution) and several foci, re-examining structures, processes, and attitudes (in this case, only minorly). The content of the change initiative raises few political red flags on this campus and is well aligned to strategic plans.

While this change fits in well within the campus's priorities, a variety of contextual issues require Ken's attention. State policymakers have expressed concerns about spending public tax dollars to educate people in other countries, particularly during a period when state budgets are constrained and there is not capacity at home to admit every in-state student who wants to attend a public institution. And, while the school of business enrolls mostly graduate students, there are some tricky politics to consider in terms of the campus's focus on undergraduates and the additional expenditures often associated with business programs. Overall, alumni of the school of business have not been excited about the direction of the school, either. While a global business focus is acknowledged as a priority, the proposal to establish the branch campus has been the focus of some incendiary letters from alumni. Accreditation agencies have been looking into determining standards of practice for branch campuses, but these have not been finalized and are in flux. Ken recognizes that there are some preliminary guidelines he should continue to monitor. There are also groups on campus, specifically the humanities faculty, that consider the proposal to be morally precarious and have called for a committee to investigate the issue.

The campus culture is quite fast paced and decisions are made in a largely top-down manner. Ken has been searching for allies to support his efforts within the school of business and across campus, who can also help by taking a lead on various aspects of the initiative. He has created an advisory group that includes faculty, staff, students, and alumni who have shown interest in global issues. Additionally, he has created an informal network of individuals with whom he communicates and shares plans on a regular basis. He recognizes that his formal authority allows him to utilize certain strategies that are at his disposal. Ken has been continually taking the pulse of the campus to monitor contextual factors that might affect the progress of his change initiative. He has also been analyzing conditions to determine the type of change, its fit, and has organized a leadership team to support his initiative. Now what?

Ken will be well served by the efforts he has already undertaken. He has the leadership in place to support change, understands the tools that are available to him to create change, and has continued to analyze the type of change and context. Now he needs to decide upon a strategy for moving forward in conjunction with his leadership team. In this chapter, I review how change agents like Ken can move to the next step, developing a customized approach for change through intentional reflection and use of the theories described in Chapter 2. One of the key findings in the literature on change is that creating a complex strategy and aligning it to the change situation and type of change, often called a multi-theory approach, stands a better chance of succeeding (Bolman and Deal 2007). In order to make the multi-theory approach described here more visible, I review five cases that serve as examples of how to apply the theories and concepts reviewed in the framework in previous chapters to change processes. I have italicized theories and related concepts contained in the examples throughout the chapter. In the cases that follow, I highlight several different types of changes, change contexts, and kinds of change agents to demonstrate how the approach varies, using the principles outlined in the previous chapters.

One can use theories to *analyze* the type of change, contextual features, agency of change agents, and leadership situation, but the theories can also be used to formulate change tactics and strategy (or approach to change)—moving toward action. Using theories, change agents need to analyze the type of change, context, and agency to understand which theories might be useful and how to execute the various strategies associated with each. However, strategies cannot be developed until a careful analysis of the type of change, context of change, and leadership available is developed.

Table 7.1 offers details about the methods of analysis each of our change agents will undertake. The narrative sections describe their approaches to change. With each case study below, I will also introduce a diagram that captures their specific approach and means for conducting analysis. To provide a reminder of the strategies presented in Chapter 2, Figure 7.1 summarizes some key strategies associated with each theory of change. While certain theories— *scientific management* and *political theories* —offer many specific change strategies, others— *institutional* and *evolutionary theories*—offer more for analysis and less in terms of guides for action.

Case 1b: Creating an International Branch Campus

Ken's international branch campus provides an interesting case to examine. In this section, I use the following framework to analyze Ken's situation and offer a way forward toward change (see Figure 7.2).

TABLE 7.1. Key strategies for change within each theory

Scientific management theories	Strategic planning; restructuring; rewards and incentives; vision setting; examination of organizational infrastructure; professional development; hiring consultants; benchmarking
Evolutionary theories	Creating infrastructure or additional capacity; establishing a strong steering committee; having nimble and flexible structures; proactive, rather than reactive approaches; incorporating broad team input; priority-setting entrepreneurialism
Political theories	Creating coalitions; identifying allies; building an agenda; creating a collective vision; negotiating; mapping power; persuasion and influence; building relationships; mobilizing people and resources; raising consciousness
Social cognition theories	Forming data teams; building data infrastructure; enhancing systems thinking through training; facilitating interaction to encourage sensemaking; using dialogues to encourage sensemaking
Cultural theories	Appealing to values; examining history and context to better understand underlying values; altering mission; creating new rituals; telling stories to recreate values and understanding
Institutional and neo-institutional theory	Understanding external forces and buffering the institution; analyzing existing schemas and norms; aligning external interests in support of a direction

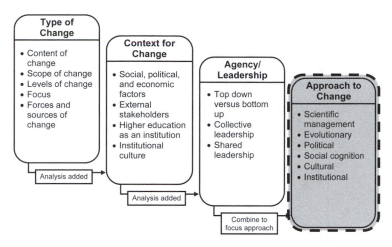

Figure 7.1. Change macro framework: approach to change.

Type of Change

Regarding the type of change, in Ken's situation deep or second-order change is not required. Most campuses constituents are already familiar with the values of a global or international education and its benefits. So, sensemaking and learning are not a main strategy. Instead, first-order change strategies are likely to be drawn from *scientific management, evolutionary* and *political theories* of change. In terms of the content of the change, there are many concerned stakeholders and the emerging politics suggests *political* and *evolutionary theories* will be very important. Because of the many state, institution, and community stakeholders who are involved, the levels of change involved are extensive. Ken will need to work across the group (*political theories*), organizational (*scientific management*), and state levels (*evolutionary theories*). Regarding focus, organizational structures and processes will be targeted for change more than attitudes, again suggesting *scientific management theories*. While the source of the change is internal and campus based, there is external resistance—making *evolutionary theories* important to consider.

Context of Change

By using *evolutionary theories*, Ken can assess that there are social, political, and economic factors and external stakeholders who are shaping the progress of the change initiative. Since members of the state legislature are concerned about the use of tax dollars, Ken needs to consider both the political and economic forces that are working against his change initiative. *Institutional* and *cultural theories* will be less important for Ken, since this particular change does not challenge the mission or structures of this institution fundamentally. The particular campus context (understood by using *cultural theories*) is one in which changes are typically enacted

---

Type of Change

- Content of change: politically charged academic change; values dissonance
- Degree of change: first order
- Levels of change: institutional, community, state
- Focus of change: structures and processes
- Source of change: internal change

 Analysis added

Context for Change

- Economic factors: use of tax dollars
- External stakeholders: state legislature, alumni
- Institutional status: challenging some traditional assumptions of institution; physical location
- Institutional culture: top-down leadership, quick decision-making, faculty resistance, reputation as a leader in internationalization
- Capacity and readiness: substantial capacity and readiness

 Analysis added

Agency/Leadership

- Top down versus bottom up: formal authority and agency
- Collective leadership: advisory board, but limited
- Shared leadership: not shared; many internal groups (e.g. faculty) and external groups do not support the initiative

 Combine to focus approach

Approach to Change: Summary of Main Theories Only

- Scientific management theory: using data, benchmarks, consultants, and planning
- Political theory: create coalitions, negotiate, and map differing interests
- Evolutionary theory: draw upon resources and reputations of external organizations that support internationalization

---

Figure 7.2. Ken's approach to change.

quickly. Also, the top-down nature of the organization makes this change harder to facilitate. This change involves many politics and in order for it to be successful each stakeholder's concerns need to be addressed, which means slowing down the change. It is important for Ken to recognize the conflict between the institutional culture (e.g. fast paced change) and the approach needed to effectively implement the change he is trying to create (e.g. a slow approach, working through the politics, and gaining buy-in). Holding these two opposing processes in place will be challenging for Ken. In addition, the campus is largely ready for this type of change and has the appropriate value set and an emerging infrastructure (e.g. curriculum, resources, advising) to support the change. Thus, he does not need to utilize strategies that are intended for preparing the campus for a change. Instead, Ken and his allies need to focus on addressing external politics and sources of resistance.

Leadership and Agency

As noted above, Ken has formal authority within the organization as an associate dean, so he can leverage many of the strategies offered through *scientific management theories*. He recognizes that the politics around his initiative and many external stakeholders' concerns suggest the need for a shared leadership process in which he secures buy-in from others who are situated above and below him in the hierarchy. To advance this effort, Ken has already created an advisory group that includes faculty, staff, students, and alumni, as well as an informal network across campus. While Ken has a great deal of agency as an associate dean, his agency is constrained because of the wide range of external and internal stakeholders who have an interest in the issue and the politics that have emerged. So, in examining his leadership agency, Ken has identified some of these constraints and needs to address them in his overall approach to change. This suggests the need for and use of *political* strategies that might not be necessary in changes he has been involved with in the past.

Approach to Change

Based on the assessments above related to the type of change, context of change, and change agency that Ken has, we would expect him to draw largely upon *scientific management* and *political theories* of change. In fact, many of the *scientific management* approaches, such as using data, benchmarks, consultants, and planning, are ways to mitigate the impact of the politics that have emerged within this case. However, we would also expect Ken to draw upon recommendations from *evolutionary theories* about how to handle external forces and ways to buffer the institution. Also, while strategies from *scientific management theories* can help diffuse some of the politics, *evolutionary theories* offer additional strategies for mitigating the impact of external forces, as well as for using external forces to support the change. For example, *evolutionary theories* suggest that Ken can draw support from important external organizations that advocate for international education to provide logic, legitimacy, and endorsements for this initiative. The underlying politics are unlikely to go away completely, so Ken will need to continually draw upon *political theories* for creating coalitions, negotiating and mapping different interests as they evolve. I now review a potential way that these theories might be drawn upon to move Ken's change initiative forward.

Evolutionary theories would recommend that Ken should not ignore the political issues in his state. He should be proactive, letting campus administrators at higher levels know about the concerns that have been registered by lawmakers, alumni, and others. However, given the fast moving, top-down culture of the campus, Ken needs to formulate a plan before going to these administrators so they are not compelled to shut down the initiative. A helpful step would be to consult with other business schools or even other units at any of the other institutions in the state where similar proposals for branch campuses are being considered to see if an alliance or coalition could be formed (*political theory*). Because Ken's institution is a pioneer and out in front on this issue, such alliances within the state may not be possible, though. This may require Ken to look to institutions in other states or to other frontrunners to identify any logics they have formed to combat similar concerns (*political theory*).

While Ken is checking in with these other campuses, he can also identify data demonstrating the successes or benefits of other branch campuses to support his argument for the expansion. For example, Ken can use data from the Association to Advance Collegiate Schools of Business (AACSB) on research suggesting the need to internationalize business school curricula and trends toward establishing branch campuses (*evolutionary theories*). In fact, a book recently published by AACSB, *Globalization of Management Education: Changing International Structures, Adaptive Strategies, and the Impact of Institutions*, provides models, examples, and data about trends in the United States and internationally. There are many national organizations that support the development of branch campuses and promote the benefits of educating students globally, not just in the jurisdictions where tax dollars are collected (*evolutionary theory* and *scientific management*). Being a pioneer on an issue often means there is less research and fewer models are available to support the direction of an initiative. Still, Ken prepares data to share in his meeting with administrators, who also point out that aspects of the campus's mission addressing innovation might also be used for supporting his proposal. He has also collected recent articles and op-eds from the *Chronicle of Higher Education* documenting issues faced by other institutions establishing branch campuses, where there are different values and factors at play. He distributes these articles to faculty and administrators and suggests that a campus forum be held to discuss them (*political theories*).

As noted above in chapter 6 on leadership agency, Ken recognizes that he will need to utilize *political* approaches to move his initiative forward. He identifies three key *political* strategies. First, he acknowledges a need to create a public report describing the benefits of branch campuses and models of success at other institutions that can be used by his superiors in addressing the concerns of various groups, particularly alumni but also policymakers, as needed. Second, Ken has determined he should develop an alliance of concerned educators, which will lobby state officials informally and try to meet with key legislators to persuade them about the value of the proposal. Third, Ken and his partners can bargain with the state, framing the branch campus as a test site and proposing that if the effort proves unsuccessful after a certain amount of time and under certain conditions it can be closed.

Also, Ken's analysis regarding the focus of change suggests that many on-campus processes and structures may need to be amended in order to support the new branch campus (*scientific management*). This will require Ken and others to identify each of the campus processes (e.g. budgeting and facilities planning) and structures (e.g. admissions criteria and policies) that will need to be considered, rethinking them in the context of an additional, branch campus. Decisions need to be made about which structures and processes will be moved completely to the branch campus, being made autonomous from the home campus. He can use principles from *scientific management theories* of restructuring to aid him in these choices. For example, McNulty and Enjeti (2010) recommend that recruitment, scholarship programs, and student support services should be offered on the branch campus. They also recommend that the quality of education offered at branch campuses be equivalent to the quality that exists on the home campus. In order to maintain a consistent standard for the quality of education, academic affairs should be managed from the home campus, whereas budgetary and planning operations should be split between the two locations. AACSB's recent report also offers various models for effectively thinking about the structure and processes necessary for supporting branch campuses.

Given Ken's campus culture is top down and fast paced in nature, Ken recognizes that his efforts to collect data and models of successful campuses in order to persuade external groups of the value of these branch campuses must be balanced with making progress on planning the branch campus (*cultural theories*). While he would prefer to focus on implementing the branch campus, he realizes he needs to engage in the political work at the same time as he is continuing to plan for opening the campus so campus administrators do not become frustrated with what may be perceived as a lack of progress. Yet, if the alumni or humanities faculty who have expressed concerns feel that Ken and his allies are moving forward without considering the issues they have raised, the whole process might backfire. Thus, while acknowledging there are problems to be worked out, he invites some of his key naysayers—mainly representatives from the humanities faculty and alumni—to join the planning team. While the culture might support Ken working unilaterally, without including individuals and groups who oppose the initiative, he realizes that they might create significant roadblocks later on if they are not included in the process. So, he follows advice from *evolutionary theories* to be proactive about scanning and addressing external and internal sources of influence and pressure, even when those adaptations are toward homeostasis and away from change. Ken continues to focus on addressing the politics around the initiative, incorporating the perspectives of different stakeholders, but also strives to make progress with planning to maintain support for his efforts among the administration, who expect to see progress. So, his strategy blends input from *political theories*, as well as understanding the institutional context through *cultural theories*.

Thus, in the end, Ken will have utilized many different theories of change—*political, evolutionary, cultural,* and *scientific management* —to advance his initiative. Had he only focused on the politics, then campus structures and processes may not have been altered to support his efforts. Had he worked only within the campus culture and ignored the prevailing politics, his efforts might have been stalled. These four very different change dynamics—politics, institutional culture, alterations to campuses' processes and structures, and engagement of external support levers—were all needed for managing a successful change process. Let's take a look at another, very different scenario and examine how it might be approached using a multi-theory approach.

Case 2: External Mandate for Improved Graduation Rates

Phyllis is the provost at a community college, where there is significant pressure from state officials to increase completion rates. The college president has just returned from a series of discussions with local and state officials, who have made it clear that they are considering measures to tie funding to some measures around completion. State officials note there is concern about dropouts and steps toward accountability that need to be instituted. If the institution does not come up with its own criteria and plan, the state will be forced to do so. While the state and local officials recognize graduation rates are not a good measure of success at community colleges, they have told campus leaders that they need to do more to convince officials that the taxpayers' money is being well spent. Phyllis has been tasked by the president with developing a response and approach to address this problem. Failure to satisfy officials' concerns could lead to mandated change, so Phyllis's efforts will be critical for helping the college to dodge imposed changes.

Phyllis recognizes that completion rates are actually a symptom of a larger accountability problem. She realizes that there is a large gap between policymakers' views of accountability and the views of campus constituents. Policymakers think about accountability in terms of outcomes, whereas Phyllis knows most people on campus think about the related processes. There is a deep cultural divide here. The change proposed by the state will not really address the problem it is concerned about solving—whether the state money being invested to support student success is well spent. If officials end up tying public funding to completion rates this could devastate the campus, throwing it into a financial crisis from which it may never fully recover. The campus is unionized, but faculty and administrators generally have a strong relationship and recent collective bargaining agreements have been quite successful. (See Figure 7.3 for a summary analysis of the case.)

Type of Change

- Content of change: external threat; values dissonance
- Degree of change: unclear — could be first or second order
- Levels of change: state and institutional levels
- Focus of change: unclear
- Source of change: external

 Analysis added

Context for Change

- Economic and political factors: public and legislative accountability concerns
- External stakeholders: state legislature, public
- Institutional status: not challenging traditional assumptions of institution
- Institutional culture: institutional values differ from external values and priorities around completion; strong relationships between faculty and administration; resources constrained
- Capacity and readiness: strong capacity and some readiness

 Analysis added

Agency/Leadership

- Top down versus bottom up: formal authority and agency
- Collective leadership: engagement among all state community college leaders
- Shared leadership: shared interests between faculty and administration

 Combine to focus approach

Approach to Change: Summary of Main Theories Only

- Political theory: create coalitions, negotiate, and map differing interests
- Evolutionary theory: proactive task force, data collection, bringing campus constituencies together to problem solve, building on internal trust and existing capacity to face threats

Figure 7.3. Phyllis's approach to change.

Type of Change

Phyllis is responsible for managing a distinct type of change, buffering the institution from a potential change that would threaten its livelihood and sustainability. This change mandate originated from outside the institution. The president has given Phyllis two months to develop a thoughtful response that can be communicated back to the system's office, so she has very little time to act. The type of change Phyllis has encountered is very typical among the literature on *evolutionary theories* of change. The strategies focused on unplanned change described in Chapter 3, in particular, will be applicable to this case. The content of the change is very political in nature. Phyllis recognizes that policymakers and campus constituents have very different beliefs and understandings about accountability, college completion, and potential reasons why students do not complete their degrees. The degree of change is unclear; it could be either first or second order depending on her response. The level of change is much more at the enterprise or state level, suggesting the use of *evolutionary* tactics and means for analysis. At this juncture, the focus of change is not quite clear, so it will need to be analyzed further throughout the change process.

Context for Change

Using *evolutionary theories*, Phyllis has recognized that political and other external factors are heavily shaping this case. The public is demanding greater accountability and officials are attempting to hold institutions responsible for improving graduation rates. The stakeholders that are most directly related to this case are the policymakers, but the general public (and in the case of community college, the local community) and its concerns must also be considered in this case. Using *cultural theory*, Phyllis, who has been provost for a while, understands the faculty's beliefs and values about facilitating completion and knows that these views differ from policymakers'. Phyllis will have to capitalize on the strong relationship between the faculty and administration to help facilitate making changes at a rapid pace. She recognizes that if the relationship between the faculty and staff was strained, there would be additional layers of complexity and difficulty involved. Thus, as *evolutionary theories* would predict, their earlier work to create an organization with the capacity for change by having a solid infrastructure and functional relationships among groups on campus enhances their ability to respond to change.

Leadership and Agency

Phyllis is lucky to have a great degree of agency as provost and many strategies and tactics at her disposal. However, because of the urgency of this crisis, her agency is also limited in some ways. She will need to utilize relationships that are already in place. Given the short time frame for action and crisis conditions, Phyllis will need to rely on *evolutionary theories* of change and the strategies within them. *Scientific management* tactics (e.g. planning, consultants) that normally would be at her disposal may be less helpful within this particular initiative. She also recognizes that she will need to work with leaders at colleges across the state because the type of change proposed by state officials will not just affect her own institution; it will affect all other community colleges within the state. From a *political* perspective, she also recognizes that by working collectively with the other colleges, they can all have a much stronger voice and greater agency.

Approach to Change

While Ken's process at the start of this chapter required the use of multiple theories of change, the type of change and context here suggest a more focused approach is needed, drawing largely on *evolutionary* and *political* strategies and tactics for change. While you'll see below that Phyllis uses *cultural theories* to evaluate the differences in views and values between state officials and campus constituents, she also uses *political* strategies to overcome those differences.

Luckily, Phyllis is familiar with *evolutionary theories* of change and recognizes that when there are external threats it is important to have a strategic and measured response. But *evolutionary theory* suggests that she will need to respond quickly, yet thoughtfully. In order to be responsive, Phyllis knows some of the steps she needs to take. They include obtaining data from the institutional research office about dropouts, trying to better understand the reasons for attrition, and exploring the ways that the institution can respond to these issues. By better understanding the underlying causes, Phyllis might be able to create a more focused plan to be proposed to state policymakers, which will measure completion rates and address their accountability concerns. She also obtains data about the number of students pursuing degrees versus those who are non-degree seeking. Additionally, Phyllis creates a cabinet-level task force to help her collect and analyze the data needed to inform the president and to provide to the state—having a strong, newly formed governance body or steering core helps change agents to respond quickly to external challenges (*evolutionary* and *scientific management*).

Of course, this problem is not isolated to Phyllis's community college. Luckily, she is aware of the importance of networks and collective leadership for change in a political process. As a result, she has already been meeting with the leadership of other colleges over the past five years, so there is already a sense of trust in working together. Phyllis reaches out to provosts she has already been working with at several other community colleges in the state to discuss creating a unified response, informed by an examination of their own unique campus contexts. By working together through a coalition, she knows the institutions will have a much better chance of achieving success (*political theories*). So, each campus is tasked with checking in with their faculty and staff. The provost's team will gather at a meeting in one month to review various proposals they might offer to the system office. If disgruntled faculty or staff go to the media because they are not included, this could derail their plan.

Also, she is adept at seeing that campus constituents' and state policymakers' views on accountability are quite different and any response will require that each group better understand each other's perspectives. *Cultural theories* of change focus leaders' attention on the value systems and beliefs of different groups in change processes. In order to bridge the different perspectives between policymakers and campus constituents, she needs to not only offer up data, but engage in strategic communications with both groups. So, she calls for a town hall meeting with faculty and staff to discuss the potential state mandate and to call for creative thinking and responses. *Evolutionary theories* point to the need to bring campus constituents together to help problem solve and to create buy-in for potential plans for addressing external threats. She cautions faculty and staff to think about accountability as more than just ensuring that programs are in place to support retention and to recognize that policymakers think about accountability in terms of outcomes. In the short amount of time that she has, she cannot change value systems, but can try to shape the more immediate climate to be more supportive and think about how to formulate a measured and thoughtful response that draws on the collective expertise of her campus. The town hall meeting produces several proposals that are much stronger than Phyllis's original ideas. She shares these new ideas at a system-wide meeting of provosts and presidents.

At the same meeting, each campus shares data and ideas and the leadership teams from each campus agree to a joint plan. Together, the presidents go to the state higher education committee to propose some proven approaches for improving completion and provide more accurate data related to retention, taking student motivations into account. They offer a plan with measurable goals and targets, ideas for implementation, and recommendations and processes to measure improvement. The state higher education committee staff agrees to the new approach, but asks for more aggressive goals. With some hesitation, the presidents agree to negotiate (*political theories*). *Political theories* suggest that rather than taking a hardline approach that might alienate the legislative staff, the campus leaders should compromise, particularly given the progress they have already made from the original plan. The presidents feel that the new plan is much better than what was initially proposed by the state, but also more ambitious than what they had put forward on their campuses. So, there will still be work to do once they return to their colleges. But, because they negotiated, they are in a much better position than they were when the state originally proposed tying funding to graduation rates.

Case 3: Implementing Family-friendly Policies

So far we have focused on two individuals in positions of power. Now, we move to three bottom-up leaders on campus with varying amounts of agency. I will also introduce a new set of interesting change initiatives, identifying how a multi-theory approach is needed and drawn upon to address the issue at the heart of each case.

> *Jeff is a faculty member at a technical college who is interested in creating more family-friendly policies. Over the years, Jeff has witnessed many faculty, particularly women in the sciences, who have had to choose between family and career. The institution has not been supportive in*

*any way. He has watched many women colleagues leave the profes-
soriate out of frustration, as a result. He has also witnessed many tal-
ented women staff members leave because they could not get part-time
hours after having children. The technical college where Jeff works has
a history of enrolling male students and has a predominately male faculty. While more women students are enrolling at the college and some
women have been recruited and retained in the faculty, it is still largely a
male domain. Having been on the campus for many years, Jeff has had
a chance to appreciate and understand many of the norms that have
prevented women faculty and students from being successful. Some
of the earlier efforts to support and diversify women faculty were met
with resistance and apathy. But, in more recent years, new faculty have
been hired who are from a new generation and have slightly different
values. Jeff might be able to capitalize on these values this time to make
changes that were not possible before or were much more difficult to
achieve in earlier times. While Jeff has no formal power or authority as a
faculty member, his years of working on the campus have allowed him to
develop a pretty vast network of colleagues. (See Figure 7.4.)*

Type of Change

Because Jeff recognizes this is a transformational or second-order change, he will
need to develop strategies that help people on campus to rethink their existing and
unrecognized patriarchal value systems. Given the second-order nature of change
in this case, *social cognition* and *cultural theories* will be drawn upon heavily to
move forward. The content of the change is likely to be resisted, not only because
of the current value system, but because of the history of the institution and the
current lack of support structures and processes. The known resistance suggests
that *political theories* of change will be important within this process. The level of
change is focused at the individual and organizational levels, so will need to draw
upon *social cognition* and *scientific management theories* of change. The focus of
the change will be processes, structures, and attitudes and, given the comprehensive nature of the focus, will draw upon multiple theories of change. The source of
the initiative is a faculty member at the institution, so it originated from within,
but since there are sources of resistance, mostly internal, *political theories* will be at
the forefront, rather than *evolutionary theories*.

Context for Change

Jeff knows from his prior efforts that this will be very difficult and that there are
some strong sources of resistance on campus. Again, this suggests *political theories* will be particularly important. But, he has spent time getting to know the
new faculty and staff on campus, whom he sees as potential supporters for his
initiative. While there is minimal organizational support for the initiative, using

---

Type of Change

- Content of change: politically charged and largely not understood — requiring sensemaking
- Degree of change: second order
- Levels of change: institutional and group (faculty) levels
- Focus of change: processes, structures, and attitudes
- Source of change: internal

 Analysis added

Context for Change

- Economic and political factors: social pressures from business to diversify faculty
- External stakeholders: NSF
- Institutional status: challenging organizational values
- Institutional culture: climate shifting from unsupportive to some valuing of family friendly; long-standing sexism
- Capacity and readiness: some capacity and readiness

 Analysis added

Agency/Leadership

- Top down versus bottom up: no formal authority; long time on campus and existing relationships builds agency
- Collective leadership: builds collective leadership among the administration, faculty, and staff
- Shared leadership: shared interests between faculty and administration

 Combine to focus approach

Approach to Change: Summary of Main Theories Only

- Social cognition theory: speaker series, public speeches, materials and articles, learning from women
- Political theory: co-chair for task force, incremental changes, map differing interests
- Evolutionary theory: draw upon NSF support, external speakers

---

Figure 7.4. Jeff's approach to change.

analysis from an *evolutionary* perspective regarding the context for change, Jeff knows there are larger external forces that he can draw upon for additional support such as the National Science Foundation. He also knows there are increasing social and political pressures to diversify the faculty in STEM fields and that business leaders want a more diverse workforce. But, changing organizational values supporting more family-friendly policies run counter to the structures and processes of higher education. *Institutional theories* suggest that this change will be particularly difficult as a result, requiring a deep and thorough strategy for change. Jeff has seen earlier initiatives attempting to create family-friendly policies fail, but he feels that recent hiring and leadership changes may make the institution ready for change at this particular point in time. Based on this assessment, he feels confident about moving forward with a complex strategy that acknowledges and addresses this type of multi-faceted second-order change.

Leadership and Agency

While Jeff has limited agency and no formal leadership role, he has developed a network of colleagues to draw upon to create a collective leadership process. He is aware of the need, but also the potential for shared and collective leadership for this effort. Luckily, Jeff has a good relationship with his dean and has met with him to discuss some of his ideas related to this change initiative. By testing the waters with the dean and others in positions of authority, as well as determining he has support among some new junior faculty members, Jeff is working to create a shared leadership environment, which is particularly important for creating deep change.

Approach to Change

Like in Ken's case, Jeff's change effort will require a multi-change theory approach, utilizing tactics and analysis from most of the theories presented in this book. Using the analysis of content, context, and leadership agency, I described how Jeff can draw upon multiple theories to advance his initiative. Yet, given this is a second-order change, Jeff will foreground *cognitive* and *cultural theories* of change in his approach to be successful, which are best for moving forward second-order changes. It is important to note that this initiative would be unlikely to move forward because of the difficulty of this type of change unless Jeff had formed a complex strategy addressing the politics, values, and underlying institutional assumptions.

Drawing on *political theories*, prior to his meeting with the dean, he has lunch with several colleagues he believes will be supportive of the creation of family-friendly policies. He asks them if they would be willing to serve on a campus-wide task force if he is able to get one started. He also asks for their support for creating a speaker series that he wants to get off the ground. The meeting with the dean goes really well and the dean says he will champion the idea of setting up a task force with the provost. However, using his knowledge of *sensemaking theory* and *cultural theories* of change, Jeff cautions the dean that additional groundwork needs to be completed before a higher-level task force can be established. Instead, he asks for a small amount of funding to create the speaker series. Members of the campus need to wrestle with the ideas and concepts first. Jeff quips to the dean, "We need to start slow to move fast."

Through his lunches, Jeff obtains the names of several scholars and speakers who are experts on family-friendly policies. He decides that in the next academic year he will sponsor several speakers to come to campus to discuss the need for family-friendly policies, as well as different approaches or models for creating a more family-friendly campus. He invites high-level scientists, ones he knows can influence people on campus. Jeff recognizes that few people will probably attend these events, so he uses faculty meetings and events to promote the speakers series and asks administrators to also mention the talks in their meetings (*sensemaking*).

In applying *cultural theories* of change, Jeff recognizes that he needs to change the communication, language, values, and thought patterns on campus. He provides leaders with prepared messages to include in their speeches, which will help introduce new values and make them a part of ongoing communications. Thus, even if faculty and staff do not attend the events Jeff has planned, the same kind of ideas can be circulated and capitalized on to start changing norms. Jeff also recognizes that this change is more likely to receive support if it is seen as part of a national initiative, so he and his team apply for and obtain an ADVANCE planning grant from the National Science Foundation. ADVANCE is a National Science Foundation initiative focused on getting more women and underrepresented minorities into the science, technology, engineering, and mathematics fields. By drawing upon impactful, external levers from national organizations, Jeff uses principles from *evolutionary theory* to persuade others to support change. Guided by *cultural* and *evolutionary theories* of change, he recognizes that a campus as entrenched as his will require pressure from outside forces to create motivation.

Having successfully started the speaker series and garnering new attention through the ADVANCE grant, Jeff decides to meet with the provost about creating the campus-wide task force. He feels it might be met with less resistance now that people have a better understanding of the need for change. The provost assigns a high-level faculty member who had previously been fairly resistant to implementing family-friendly policies, but has recently had a change of heart, to be Jeff's co-chair on the task force. The provost makes sure that advocates are assigned to the committee, but includes several individuals who disapprove or have raised critical questions, as well. Both the Provost and Jeff recognize that they need to acknowledge different interests and respect them throughout the process so that people do not feel they were excluded or rolled over. This response demonstrates attention to campus politics and draws upon *political theory*.

However, Jeff realizes that a task force comprised of members with divergent interests may get bogged down in conflict. So, he meets with each member prior to their full task force meeting to ask them to keep an open mind and support the process (*political theory*). Additionally, he schedules a retreat for the group so they can spend a substantial amount of time discussing the issue at their very first meeting, rather than having a more superficial meeting where they may not be able to create a shared understanding or sense of purpose. As described in the earlier chapter on sensemaking and organizational learning (Chapter 4), shared cognition is critical for advancing change (*social cognitive theory*). Jeff also provides many materials about family-friendly policies to try to bring everyone closer to being on the same page. All of this attention paid to making meaning is a purposeful part of Jeff's strategy to shift campus norms and values. His attention to meaning making, communication, and influencing shifting mindsets continues over the following year; it continues until Jeff feels that campus administrators, faculty, and staff have reached an appreciation for the issue and an approach to creating family-friendly policies that will meet the needs of this particular campus (*social cognitive theory*). At a major meeting a year and a half into the process, Jeff decides it is time to begin talking about implementation of the plan, which he has previously worked to slow down until he could tell that there was sufficiently broad support for the task force's recommendations.

Campus conversations about the ADVANCE grant provided a good avenue for beginning a broader discussion across the campus about supporting women and underrepresented minorities. *Cognitive theories* help demonstrate the importance of ongoing learning during the change process. Through the task force meetings and deliberations, even Jeff's perspectives and those of several other task force members have been changed by the insights and ideas raised. Jeff came to realize that he had actually overemphasized the potential impact of family-friendly policies. Conversations with women on the task force, for example, made him realize that these policies would only partly ameliorate the problem. Many other practices and policies also needed to be addressed, such as recruitment and hiring processes that were biased toward white male candidates, campus socialization and mentoring opportunities that often exclude women, and an overreliance on women for service on committees and student advising. The women on the task force bring in research and data about these other problems to broaden the discussion and properly diagnose the true nature of the problem at hand. While family-friendly policies are certainly helpful for addressing some of the problems that have prevented women from being as successful as possible, Jeff had not realized the wide range of other issues that needed to be considered as the task force developed an implementation plan. The task force process described here demonstrates the importance of individual and organizational learning, another key change theory.

Jeff can now move forward by working with the task force to analyze campus structures, processes, human resources, and symbols that can support family-friendly policies and create a plan for change (*cultural* and *scientific management theories*). Following best principles offered by the ADVANCE initiative and informed by the women on the task force, the implementation plan includes training sessions for department chairs on issues such as recruitment, hiring, and maternity leave, as these typically take place at the department level. These many process and structural dimensions reflect the changes noted as being critical within *scientific management theories* of change. The plan also includes a mentoring program, which will be supported by funds from the provost's office. Many campuses have found that women do not make use of family-friendly policies for fear it will affect their tenure and promotion. So, campus leaders will be encouraged to openly discuss their support for the new policies so department chairs and faculty understand they are available. While the plan includes several other tactics, the approach is multi-faceted and draws on ideas related to restructuring, training, how support is offered, and encourages paying attention to symbols and language (*scientific management* and *cultural theories*). I will now move on to an example from student affairs, which also describes how staff can create change.

Case 4: Using Social Media to Reach Diverse Students

Hector is a new professional in student affairs. In his masters program, he became very interested in examining the ways that social media might be used to connect with students who sometimes become isolated on campuses and may have difficultly finding support networks, as a result. While his initial interests were focused specifically on transgendered students, he has begun to think about other groups such as veterans, a group with growing numbers on campuses, but whose members sometimes find that campus services and support functions are not designed to best serve them. Using social media, infrastructure can be created to better support students who may become disconnected, with a fairly modest investment and often much more quickly than other types of programs or services can be mobilized. Additionally, some students encounter stigma. Hector's research suggests that enabling such students to connect through social media will make them more comfortable reaching out to others and increase the likelihood that they will make use of available support services.

As a graduate student, Hector worked with a prominent scholar in student affairs and worked on creating a mock-up of the kind of services and programs that could be enhanced through social media. He even created an organizational plan for staffing the social media program by making use of volunteers. His innovative ideas and work were recognized through a prize awarded by a major student affairs organization. In general, student affairs organizations broadly embrace the use of social media for engaging and connecting with students. Hector's graduate advisor encouraged him by telling him this was an important innovation and hoped he would continue this work when he entered the workforce. Hector is currently working at a large, public comprehensive masters-granting institution in an urban area. His supervisors are generally supportive of fostering an outreach mission and meeting the needs of an increasingly diverse and changing student body. However, Hector often hears from administrators that they are concerned about budget cuts and cannot afford to focus on much else right now. Many of the long-term staff talk about the days when these same leaders were innovative in their work and helped create all sorts of changes on the campus, such as a commuter student center, multicultural centers, and community outreach programs. Yet, these recollections seems to only be nostalgia at this point in time; few among the staff believe that the same types of changes are attainable in increasingly difficult financial times. Hector explains that his idea will cost the institution very little money, but other staff are always telling him how difficult it is to get anybody's attention, even for ideas that cost virtually nothing. Fellow staff are disheartened, describing how difficult it will be to get members of the administration to allow technology staff to work with Hector to update some of the institution's existing social media sites and technology to integrate his ideas. Furthermore, staff note how the technology expertise on campus is limited when it comes to social media and that there is insufficient infrastructure in place anyway. The climate for innovation and quality improvement seems stagnant. Yet, Hector's supervisors are very active in national student affairs organizations, so he wonders if there is potential for influencing them.

At first, Hector thought his focus would only need to be on the social media project, but as he talks to other staff members, he begins to see an even larger agenda that might include the need to reinvigorate a sense of innovation and possibility on a campus paralyzed by budget cuts. But, can a new professional just beginning his career achieve such a lofty goal? (See Figure 7.5.)

Type of Change

The content of the change is aligned with the institutional mission and will likely surface few political concerns. Hector's institution has conveyed its commitment to meeting the needs of an increasingly diverse student body. The nature of the change is first order within this institution, since there is already an understanding of the importance of supporting students from diverse backgrounds and the changes are not outside of the existing value system. Given this is a first-order change, the process will likely draw upon *scientific management* approaches. The campus is already engaged in using some social media, although only superficially. The change Hector proposed involves working with people within his unit (e.g. group level), but also with the broader administration that provides funding and oversight for the technology infrastructure on campus. Given the budget constraints and difficulty gaining the attention of leaders, Hector's having to work throughout the broader organizational level makes this change more challenging than it might otherwise be if social media were decentralized among the various units. *Evolutionary theories* suggest that Hector will have difficulty creating any sense of priority for his agenda item; they suggest that the budget will overwhelm leaders at the institution, which certainly appears to have happened. The multiple levels of change involved complicate this change process slightly.

Type of Change

- Content of change: not politically charged, no values or cognitive dissonance
- Degree of change: first order
- Levels of change: institutional and group levels
- Focus of change: processes and structures
- Source of change: internal

 Analysis added

Context for Change

- Economic and political factors: recession created budget strain and lack of motivation
- External stakeholders: state legislature, national student affairs organizations
- Institutional status: not challenging organizational values
- Institutional culture: long-standing innovator and leader in student affairs; climate currently unfavorable due to budget
- Capacity and readiness: limited capacity and some readiness

---

 Analysis added

Agency/Leadership

- Top down versus bottom up: limited agency as new professional; no formal authority, so bottom up; status from graduate advisor
- Collective leadership: developing relationships with technology staff and administration; no collective leadership at present
- Shared leadership: currently, no shared interests between staff in technology and student affairs and the administration

---

 Combine to focus approach

Approach to Change: Summary of Main Theories Only

- Political theory: build upon relationship with powerful advisor, create clout with administration, develop common interests with the technology staff
- Scientific management: review campus technology infrastructure, joint planning between technology and student affairs

---

Figure 7.5. Hector's approach to change.

The focus is mostly on processes and structures, rather than attitudes, again suggesting *scientific management* approaches to change would be appropriate.

If Hector decides to take on broader changes amid a campus culture of stagnation, rather than innovation, he might be engaging in more second-order change because he will need to attempt to change people's underlying values. But, for the purposes of this case, we will focus on Hector's social media plans as a first-order change process.

Context for Change

The type of change is less problematic for Hector than the context for change. The broader political context, characterized by decreasing funds, has created disequilibrium on the campus, making it more difficult to provide quality programming and support than in the past. *Evolutionary theories* suggest that unless the leadership of this campus can buffer the institution from the onslaught of external challenges an increasingly negative culture will take root on the campus. The history of the campus, its more long-standing institutional culture, is one marked by innovation and leaders' support for change, though, which suggests that there is a value system in place to tap into (*cultural theory*). In addition, student affairs leaders have been very involved with national student affairs organizations and have not only influenced national trends, but tended to be on the cutting edge of new practices. Hector can also look to external stakeholders such as national student affairs organizations for support on integrating social media (*evolutionary theory*). The context suggests a sort of mixed bag; if Hector can effectively draw upon and appeal to the campus's history of innovation and reconnect faculty and staff to the broader national dialogue, he might be able to pull them out of the downward spiral they are in with regard to *evolutionary* forces, particularly the budget cuts.

Leadership and Agency

Remember that Hector is a new professional, so he has very limited agency within the institution. However, his connection to a prominent scholar in student affairs through his graduate program, as well as the fact that he received a prestigious award for his innovative ideas from a national student affairs organization, provides him some avenues for empowerment and agency. Given that he is fairly new and his colleagues do not appear interested in going out on a limb for his plans right now, it may be difficult for Hector to create more collective leadership. His best opportunity is to try to partner with some other student affairs leaders on campus who know and respect his graduate advisor. Given his bottom-up positioning, he should likely use *political* strategies to advance his ideas.

Approach to Change

Hector's approach to change will rely primarily on *political theory* and *scientific management* approaches. Yet, the many significant constraints and changes in context will make *cultural theories* important to consider throughout the change process. Given his limited agency on this campus, Hector decides to contact his former graduate advisor to ask about how he might go about influencing the vice president and dean for student affairs (*political theory*). His advisor agrees to contact them to describe his innovative work in graduate school and let them know about the award that he received. While some of these matters have already been discussed during the hiring process, it is hard to know if anybody really thought about the potential of Hector's social media work and how it might improve the campus. His advisor suggests asking student affairs administrators to participate in a session at a national student affairs conference that is planned to focus on the issue of social media and its potential within urban institutions to meet diverse students' needs. His advisor notes that she will appeal to their history as an innovator, as well as their mission and commitment to reaching out to students who are often marginalized (*cultural theory*). Hector is excited about the possibilities.

While he waits to hear back from his advisor, Hector recognizes that he also has to explore and potentially address the limited expertise and infrastructure for social media (*scientific management*). Using his political skills, he decides to take several staff members from the technology office out for lunch under the auspices of sharing some of the ideas that he is generating for social media with them, but more just to connect with them about similar interests and ideas (*political theory*). He also helps to expand their thinking by introducing his new social media ideas (*social cognition*). He does not mention that he has an interest in moving the ideas forward at the institution yet, but tries to determine whether there is any interest in building the social media infrastructure. He also wants to further develop his relationships with them, so he might call upon them later if student affairs administrators decide that they want to pursue his ideas.

He hears back from his former advisor, who tells him that the student affairs administrators have agreed to be on the conference panel. She also mentions that she provided Hector's name as a resource for their presentation and indicated she would ask Hector to follow up with them. Hector contacts the two administrators, but doesn't hear back from them. He begins to become dismayed. He e-mails his graduate advisor again; almost a month has passed since his original e-mail and he doesn't know how many times he should reach out to them. She suggests that he contact their administrative assistants and set up a meeting through them, instead. The administrative assistance responds to Hector immediately with some possible meeting dates and times. Hector simply wasn't aware how busy senior administrators are and that they often don't manage their own calendars or respond to e-mails, particularly on larger campuses such as this one (*cultural theory*). Hector's only work experience so far has been on smaller liberal arts campuses where people, even senior administrators, were typically very responsive. Even the rather small details of institutional culture—like how to schedule a meeting—can shape the progress of a change process. Hector almost gave up on moving forward when he did not hear back from the administrators (*cultural theory*).

Hector speaks with his advisor a few days before the meeting and asks whether he should present his proposal for the new social media program to the administrators. Hector notes that he is not sure whether he will get another opportunity to meet with the senior administrators. She recommends that he should not plan on presenting the proposal, but instead focus on helping them to develop their presentation. If, for some reason, the mood seems right, she said it would be alright to bring a copy of his proposal and to be prepared to discuss it, but cautioned it probably wasn't a good idea. She noted, "You need to get to know them first and be seen as an asset." She recommends that it might be a good idea to ask them questions about some of their earlier programs, which received national attention, to bring those innovations back into their consciousness. Hector's continued discussion with his advisor is a strong illustration of *political* leadership towards change. Through his interactions with her, he is mapping power structures, gaining influence, developing insight into stakeholder interests, and garnering greater access to power.

The day arrives for his meeting with the vice president of student affairs and the dean. Hector provides some ideas for their presentation and they all do a lot of brainstorming. He finds that the administrators are quite excited to engage in the discussion. In fact, they are much more excited than he had expected. He takes the opportunity to ask about their previous initiatives like their community engagement efforts and commuter center, as well as whether they had any other ideas for changes they might pursue in the future, noting the challenges faced by groups like transgendered students and veterans. Both administrators looked a bit dismayed at first, apparently reminded of the difficult circumstances they find themselves in with regard to the budget. Hector connects the presentation they are creating with other possibilities for making changes on their campus at virtually no cost.

A lightbulb goes off for the administrators. They suggest that they schedule another meeting where they can discuss this particular issue in more depth. At the second meeting, Hector presents his proposal. The administrators note their approval for Hector's idea and he asks them if they will work to provide support through the technology office to enact his ideas. They enthusiastically agree to contact the business division to help support his plan. He describes some of the basic infrastructure and expertise issues that may need to be addressed using his earlier scanning of the campus infrastructure (*scientific management*). They ask him to write up some of the needed or suggested changes, which will be brought to a joint meeting between student affairs staff and the business division and can inform planning for the central technology office (*scientific management*). The joint meeting of these offices results in an even broader meeting to discuss support for social media across the campus. Hector is also invited to a series of meetings to provide input and ideas for an emerging social media strategic plan. All of this occurs over the next academic year. The changes don't happen overnight; a year has passed and he is still just in the process of getting the approvals and infrastructure in place to execute his plan. However, a year ago he couldn't imagine any change could occur at all. Hector also learns the value of multiple approaches to change. Had he focused only on the technology infrastructure, which had been his main focus at the start, he would have missed the opportunity to use political strategies to shift campus priorities and interests, which were essential to creating his change.

Case 5: Disseminating Process-oriented Guided Inquiry Learning

We now turn to our final example of this chapter, featuring Sylvia, a faculty member who is working with a consortium of institutions to create curricular changes.

Sylvia is an assistant professor in chemistry who is interested in working with several institutions as part of a consortium of liberal arts colleges to integrate process-oriented, guided inquiry into the curriculum across the sciences. She has been to several professional development programs offered nationally about process-oriented guided inquiry learning and has joined a national network called POGIL (Process-Oriented Guided Inquiry Learning). Through POGIL, she has met faculty from several other campuses who are part of a consortium of liberal arts colleges that her campus belongs to. Few faculty members on her own campus use process-oriented guided inquiry learning, but Sylvia notices that it is becoming very popular in chemistry and was the subject of several sessions at the last few disciplinary conferences she attended. There is currently a new president on campus, who is promoting service learning and civic engagement, which Sylvia does not know much about. But, she does know that the faculty have not embraced many curricular changes and that there is some grumbling about the new president. Jokes are circulating about whether service learning is a fad they are being asked to support. There has been tremendous turnover in leadership over the years, making it difficult for innovation to occur on the campus throughout the last 20 years. In addition, the faculty have been very resistant to top-down changes that have been put in place by administrators over the years. Sylvia wonders whether if she tries to bring up process-based guided inquiry, it will be met with the same response as service learning. She meets with a colleague who is part of the consortium interested in integrating process-based guided inquiry on a nearby campus and is also a member of the POGIL network to discuss the issue. In her discussions with this colleague and others, she finds out that on other campuses process-based guided learning is seen as a foundational technique. While it is different from lecturing, it is not seen as a more radical pedagogy, as service learning is often characterized. (See Figure 7.6.)

Type of Change

- Content of change: not seemingly politically charged; some values dissonance
- Degree of change: first order
- Levels of change: mostly individual and group levels but also institutional
- Focus of change: processes, structures, and attitudes
- Source of change: internal and external through the consortium and national groups such as NSF

 Analysis added

Context for Change

- Economic and political factors: support from national organizations like NSF, private sector's desire for competent science graduates
- External stakeholders: consortium, NSF, disciplinary societies, foundations
- Institutional status: not challenging organizational values
- Institutional culture: new president, leadership turnover, lack of stability for innovations, cynicism about curricular changes
- Capacity and readiness: limited capacity and readiness

 Analysis added

Agency/Leadership

- Top down versus bottom up: limited agency as an assistant professor; no formal authority
- Collective leadership: consortium
- Shared leadership: currently, there are shared interests between administration and faculty

 Combine to focus approach

Approach to Change: Summary of Main Theories Only

- Social cognition theory: workshops, ongoing professional development, sensemaking through ongoing meeting group
- Political theory: engineers and department chairs to provide support, leverage support from consortium
- Evolutionary theory: draw upon external support from NSF, consortium, and disciplinary societies
- Scientific management: create incentives

Figure 7.6. Sylvia's approach to change.

Type of Change

For Sylvia, the integration of process-oriented guided inquiry learning may not raise as many political alarms as service learning has among the science faculty. The National Science Foundation has funded many problem-based learning projects and POGIL is a large and well-supported network nationally. There is a great deal of legitimacy to draw upon from this national network (*evolutionary theory*). There is no moral component, as there is in service learning, which is often a trigger for concern among science faculty. The scope of change is more first-order change, requiring people to rethink their pedagogical strategies to be more inquiry based and active. While on some campuses this might be a second-order change, at a small liberal arts college where many faculty utilize active learning strategies, this is merely a difference of kind than a whole new pedagogical philosophy. The focus of the change will be expansive, though, as it will require rethinking of campus classrooms and resources to support this type of learning, as well as professional development. Thus, the focus is broad and involves reshaping various processes and campus systems. The change comes from both internal and external sources, with the consortium providing external support. The level of change is more directly focused on the individual, but also requires some change at the organizational level to support the more individual pedagogical changes. Thus, *scientific management* strategies (aimed at the organizational level) will be needed, as well as *social cognition* strategies aimed at creating individual-level changes in thinking.

Context for Change

Using *cultural theories* related to institutional culture to assess the campus, an important context feature for Sylvia to consider is the new president on campus, as well as the ongoing turnover in leadership that has made it difficult to create support for changes and innovative. The campus context historically has not been characterized and still is not innovative; the campus is quite conservative. Since there have been so few changes over the years, Sylvia is having problems even identifying what the campus culture is with regard to change. It is also important for her to consider that she does not know how the faculty members on her campus feel about this new type of teaching and whether they will be supportive. Given their lack of support for service learning, which is advocated for by the new president, there is reason to believe that faculty may be resistant. However, it is also important to recognize that resistance often arises because changes have been implemented from the top down. On the small campus, bottom-up changes are perceived as being much more acceptable. Given that her change initiative is bottom up in orientation, Sylvia recognizes that her initiative may not be met with the same resistance. However, she notes that the lack of ongoing leadership might make implementation and sustaining of this new form of teaching difficult. She wonders how she will get the institutional support for classroom changes or resources given the instability of leadership.

There does not appear to be organizational readiness for change, so Sylvia will need to work to provide the attitudes, structures, and processes to support change.

The proposed change, though, is aligned with traditional higher education values, so it is unlikely to lead to great resistance. It is important to note that there is broader environmental support (through the consortium) for her change initiative and that important external stakeholders such as the National Science Foundation, disciplinary societies, and other regional consortia support and are advancing this change. *Evolutionary* and *institutional theories* would suggest that having support from these many external stakeholders for this type of change would make it possible for Sylvia to implement the change she is pursuing.

Leadership and Agency

As an assistant professor, Sylvia needs to be careful about rocking the boat too much or being perceived as being too far outside the mainstream. She also has very limited contacts on campus since she is fairly new. She does not yet know who can be counted on or who has influence. Her goal of trying to work across a consortium of campuses is ambitious, but the plan also alleviates some political pressure since she is working in a collective with others who have a great deal of agency and clout. Not only does the consortium provide collective leadership, it provides her agency for her efforts. She is not isolated or alone; the consortium provides her legitimacy. Additionally, as noted above, there are a variety of external organizations that provide support for her efforts (*evolutionary theory*). Using *political theories* to assess her agency, she notes how several full professors who are quite esteemed are part of the consortium's planning group. This provides her with some extra support and suggests that she should consider moving the initiative forward.

Approach to Change

Sylvia's change requires her to use most of the theories to some degree, but her strategy draws largely on *social cognition theory*, as she is working on creating individual changes in pedagogical practice, and *evolutionary*, *political* and *scientific management theories* to persuade and provide rationale for the change.

While originally she felt unsure about how to move forward, Sylvia attended a session on leadership and change theories hosted by the POGIL network, which has provided her with several ideas for how she might consider moving forward. The analysis above suggests that *evolutionary theories* can provide support for her change. While her campus is conservative, the changes she is promoting are supported by many powerful external organizations. She also recognizes that because this is a fundamental change in practice it will require *social cognition* approaches to change, which will be a major focus in this initiative. She will also need to get the infrastructure and incentives to support faculty in this new approach, so *scientific management theories* will be important. While Sylvia uses some ideas from *political* and *cultural theories*, they are not a major focus. She is, however, conscious of them, even though they are not in the foreground.

Using *evolutionary theories*, Sylvia recognizes the advantage she has from the support at multiple levels—NSF, disciplinary societies, POGIL, and the consortium—there are many networks to draw upon, which increases her agency and collective power. Also, her conversation with her senior colleague in the consortium has helped her realize that, while she may feel that few people on her campus are interested, there is not only lots of external support, but the issue may be less controversial on her campus than expected and could be seen as less of a fad than the president's service learning initiative. She tests the waters by talking to a few faculty on her campus, noting her recent work with the consortium and POGIL. She also describes the changes in her disciplinary society, making an even stronger case for her colleagues for why they may want to pay attention to this pedagogy (*evolutionary* and *institutional theory*). Sylvia finds her colleagues interested. In fact, they appreciate her desire to improve teaching with research-based methods. Sylvia provides her colleagues with links to POGIL and resources describing some National Science Foundation sponsored projects that have used process-oriented guided inquiry, and several of them visit the POGIL website afterward. By drawing on these external groups and their legitimacy, she garners immediate support.

Sylvia notes that the consortium will be offering professional development and asks if any of the faculty are interested in attending. Several people comment that they would be willing to go and to learn more (*social cognition theory*). Sylvia is encouraged. Understanding their concerns about changes pushed by the administration through the lens of *cultural theory*, focused on institutional culture, Sylvia reminds her colleagues how the consortium is led by faculty. The reputation of the consortium as well as the fact that its projects are largely driven by faculty, rather than administrators, leads faculty on Sylvia's campus to be more comfortable supporting the change.

Sylvia joins the consortium's planning team and helps create professional development programs. But, one issue arising from her national experience with process-oriented guided inquiry keeps bothering her. It is not enough to hear about process-oriented guided inquiry, you need to see it modeled, and often among different disciplines. *Social cognition theory* reminds change agents that learning is necessary for changes to be understood more deeply, particularly as it comes to changing fundamental practices like teaching. She suggests that the consortium should create several modules of the course that can be recorded, allowing the techniques to be learned through professional development that can be readily shared across the various campuses. As the professional development programs are about to kick off, she sends an e-mail to the faculty members she met with earlier and asks them if they would be willing to attend and encourage their colleagues to come along, too. Through this effort, Sylvia gets 18 faculty members from many different disciplines to attend the first professional development workshop. This is more faculty than have attended any of the workshops on other campuses in the consortium so far, so she can see her early legwork is paying off.

She meets with several department chairs after the meeting, reports what happened at the professional development, and asks if they will encourage other faculty to use the new pedagogy. She had not met with department chairs, specifically, before, as she did not want faculty to feel they were being coerced to get behind the changes (*political theory*), but chairs might be able to provide course releases or incentives that could help to continue to build helpful support (*scientific management theory*). Providing incentives is a strong *scientific management* practice for encouraging new practices. The chairs offer faculty access to summer salary to try out the pedagogy in a course. Ten faculty members decide to integrate the pedagogy and obtain the summer stipend.

Sylvia starts a campus support group for those using the new pedagogy, which meets twice a semester to discuss issues that have arisen and to troubleshoot as a group. Her familiarity with *social cognition theory* reminds her that one training will not be enough for people to truly change their practices; they will need ongoing support. The 10 faculty members who integrated the pedagogy over the summer attend, but other interested faculty also start to join in. By the end of the first year, there are 19 members in the support group. In the next year, when the consortium offers another training session, 12 new faculty attend and join the campus group. At this rate, within four years they will have most faculty in the sciences using the new pedagogy. She is excited; this is more than she hoped for when she got started.

Through the consortium, Sylvia continues working with the planning group, which is seeing results on some campuses, but not all of them. The group begins to discuss how the change process is emerging on different campuses to try to identify ways to help others facilitate the process. For example, on one campus, there are severe constraints on resources that make offering any incentives, even funding to attend the consortium training, an impossibility. So they are considering an online version of the training that can be used to support this campus and others. Sylvia learns that thinking about the type of change, external supports, and being careful to read institutional culture is a step in the right direction.

Summary

Through these examples, I have illustrated the way change can happen—even on vexing issues—when change agents are armed with the macro framework on change drawing upon proven strategies and advice from research and theory. I showed how the change agents carefully identify the type of change, context within which the change is taking place, and analyze their own agency in order to craft an approach that draws on the theories from Chapter 2.

The intent of this chapter was to demonstrate how the theories of change and framework reviewed in earlier chapters can be used to analyze and create a multifaceted approach to change. However, the ultimate goal is not to have change agents explicitly undergo a process of reviewing theories or applying the framework to various situations. Instead, over time, as change agents use the theories and framework, they will become implicitly embedded into their knowledge base and used effortlessly.

eight
Change Implementation
Encounters with Resistance and Obstacles

Sylvia, who was featured at the end of Chapter 7, finds herself in a very different situation a year later. Her own department chair leaves and the incoming chair does not support her innovative ideas about teaching. Instead, the new chair wants faculty to focus much more on conducting research and feels the effort toward teaching is taking time away from other important initiatives, such as applying for grants. The department chair is really interested in improving the department's placement in the rankings and does not see problem-based guided inquiry learning as advancing that goal. Facing pressure from her department chair, Sylvia finds she has little time to participate in the consortium, and the support that her campus received through the consortium begins to wane without her active leadership and involvement. While other faculty members are still continuing to use problem-based learning in their courses, the effort has definitely slowed down on their campus.

Ken, Phyllis, Jeff, Hector, and Sylvia (all featured in Chapter 7) are all off to a good start in terms of their change processes, but issues often emerge along the way when leading complex and long-term initiatives. The short vignette about Sylvia above describes some of the kinds of challenges, obstacles, and forms of resistance that change agents can face and often must wrestle with over the course of implementing their changes. This chapter will begin to examine and provide ideas for how to address obstacles and resistance that are an ongoing and perennial part of change processes. As noted at the beginning of Part II, careful analysis of the type of change, context of change, and leadership resources helps to alleviate many of the common obstacles and sources of resistance to change. But, as change processes unfold, obstacles will always emerge that need to be overcome. The theories of change reviewed in Chapter 2 provide ideas for how to approach these perennial struggles.

Each of the theories offered in Chapter 2 suggests certain types of obstacles and forms of resistance that are likely to emerge and can be anticipated, as well as ways to address these issues once they arise. I also set these challenges in the context of a framework of implementation of change. While not all changes go through particular phases, most change initiatives progress through these phases, which helps change agents to anticipate particular challenges and how they might need to align their activities. Change agents are better prepared when they recognize that changes typically advance through a common set of stages.

Theories of Change and Ideas about Obstacles and Resistance

In this section, I review each of the theories of change described in Chapter 2, paying particular attention to how these theories inform our understanding of obstacles that are sources of resistance to change. I review the theories that offer more detailed advice first and review those with less specific advice last.

Social Cognition Theories of Change of Obstacles

Social cognition theories suggest that resistance and obstacles will emerge because people often do not fundamentally understand change initiatives. Because organizations and change agents do not always invest the time and energy to help people to understand proposed changes, individuals aren't sure how to incorporate them into their work and roles. Also, proposals for change, by their nature, suggest that the status quo is not working. Most people have invested their identities in the way the organization is currently working, so recommended changes might suggest that in some way they are not doing their jobs correctly, or at least that their work is suboptimal. In fact, social cognition theories emerged out of studies about resistance and obstacles that sought to better understand what prevents people from engaging in change initiatives and what type of meaning making needs to occur for changes to be more successful.

Studies from this perspective identify mental models that people hold, which are fundamental. If they are not exposed and examined, mental models can prevent people from engaging with change because they are unable to reconcile the new ideas with their old mental models. Social cognition theories suggest that deep and meaningful opportunities for creating sensemaking help to overcome resistance and obstacles. Chapter 4 is devoted to the process of facilitating sensemaking and organizational learning—two key strategies to overcome this particular obstacle. Studies demonstrate that carefully constructed opportunities for interaction among individuals involved in a change initiative can help to spur both sense-making and organizational learning, opening people's minds to change (Kezar 2001). Often, people focus on meaning making as it relates to change processes in the early phases of change, but forget that new employees are constantly joining organizations and leadership turns over. So, the process of helping people to understand the change being implemented and overcoming resistance is an ongoing process.

Integrating online learning on college campuses is an example of a change that often reflects the importance of social cognition theories because faculties' traditional mental model for teaching is tied to the physical classroom, in-person interaction, dialogue, and intuition and feelings that come from interacting with other people face to face. To move teaching and learning completely online reflects a major shift in the faculty mental model because these same physical cues are not available, the physical classroom environment is lost, and the shift to this new approach is akin to shifting paradigms. Social cognition theories help explain and understand why the movement to online learning is so difficult. They also help to understand the barriers that are likely to emerge even as people start to use the related technology, which does not necessarily mean that their mental model has been fully altered or that resistance will not emerge over time.

Cultural Theories of Change and Obstacles

Like social cognition theories of change, *cultural theories* emerged from studies about the difficulties of creating change, providing particular insight about obstacles and resistance. *Cultural theories* suggest that the major obstacles to change will emerge when the values and underlying beliefs associated with change initiatives violate existing cultural norms or fall outside of them, making them harder for people to understand. The way to overcome such sources of resistance and obstacles is to help people to appreciate and understand the new values and beliefs that are being introduced and to reconcile them with existing values and beliefs that may conflict with them. However, *cultural theories* of change also underscore how difficult it is to shift or change values because they are fundamental beliefs that people hold. Simply having a conversation with someone about the way you see values differently or providing research to support your argument is unlikely to sway individuals who hold deep and abiding values. In addition, people are not consciously aware of their underlying values and beliefs, so surfacing them to create changes is a laborious, time-intensive process.

Various scholars suggest that resistance based on people's deeply held, underlying beliefs and values are quite difficult to overcome (Dawson 1994; Kezar 2001). These studies suggest that careful attention to messaging early on, particularly how it is delivered and which values underpin it, makes a significant difference in how much resistance emerges and whether the initiative will be successful. To overcome resistance, the value system needs to be slowly adjusted. Each of the mechanisms described in the next section can help in altering people's ideas or facilitating their re-examination. Strategies for overcoming this type of resistance include modifying the mission and vision so it is aligned with the new values, creating new myths and rituals, leaders performing symbolic actions, using metaphors and language to guide new thinking, ongoing communication with the new values, and refining or revising values and beliefs statements (Chaffee 1983). Change agents can reinforce and reiterate the need for new values as well as trying to attach them to the current culture or emerging vision for the organization.

Let us consider a campus that has long been focused on the traditional liberal arts curriculum, but has decided to expand its mission to offer additional professional masters degree programs. This new orientation is likely to create a culture clash among faculty, who are strongly committed to a liberal arts education and do not see professional degree programs as aligned with the underlying values of the institution. In this situation, it is likely that much work will need to be done by leaders to realign the mission to embrace professional education. Change agents will need to take care that the way they speak about the new programs does not make them sound too distinctive from the original goals of providing a liberal arts education and will need to connect the expansion to the long-standing mission of the institution. Leaders will need to keep encouraging the new professional degrees as part of an amended campus identity. Along the way, many faculty members will likely find themselves struggling to support this new approach because their underlying values have been tied to liberal arts for such a long time. *Cultural theories* point more to the ongoing resistance and obstacles and offer less in terms of specific guidance to overcome resistance beyond understanding values, underlying assumptions, and history and trying to alter values slowly over time.

Scientific Management Theory and Obstacles

Scientific management theory suggests that changes are often prevented because important operational or structural elements have not been attended to, which creates problems for implementation. Most change agents will be familiar with *scientific management*'s notions about obstacles and resistance. A classic type of resistance that *scientific management theory* addresses is the lack of incentives or rewards that are in place to support a change. Because these incentives are missing, people do not move toward embracing a proposed change, whereas if incentives are put in place resistance will be overcome. Other commonly identified examples of missing elements that result in obstacles and resistance are a lack of professional development, training, policies, procedures, financial support, human resource support, administrative support, proactive planning process, good working relationships, information or data, or other aspects of organizational infrastructure that are critical to enacting changes. *Scientific management theories* also suggest that when leadership wanes, change initiatives can face new obstacles and resistance.

The main strategies for addressing sources of resistance and obstacles within *scientific management theory* is to engage in careful evaluation of implementation processes so that various infrastructure elements that are missing can be identified and added to ensure smoother implementation and institutionalization of the change. In addition, these theories suggest the need to ensure proper leadership, even recommending succession planning so that change agents and champions are always available to keep a change initiative moving forward. A void or lack of leadership is often a serious obstacle within *scientific management theories*. Also, strong leadership and management practices, such as employee involvement, appropriate communications, and inviting participation and involvement along the way, have been identified as ways to lessen resistance, overcoming obstacles, and increasing buy-in among stakeholders.

An example of how *scientific management theories* can help in overcoming obstacles is when an organization implements a new accounting system without systematically integrating the system across all units. Change agents realize they have a problem when many people cannot use the new accounting system because as they interact with other units they recognize the older accounting systems are incompatible with the new one. So, employees retreat to using the old accounting system. It is only through conversations with people over time that change agents discover why they were unsuccessful and appreciate the need for full integration of the accounting software throughout the campus.

Political Theory and Obstacles

Political theory suggests that resistance and obstacles will keep emerging as individuals with different interests continue to see a change as being at odds with their own agenda. As long as there are opportunities for this type of resistance to emerge, the opposing viewpoint will continue to exist. Obstacles identified within the literature on this theory are typically connected to the use of *political* strategies used to hinder a change initiative, including the development of alliances, articulating different agendas, establishing a competing power base, and fostering resistance through networking, for example. Perhaps the most common obstacle within *political theories* is when a coalition or alliance opposed to a change initiative emerges and gains momentum. Political resistance and obstacles can certainly be addressed through the use of the same *political* strategies, carefully building an agenda, creating stronger alliances and coalitions, developing a stronger power base, more aggressive networking, and using bold bargaining strategies.

Others suggest that political resistance can be overcome through relationship building, attempting to break down political dynamics rather than addressing them head to head (Kotter 1985, 1996). Still, another perspective suggests that politics can be addressed by helping individuals to understand that a change is not opposed to their interests, connecting it to their values and identity using *social cognition* or *cultural* strategies (Kezar 2001). However, there are factions of political theorists who find the presence of obstacles, resistance, and opposition to be a natural, inherent part of change processes. These scholars advocate for spending little time trying to alleviate these oppositional factors and focusing more on maintaining movement forward. Oppositional forces are natural and should be monitored, but should not be ascribed too much influence or given too much attention.

An issue that might invoke political resistance on campuses is sustainability or environmentalism. There are many people who feel strongly that campuses should watch their carbon footprint and develop practices that help to model environmentally sustainable practices and behaviors for students. However, others strongly believe that sustainability is a hyped-up, liberal myth that can hurt an organization's business and economic interests. Because people may be on different sides of this issue, it is likely that competing coalitions or interest groups may emerge. The opponents of sustainability might conduct their networking underground, while the proponents are trying to get their initiative off the ground, causing resistance to emerge down the line at a time when the opposition has developed its power base.

Evolutionary Theories and Obstacles

Evolutionary theories suggest that the main obstacles and sources of resistance emerge because many change initiatives originate outside organizations and may violate existing norms and habits. Given many of the changes that emerge out of evolutionary theories come from outside stakeholders and reflect outsiders' concerns and interests, some concern among internal stakeholders is likely a natural reaction. *Evolutionary theories* predict that the amount of obstacles and resistance depend on the dissonance between the internal norms and the external norms being imposed. *Evolutionary theory* presents resistance and obstacles as being natural parts of change processes that involve varying stakeholders' interests. Yet, because changes are often pursued in the service of the survival of an organization, *evolutionary theory* suggests that resistance often dissipates, particularly as leaders can show the necessity or inevitability of a particular change.

Student learning outcomes assessment is a good example of an imposed change wherein many external stakeholders support the notion and assessment has now been integrated into the accreditation process. Faculty continue to resist notions associated with assessment, but there are well-developed arguments for its necessity and it seems inevitable that campuses will have to perform this work at some point, if they are not already. While *evolutionary theories* help to explain obstacles, they provide few mechanisms for navigating around resistance. Some theories suggest that leaders' roles are to buffer their organizations from changes that are seen as problematic, instead proposing ways to meet a mandate through making superficial changes that do little to alter internal, core processes. The concepts presented in Chapter 3 about adaptation to imposed changes provide other ideas for addressing resistance and obstacles. For example, campuses can adopt learning teams or task forces that are prepared to respond to external changes on an ongoing basis. Alternately, a steering core (e.g. a group of key administrators and faculty who work together in a shared fashion) can be formed to help address issues and integrate changes.

Institutional Theories and Obstacles

Institutional theories suggest that new ideas will be met with resistance and obstacles. Institutional theory predicts that changes in the normative schema of individuals within organizations that have strong institutional norms will almost always be resisted. However, institutional norms are constantly being shaped by powerful external fields that are part of a dynamic environment and increase the possibility that changes (and resistance) will emerge. One way that resistance emerges is seen when the different fields shaping higher education have contradictory stances on a particular change initiative. To take the issue of student outcomes assessment again, accreditation agencies, government entities, and other powerful groups have been pushing for the need to measure student learning and having a particular standard for determining institutional quality. Disciplinary societies, another organizational field shaping higher education, often present an opposing view of student learning outcomes assessment, suggesting that the processes identified by the external groups calling for this change are oversimplified and problematic. A number of disciplinary societies have raised concerns about student learning outcomes assessment. A faculty member might be confused or unsure about which message to follow; this conflict may result in resistance as individuals consider the change. Later, individual resistance may become organizational resistance if a faculty member decides to align with others who are concerned about student learning outcomes assessment. *Institutional theory*, like *cultural, political* and *evolutionary theories*, suggests that resistance and obstacles are part and parcel of most change initiatives. Yet, these theories also help explain why certain changes that have little internal support often are institutionalized and why few obstacles may emerge (e.g. the confluence of many external powerful fields).

Institutional theory offers little advice for how to navigate resistance and obstacles. A few recent versions of *neo-institutional theory* have focused more on the potential for change agents (both inside and outside institutions) to create resistance to powerful external forces, but mostly in rare situations when stakeholders become aware that external forces are having a detrimental effect on an organization. In these cases, the situation becomes dysfunctional and the problems with the logic come to be so obvious that resistance can emerge. However, the theory reinforces that a high level of contradiction must be experienced for resistance to have much success in blocking changes. Next, I will present a three-stage model of implementation and then describe how various obstacles and sources of resistance noted in this section emerge as a change initiative unfolds.

Change Institutionalization Framework

The goal of most change processes is to become institutionalized, in other words to become part of the day-to-day operations. Institutionalization is defined as establishing a standard practice or custom within a human system (Curry 1992; Kramer 2000). The following characteristics are typically associated with an institutionalized practice: routine, widespread, legitimized, expected, supported, permanent, and resilient (Kramer 2000).

Before a practice is institutionalized, it proceeds through a series of phases that appear to have some predictable elements (Goodman 1982; Kramer 2000). A three-stage model of change has typically been identified in studies examining how change processes evolve:

1. Mobilization: "the system is prepared for change";
2. Implementation: "the change is introduced"; and
3. Institutionalization: "the system is stabilized in its changed state."

(Curry 1991 as referenced in Curry 1992: 5)

In much of the change literature on institutionalization, different labels or names are given to these three stages.[1] However, despite the different terms used, all of the labels indicate three stages of progression that follow similar, relatively linear patterns.

Mobilization is the first stage of the model. In this stage, the organization is beginning to prepare for change. Preparation ranges from fostering initial aware-ness of a problem, mobilizing, raising consciousness, and laying the foundation for a change initiative to be implemented (Curry 1992). In this stage, people begin to gather around a common cause or reform. It is in this stage that change agents begin to question and challenge the status quo—the practices and policies that are enmeshed in the current institutional culture. This stage includes two parts, galvanizing members and initial structural changes to the organization. Galvaniz-ing members toward action can occur through raising awareness or disseminating information. Structural change occurs when "innovations are reflected in a con-crete fashion throughout the organization" (Datnow 2005: 124). Initial structural changes can range from setting up agendas and priorities at meetings to changing mission statements. Several researchers of institutionalization describe how the process begins by focusing on establishing concrete ways that the innovation is represented through organizational structures—the *structural level.*

Implementation is the second stage, focusing on the creation of infrastructure and support for the reform. During this stage, initiatives begin to materialize in the organization and people develop support for the structures to maintain momen-tum (Curry 1992; Kezar 2007d). These initiatives may take the form of rewards, incentives, or sanctions for behaviors (Curry 1992; Fullan 1989). During imple-mentation, various groups and individuals begin to cooperate and new members may join, providing additional support (Fullan 1989). Technical assistance is pro-vided for any needed troubleshooting or to solve logistical issues. At this stage, policy and behaviors are becoming part of the standard operating procedures of the organization (Curry 1992). Members are conducting new work, but have not fully accepted the procedure. People begin to have a preference for the behavior or practice. The policy and behaviors start to become more commonplace and part of the standard operating procedure (Curry 1992). This phase is often focused on the *procedural* or *behavioral level.* At this stage, they have not formulated an evaluation of the innovation or think about it as part of ongoing planning; it is still an innovation.

Institutionalization is the final stage of the process. At this point, a change moves beyond having become part of the standard operating procedures, becoming embedded in the actual value system of the organization. Members come to a consensus, accept the value of innovation, and see it as a normative behavior in the institution. At this stage, authors connect institutionalization with the changing of the culture and core understandings about the culture (Curry 1992; Kezar 2007d; Kanter 1990). The innovation has maintained stability within the organization and has become virtually indistinguishable from the rest of the institution. In a bit of irony, an innovation reaches the institutionalization stage and is successful when it is no longer seen as an innovation. Rather, it is just a part of the organizational framework. This is often referred to as the *cultural level.*

Since organizational evolution is a process that occurs over time, these three stages occur along a continuum rather than through set, delineated levels (Curry 1992). This three-phase model provides a useful framework because it allows for an understanding of how leaders establish permanent innovations at their institution. These three phases also anticipate different types of obstacles and resistance.

Institutionalization also provides an important theoretical framework for understanding the role of leaders in creating change (Kezar 2001). Scholars of change who have focused on institutionalization suggest that leaders need to utilize different strategies when an initiative is new to an organization than when an initiative has already begun to be incorporated into the organization or has been institutionalized. Curry (1992) hypothesizes how early on leaders need to help people on campus to recognize the need for change, mobilize, and energize individuals for change. Later, they proceed to implementation and developing programs and initiatives. Lastly, they work to stabilize the change and make it part of the ongoing operations of the organization, including it in processes related to evaluation and the budget, for example.

In reflecting on these three distinct phases of institutionalization, it becomes apparent why different leadership might be needed within each stage. For example, researchers have described the importance of the leadership of attention or priority setting within the first stage—mobilization (Kotter 1988). Within this phase, leaders focus on developing and setting a vision or direction. It is also important here to focus on the management of meaning, where leaders communicate their vision and help others to see its value and importance. Thus, leaders are likely to draw upon *social cognition* and *cultural theories* to overcome resistance and move changes forward during mobilization.

In phase two—implementation—leadership focuses on building momentum. Leaders need to create incentives and opportunities for people to become involved (Curry 1992; Kanter 1990). They also need to play the role of inspirational leader and help people to want to be involved through persuasion. Therefore, during implementation, *scientific management* and *political theories* will be important for overcoming obstacles.

Lastly, in phase three—institutionalization—leaders need to be cultural agents and focus more on the value and meaning of the innovation (Schein 1985). Leaders need to help build cultural consensus for the innovation. Here, leaders help people to sort out conflicting values that they might hold. For example, there may be faculty on campus who are committed to social justice and equity, but hold views about hiring criteria that are in conflict with their beliefs in equity. During phase three, leaders help bring these conflicts, which could otherwise prevent institutionalization and create barriers and resistance, to the surface. Leaders will draw upon *cultural theories* and *social cognition* to help overcome obstacles toward institutionalization.

Example of Change Agents Institutionalizing Change: A Look through the Three-Phase Model

A common challenge on many campuses today is how to provide greater support for the emerging segment of non-tenure-track faculty, which has grown to comprise more than two-thirds of the faculty. Non-tenure-track faculty often have poor working conditions with low pay and no benefits, last minute hiring, no orientation, professional development, and mentoring, and virtually no basic support, such as materials, an office or administrative support. Most of the change agents associated with this issue are non-tenure-track faculty members themselves, creating change from the bottom up. In studies conducted on non-tenure-track faculty leaders who are mobilizing for change, you can see the way these three phases of institutionalization play out as change agents work to integrate new policies in support of the changing faculty.

Mobilizing faculty is a particular challenge among non-tenure-track faculty, who are *often* disconnected from the campus, teaching a class and then moving on to another professional career that they have or teaching on another campus. Because non-tenure-track faculty are often isolated, disconnected, and may even be apathetic toward their campus, mobilizing them can require even more work than other types of changes where change agents might more easily gain focused attention on the issue. Therefore, developing an awareness about the problems faced by non-tenure-track faculty is the first step in mobilization. For some institutions, apathy toward poor work conditions was overcome by a significant galvanizing event such as a person being unfairly fired, a major grievance being filed, or when a non-tenure-track faculty member was excluded from or thrown off a governance body. A second way that campuses have created awareness is through data collection, demonstrating how poor the working conditions of non-tenure-track faculty are compared to faculty at other institutions or to tenure-track faculty members. Once change agents develop awareness, they have the opportunity to capitalize on the attention they have garnered, creating communications vehicles to disseminate information, as well as further unite individuals. The most prevalent mechanisms for communicating and connecting people have been campus-based listservs, websites, and electronic or printed newsletters. Unlike other campus groups, like tenure-track faculty, staff, or even students, these individuals are less likely to come in contact with or sometimes even to be on campus to network in more traditional ways.

One can also see in this example how the leadership of change agents in this first phase is focused on creating a sense of priority through the gathering of data or capitalizing on events to stimulate people's attention. Resistance and obstacles at this phase often stem from tenure-track faculty and administrators not understanding the experience of non-tenure-track faculty members, so strategies include helping them to shift their view of who is considered faculty and making this segment of the professoriate visible to them. With a sense of priority and the network developed to move toward action, change agents are now positioned to begin implementing change.

The second phase, *implementation*, involves creating the necessary policies and practices, as well as finding vehicles for putting them in place. The first step for change agents is to create regular meetings or a task force charged with creating better non-tenure-track faculty working conditions. This group of individuals would look at data, benchmarks, and model institutions to help develop policies and practices for their own institution. They also need to create some sort of plan of action about how the ideas generated in the group can be actualized within departments and colleges. This might go in many different directions but many change agents have relied on allies within departments, sometimes tenure-track faculty or department chairs, to help implement the policies that have been created. They can also work with campus governance to explore whether more overarching policies can be created or added to the faculty handbook to support implementation.

As noted above, leadership at this phase is focused on helping to get others involved and actualizing the change within the organizational structure and culture. Through the various processes described above, working with a task force, allies within departments, and a plan for action, change agents have been able to engage other stakeholders and begin the integration of their policy changes into campus operations. Some obstacles often faced during this phase include trouble obtaining institutional data or weak infrastructure or resources to support new policies. Campus politics can also emerge to stifle efforts, which is why change agents sometimes rely on allies within departments, as well as their broader networks, for continuing to move change forward.

Lastly, the third phase is *institutionalization*, when the change becomes a part of the day-to-day operations and the norms and values. During institutionalization, non-tenure-track faculty have become valued within the institution. Special policies and practices are no longer necessary because they are thought about the same way as other faculty, being integrated into the daily operations of the campus. Whenever any new policy emerges, the question is asked: How does this particular policy also impact non-tenure-track faculty? Instead of having to create special and different policies because they are not included in assumptions about who is a member of the faculty, they are subject to the same policies that are developed for other faculty, are considered for awards, are included when celebrations or ceremonies are held, and are able to participate and benefit from professional development and mentoring opportunities. In fact, at this point, leaders are mostly looking at the overall climate to ensure that it supports non-tenure-track faculty in all facets of their work. Members of campus now actively consider tenure-track faculty and non-tenure-track faculty as distinct, but equally important members of campus and are actively engaging in non-tenure-track faculty in campus leadership. This example demonstrates how institutionalization is centered on underlying values and mental schemas. In the next section, I describe each of the three phases in more detail, providing examples of the types of obstacles and resistance that typically occur within each, as well as the way that these theories that help leaders to overcome them.

Obstacles and Resistance Emerging during Mobilization, Implementation, and Institutionalization

In this section of the chapter, I will review the three phases, focusing on the ways obstacles can and do emerge. I will draw upon some of the case studies that have already been reviewed and will imagine ways that the change agents will contend with the resistance that may unfold over the course of the change process. I also link each phase—mobilization, implementation, and institutionalization—to the various theories that are most prevalent in helping to address common obstacles.

Mobilization

Most of the examples described throughout this book, particularly in Chapter 7, have been in the mobilization or early implementation phase. *Social cognition, cultural,* and *political theories* are particularly salient for understanding resistance and obstacles during the mobilization phase. The case involving Jeff, who was advancing family-friendly policies, provides an example of some of the challenges that can be experienced during the mobilization phase for second-order change. Jeff realized that many of his colleagues lacked an understanding of the need for family-friendly policies and that it would be difficult to mobilize them without developing an understanding and awareness of the necessity for change. *Social cognition theories* and *cultural theories* speak specifically to gathering support for and mobilizing people. So, instead of moving forward right away, Jeff spent the first year educating others about the need for family-friendly policies, drawing on national studies and research, bringing in speakers, and hosting events that provided new information to promote learning, as well as to provide opportunities for sensemaking.

The case involving Albert and his leadership development proposal demonstrates how *cultural theories* can be brought to bear to overcome resistance based on underlying values. Albert had not realized that the preliminary proposal he advanced for the leadership development program, which was based on principles from business, would result in such great resistance. Albert used principles from *cultural theories* to overcome this resistance by reframing some of the business principles as non-profit entrepreneurship, creating greater connections and alignment among the two sets of values and getting rid of some of the dissonance. He revised the proposal using language that draws upon the academic tradition more and much less on business, using standards adopted by academic professional societies. He also learned more about the institutional history associated with these concepts so he could better connect to people's emotions, concerns, and priorities for the campus. Through his shift in language, communication, and underlying values, he was able to mobilize support for his proposal.

Ken's experience with creating a branch campus exemplified the importance of *political theories* for understanding resistance and developing a strategy to move forward. A group of faculty in the humanities, external legislative leaders, and an influential group of alumni were all attempting to stop the efforts to establish a branch campus in Saudi Arabia. A variety of powerful interests were creating a formidable resistance, which Ken had to address. He recognized that he would not be able to move forward effectively if there were so many groups pressuring the administration to kill the program. Ken used a combination of strategies to overcome resistance, drawing upon *scientific management theories* to present data to the state legislatures. He also drew upon *social cognition theories* by presenting research and op-ed pieces to faculty members and bringing the humanities faculty into the planning group, so they could make sense of the change, but also so their concerns could be expressed and considered. Without addressing these many groups early on, Ken would not have been able to implement his ideas.

For externally imposed changes, like the one Phyllis experienced, evolutionary theories provide some guidance about how to mobilize. The changes imposed by the state related to tying funding to graduation rates would clearly have created a crisis for the campus. Phyllis can draw on her understanding of evolutionary theories, knowing that people prefer homeostasis over chaos, to help draw upon a sense of crisis to help mobilize people to take immediate action. She would never have had the high attendance she had at the town meeting if she had not drawn upon a sense of crisis to mobilize others. Also, evolutionary theories suggest that remaining mission centered is critical for attaining success in a volatile environment. Phyllis knows that community colleges have a particular mission and that the proposed changes will not serve this institution or its students well. She needs to fight for and preserve their original mission, while still addressing the concerns of the legislature, but in ways that respect community colleges' unique mission of providing open access. Phyllis needs to be careful to not permit values associated with four-year institutions, which legislators are drawing upon, to determine changes at community colleges. She also knows she needs to be proactive about creating a better solution to the problems that need to be addressed, rather than waiting for external forces to mount.

Implementation

Several of the change agents reviewed in this book have entered the implementation phase, including Ken, Sylvia, and Jeff. Typically, *scientific management theories* are particularly salient during the implementation phase, when infrastructure needs are critical. For example, as Ken progressed with implementing his branch campus in Saudi Arabia he experienced several challenges that *scientific management theory* would predict. First, he found that he was missing critical governance and decision-making structures that would link the campus overseas to the campus back in the United States. He only realized that these structures were missing when a miscommunication resulted in faculty on the main campus drawing up a proposal against the curriculum being developed on the branch campus because they felt they did not have an opportunity to provide their input, although this merely happened because the curriculum had not gone through a formal governance process. Ken had obtained input from faculty, but not through a formalized, participatory process that included bringing the curriculum up for a formal vote. Another major area of resistance that emerged was among students on the branch campus, who felt that faculty members were not adopting teaching models that were culturally relevant, thus alienating students. As a result, Ken realized that he needed to put in place professional development to support faculty, providing them with a better understanding of the cultural context in which they were teaching.

Sylvia's example also relates to the importance of *scientific management theories* in overcoming barriers at implementation. As a result of a turnover in leadership on her campus—a new department chair—she lost support for the process-oriented guided inquiry learning initiative. *Scientific management theories* specifically speak to the importance of leadership for carrying change efforts forward. Sylvia's own efforts at leadership were stifled by her department chair. The department chair was not providing leadership, but instead was blocking Sylvia's efforts by imposing a different set of values and rewards within the department. The departure of the prior chair, who had been supportive, resulted in a void of leadership as the new chair began to pull Sylvia in different directions. Drawing upon both *scientific management* and *political theories*, she was able to overcome these obstacles.

First, she created an alliance to influence the department chair so she could reassume her leadership in the consortium and on campus. She could also use this alliance to reshape the values and beliefs of her department chair. Sylvia met with the other faculty who were working with process-oriented guided inquiry learning to explain her dilemma and lack of support from her new chair. Each of these faculty members met with their own department chairs, across a host of disciplines, and the chairs decided that they could enlist the support of the dean. The dean saw that new pedagogies, but also the need for more research, were important. However, he recognized that chair was only focused on research, which was problematic and contrary to the institutional mission. He decided it was important to speak with the department chair about allowing Sylvia to participate and lead the effort for the whole college, providing her a course release once again. Building on her earlier political connections, she was able to overcome the obstacles presented by the new department chair and began her work with the consortium again.

Second, through her familiarity with *cultural theories*, she realized that she needed to work with the department chair to help him appreciate and understand the value of new pedagogies. So, she began sending him materials from the consortium, inviting him to the faculty professional development workshops, and forwarding research from the national network at POGIL. While she is frustrated to feel like she is circling back to the mobilization phase again, she recognizes that as new people enter an organization, change agents must sometimes return to earlier steps in mobilization to bring recent entrants on board and keep moving forward toward implementation. Some other problem may emerge before the effort is fully institutionalized, but she knows that she cannot just give up whenever an obstacle emerges.

As long as the change initiative remains in its implementation phase, there are likely to be obstacles that emerge. For example, new people come to the campus who do not understand the initiative or, in other cases, rewards structures might be in conflict with the effort. New implementation issues emerge on an ongoing basis as the change unfolds.

Institutionalization

If they are lucky, Ken, Jeff, Phyllis, Melissa, Hector, Albert, and Sylvia will all institutionalize their change efforts. *Cultural theories* are particularly salient for understanding obstacles and resistance at the point of institutionalization. For Sylvia, the major set of values that threaten institutionalization emerge from faculty who are entrenched in a lecture-based approach to teaching and learning. These individuals still make up the majority of the faculty and they find that new pedagogies violate their deeply held beliefs that classes need to cover a certain amount of material and should be presented in a linear way that builds upon existing knowledge. Sylvia recognizes that to overcome these underlying values and move toward institutionalization she needs to create a deeper appreciation among a larger share of faculty that, while based on different values, process-based guided inquiry learning still results in student learning. A strategy she uses to move towards institutionalization and broader cultural acceptance of problem-based learning is conducting an experiment where courses using both approaches are taught simultaneously, allowing student outcomes from the courses to be examined and compared. Through this experiment, Sylvia is able to demonstrate not only that students have similar learning outcomes, but also that the process-oriented guided inquiry courses are more engaging and result in more students becoming interested in continuing studies in the sciences. Drawing upon *cultural theories* of change, Sylvia realizes that she had to address this underlying set of values and beliefs if the effort was ever going to be institutionalized, having the majority of faculty teach using this new approach.

Summary

This chapter helps change agents to realize that the journey of change takes a long time and typically progresses through the three phases of mobilization, implementation, and institutionalization. Through these various phases, different obstacles and types of resistance are likely to emerge. The goal of most change agents is a sustained change process that becomes part of the normal workings of the campus. As a result, it's important to remember that a change process is not sustained if it has only undergone the mobilization or implementation phase. Unfortunately, many change agents do not recognize or forget that their effort will be fragile if they do not carry it to institutionalization. The effort does not have to be embraced by the entire institution to be institutionalized. It simply needs to become part of the division's, unit's, or group's underlying values and to be incorporated into their general operating procedures. Drawing again upon the six theories, change agents can help guide efforts toward sustained change initiatives, knowing the theories provide advice on how to address common challenges and obstacles.

Part 3

Challenges for Change Agents in Our Time

This part of the book looks at two key challenges of our time—scaling changes across the enterprise and the ethics of change. While most change agents historically have worked at the organizational level, there is research to suggest that working cross- or inter-organizationally is a stronger approach for achieving sustainable and larger-scale change. The concepts described in the forthcoming chapters speak to ways that change agents can work across organizational boundaries toward the creation of change.

The book ends by exploring ethics in relationship to change. This chapter circles back to ideas presented in Chapter 1 on the current context of change and how it presents ethical dilemmas. This chapter challenges change agents to consider the ethical underpinnings of all change initiatives and provides critical areas for reflection.

nine
Scaling Up Changes Beyond the Institutional Level

Elaine is interested in creating support services for lesbian, gay, bisexual, and transgendered (LGBT) students on her campus, but has little in the way of resources to understand how she might go about this process. She attends a National Association for Student Personnel Administrators (NASPA) conference and finds they have a community of practice for LGBT issues. She joins the community of practice and attends some sessions at the conference that help her to connect with colleagues who have all sorts of resources and strategies for creating change. The group holds meetings online throughout the year, so Elaine is able to send questions and get feedback and advice on an ongoing basis. What seemed an impossible task six months ago seems well within Elaine's reach thanks to the resources she was able to acquire through connecting with this community of practice.

Elaine and Sylvia from Chapter 7 both find support through an external network. Increasingly, people can become connected across organizational settings to support each other in changes, particularly through technology. Additionally, many change agents are interested in creating initiatives that permeate throughout higher education, not just the institutions where they work. Individual change agents are not the only ones creating changes, though. Foundations, government agencies, national associations, accreditation agencies, and other stakeholders and groups work to promote best practices and sometimes reach farther across the academy. While much of this book is aimed at understanding changes at the organizational level, this chapter explores research in higher education related to extending changes across the enterprise. Here, I will review some of the key ideas and lessons needed to create change. Scholars describe this type of enterprise-level change as scaling up, wherein a particular program or intervention is embedded within a broader array of institutions (Kezar 2011). Achieving scale is not an area that has been researched much in higher education, as the academy tends to operate in a more decentralized fashion without a ministry of education or similar centralized governing body to spread innovations.

The notion of scaling up changes is quite foreign to higher education in the United States. Higher education operates as a decentralized system, so change tends to happen more at the institutional and state levels (e.g. through multi-campus or state systems). The dominant assumption about change is that initiatives will need to be translated from one individual college campus to the next. In other countries, centralized policymaking can often have a substantial impact, but historically in the United States change has not been executed at the federal and only in limited ways at the state level. Instead, the history of changes has been one of individual institutions adopting particular policies or programs. This is quite different from other countries, where changes are often mandated through the ministry of education. This is not to say change cannot be encouraged through policy; many recent policy reports and recommendations have been issued by groups such as the State Higher Education Executive Officers, Education Commission of the States, and the Western Interstate Higher Commission on Education. Still, it is typically up to institutional leaders to implement and create changes on individual campuses. Thus, all of these state and national efforts require the response of leaders on individual campuses. Even countries with a more top-down infrastructure find that if there is not buy-in among various campus stakeholders, change initiatives are often subverted (Trowler 2009). Yet, with the increasing concerns about accountability among higher education stakeholders, will there be more top-down initiation of change in the United States to come? That remains an open question.

Assuming the climate does not change and higher education in the United States remains relatively decentralized as an enterprise, how might changes be scaled up within the system? This chapter describes the limited research on scaling up change and what it can tell us about how to successfully achieve scale for important innovations. I critique the traditional scaling models adopted from policy circles which reflect *evolutionary* models of change that have often been used in K-12 education, but with little success. The critiques that have been raised in K-12 education are also relevant for higher education. I propose several different models that are better for the higher education sector, such as learning communities and networks, as ways to scale up changes that have proven successful in the past. These approaches draw on *political* and *social cognition theories* of change. Although they have not been used widely, they show promise for creating deeper and more meaningful changes beyond the institutional level.

Change Theories and Scale-up

Evolutionary theories suggest that changes can be initiated through external pressures, particularly when they are attached to funding sources. This approach mirrors the way that many foundations or government agencies have tried to encourage changes by awarding grants and trying to shift fields by altering broad incentive structures or creating policies to drive change from the top down. The hope is that more institutions will adopt the approach and a broader change will occur throughout the sector as institutions see the value of an initiative. This approach is the one that is most common, but it has had limited success and has been strongly critiqued (Coburn 2003; Elmore 1996).

Scale-up typically involves adapting an innovation that has been successful in one setting for effective application in a wider range of contexts (Healy and DeStefano 1997).[1] As noted in this definition, scale assumes that a successful innovation is independent of the implementation setting. It is also generally assumed that the innovation can be applied to various contexts without modification or alteration. For example, the National Science Foundation creates innovations, tests them, and distributes findings and recommendations to various sites (Elmore 1996). Scale assumes that reform begins with small pilots, often within local settings. There is little investment in implementation at new sites (i.e. there is no money to support implementation). Because this is the dominant model for scaling up, I provide a few critiques of this model and suggest alternative approaches within this chapter.

In the K-12 system, where there have been many efforts to scale up changes and a much more top-down environment, scholars have identified how current notions of scale-up that have been borrowed from policy are lacking and have proven ineffective. Elmore (1996), in evaluating NSF school reform and scale-up efforts over 20 years, concluded that the incentive structure in schools works against any changes to the core activities and that reform efforts will never reach scale as long as the model continues to ignore altering basic organizational structures—the implementation context. He notes that we need to rethink scale as an issue of cultural norms and incentives "that cannot be fixed with simple policy shifts or exhortations from people with money," as is often assumed in traditional scale-up models (p. 25).

Building on Elmore's work, Coburn (2003) argued in a critique of traditional approaches to scaling-up reforms in K-12 that definitions of scale are overly simplistic and need to be expanded to include the concepts of depth, sustainability, spread, and shift in the reform ownership. In terms of *depth*, she noted that innovations must reach deep, affecting consequential change in classroom and school practice. She suggested that the depth needs to impact the beliefs of teachers and their underlying assumptions about the nature of teaching and learning; thus, depth refers to shaping teachers' values. Coburn also argued that *sustainability* needs to be a key component of bringing innovation to scale. Too many programs that are brought to scale fail over time. Even schools that successfully implement reforms have difficulty sustaining them in the face of competing priorities, changing demands, and teacher and administrative turnover. *Spread* refers to impacting more than just activity structures; innovations must change underlying beliefs, norms, and principles. Too often, practices change briefly, but the underlying beliefs that guide them remain unchanged. Hence, once pressures to use the new practices have lessened or disappeared, people may be inclined to return to their old habits. Coburn pointed to the need for researchers examining spread to explore more than simply achieving reform in more schools. That is, one needs to examine the actual spread within each school in terms of its effectiveness in changing underlying beliefs. Researchers should chart reform principles and norms for social interaction that have become embedded in school policy and practices. Spread focuses more on the degree to which the innovation is spreading within the system by penetrating more deeply into teacher consciousness and group interactions, not just across the system. Lastly, she examined the *shift in reform ownership*, moving away from an external group toward ownership by the districts, schools, and teachers who have sustained and deepened the reform. Coburn cited research which showed that scale cannot be achieved if the internal community does not own the reform.[2]

Evolutionary theories have been heavily critiqued for relying on external pressure and incentives or rewards. While these elements are important to change, on their own they are unlikely to bring about scaled up changes. So, what do other theories of change suggest in terms of viable alternatives to the typical top-down approach to scale? *Political theories* of change suggest that initiatives can be scaled up through the development of networks, coalitions, and eventually into social movements that can affect whole societies or operate trans-nationally. *Political theories* have long studied change outside of formal organizational contexts. Additionally, the goal is to move from smaller networks to broader coalitions, then to social movements that further advance the change initiative. In this chapter, I will highlight two areas of literature that have been used in higher education to scale up change—social movements and networks.

More recently, *social cognition theories* have been expanded beyond the individual focus to consider ways that collective schema or mindsets can be changed. Out of this thinking evolved institutional sensemaking and organizational learning, which were presented in Chapter 4. However, another area that has emerged, which is less bounded by the organization or campus, is communities of practice/learning communities.[3] Communities of practice are made up of people who have shared occupations such as faculty or student affairs practitioners. Changes might be implemented by impacting a particular community of practice that works across many different institutions throughout the entire sector. An example is provided at the beginning of this chapter through the vignette about Elaine. Instead of working at the institutional level to better support LGBT students, a group of individuals might work with student affairs practitioners through their national organizations as a way to shape the views and practices of professionals across the enterprise.

Also, *institutional theories* describe how changes become scaled up across higher education through institutional isomorphism, where institutions mimic one another. Most of the changes documented have not been positive for the enterprise, such as institutions shifting from their historic missions in order to seek greater prestige. However, proponents of sustainability have been successful in having institutions compete on which is "greener" and leaving less of a carbon footprint. Therefore, some efforts use the prestige seeking and competition underlying *institutional theory* to promote positive changes. While I do not focus on this approach, it may be a lever that change agents consider for scaling up changes. *Cultural* and *scientific management theories* work more at the organizational level, so they do not offer many ideas for scaling up changes. Social movements, networks, and communities of practice address many of the critiques raised over traditional scale-up models, so they will be highlighted in the sections below. First, though, some commonalities across these three scaling mechanisms are highlighted.

Three Common Mechanisms for Scale

Three key mechanisms are articulated within *political* and *social cognition theories* of change that are reflected in the social movements, social network, and communities of practice vehicles. They are deliberation and discussion, networks, and external support and incentives (Kezar 2011).

One of the most important findings from critiques of research on scale-up is that scale requires opportunities for people to engage in a process that helps them to understand the necessity of the change—sensemaking. As noted in earlier chapters, a variety of studies demonstrate that one of the main reasons change does not occur is that people fundamentally do not understand either the reason for the proposed change or its substance. So, they need to undergo a learning process in order to accept and implement it (Elmore 1996; Senge 1990). Another reason change does not occur is that there is no motivation or interest. In studies of K-12, *deliberation and discussion* among professionals commonly emerged as a quality that led to more authentic change. Through dialogue, norms and values are changed and people accept new ways of doing things. Deliberation provides a process whereby people come to an understanding and learn (Senge 1990). It addresses many of the challenges of scale-up by going deeper, penetrating individuals' understanding and creating ownership since people go through the learning process themselves. It touches upon underlying norms; it creates internal motivation because people come to develop the idea on their own and because dialogue is continuous. Deliberation is flexible because it allows for changes to take place during implementation, recognizing that organizations are not static and have different cultures. A common feature of social movements, networks, and communities of practice is that they allow for deliberation among professionals.

Another important feature across these three approaches to scale-up is that they involve *networks* of people who share common interests, which can enhance motivation. Networks connect people to others with similar ideas and also provide change agents with the information needed to help move the change process along. They create moral support so that people can sustain themselves and the change over time. Networks also provide incentives externally when there may not be either internal incentives or support for the innovation. By connecting individuals to others, networks overcome many of the challenges of scale in which isolated individuals or organizations are unable to sustain a change in the face of the status quo. Also, through discussions with others in a network, change agents are able to modify their strategies to adapt to contextual issues that emerge.

External supports and incentives provide the funding, awards, and recognition necessary in order to help sustain change agents in the face of entropy and even negative dynamics. Therefore, the external pressures and support articulated through *evolutionary theories* are important components of scaling up change as long as they are paired with other core mechanisms that allow for deliberation and the creation of networks to occur. Overreliance on external support and incentives alone has not been successful in facilitating the scaling up of changes. External support and incentives provide the motivation for change and enhance the sustainability of change agents. But, for scale to be achieved, other factors need to help facilitate change, such as obtaining endorsements or support from governments, foundations, and existing intermediary organizations that influence the system (e.g. accrediting agencies, disciplinary societies, and community organizations). Endorsement or support helps move acceptance of the change beyond the true believers to involve other faculty and staff members who may need more external motivation through pressure or rewards. The innovation can also gain greater legitimacy through endorsements and support. External levers contribute to the sustainability of change, as well, by making the innovation a part of the larger system of accreditation and by disciplinary groups holding the system accountable for maintaining certain norms. Traditional scale-up models have not emphasized the more systematic and comprehensive approach needed to make deep and sustained change. Social movements, networks, and communities of practice/learning communities all provide external validation for the change ideas as they are being adopted by individual college campuses.

In summary, the critiques offered by K-12 scholars, as well as by recent policy scholars such as Dede (2006) and Healy and DeStefano (1997), suggest that other approaches to scale, including a social movement, social network, or communities of practice/learning communities approach, are likely to be more profitable. These three approaches will be reviewed next. There are many ways that the three approaches overlap and are similar (e.g. their emphasis on networks, common work, and dialogue), but they tend to be described as unique approaches and have distinctions that are important to comment on.

In each section, I will review what characterizes the approach, offer examples, discuss research suggesting how change agents might use it to profitably create scaled up changes, how it addresses critiques of traditional scale-up models, and end with links to some existing examples.

Social Movement Approach

Characteristics of Examples of Social Movements

The social movement perspective on change, as advanced by Palmer (1992), suggests that when people across varying local sites decide to embrace a change, they form networks, deliberate and discuss the innovation, work collectively against opponents, and ultimately create rewards and institutional structures to make it part of the system.[4] Social movements are characterized by four main elements. The first is that they are constituted by networks of informal interaction. These networks allow them to communicate and coordinate their efforts, as well as to gain agency for change through collective action. A social movement, as compared to a social network or community of practice, has a stronger sense of shared beliefs and sense of belonging. This means they also develop a stronger sense of purpose, which drives their work together. The second characteristic is deliberation. Movements create avenues for dialogue to occur so that a shared vision and purpose can be created and strategies can be advanced. The third characteristic is a sense of opposition or the existence of something that they are moving against. A sense of opposition helps to coalesce peoples' commitment and efforts through collective action, giving them a greater sense of purpose. Some may find that having to identify an opposing party or force makes it difficult to envision various changes that might be scaled up in higher education. Yet, leaders who strive to make learning more engaging can find the lecture method an approach to oppose. Thus, a sense of opposition does not need to be antagonistic, per se. Fourth, rewards, money, and structures are often created to help sustain the movement. These various resources that help solidify the social movement are often referred to as resource mobilization. Social movements reflect the principles and concepts in *political theories* of change around allies, power, and coalitions.

Civic engagement is a good example of a social movement in the academy. In the last 20 years, service learning—a major initiative within civic engagement—went from being integrated on less than 100 campuses to being a part of over 3,000. This level of scale is noted to be the result of their social movement approach. Hollander and Hartley (2000) describe how civic engagement initiatives have operated like a social movement, involving a variety of supportive networks such as Campus Compact, the American Association of Community Colleges, the American Association of Higher Education, the Association of American Colleges and Universities, and the National Society for Experiential Education. Campus Compact, for example, created state organizations that connected institutions within states and then across states. They outline how the social movement had a clear set of shared beliefs: "The first entails the age-old desire to prepare the next generation of active participants in the democracy and the second to encourage campuses to act as good institutional citizens within their own communities" (Hollander and Hartley 2000: 353). While Hollander and Hartley note how a common set of shared beliefs is not easy to come by and that there are certainly varying views about what civic renewal looks like, a general set of shared beliefs has helped to drive the social movement around civic renewal on campuses. The authors also outline the opposition that the civic renewal movement works against, namely the notion of the academy as an ivory tower removed from real-world problems. Civic engagement also opposes the consumer model of education, instead considering higher education a public good. Civic renewal is seen as a counterweight to the excessive dominance of the market economy in American life. Lastly, Hollander and Hartley describe the ways that organizations such as Campus Compact provided rewards such as national awards or seed money to campuses to create civic engagement initiatives. Further, the statewide and national networks have created an additional infrastructure for providing information and strategy resources for individual campuses to help develop civic engagement initiatives.

In addition to civic engagement, other social movements in higher education include civil rights, affirmative action, the spread in development of ethnic and women's studies, multiculturalism and diversity, gay rights, apartheid, sweatshop activism, sustainability and environmentalism, access, and addressing faculty working conditions as we move to a largely contingent faculty (Rhoads 2005; Rojas 2012). Rhoads's (2005) work has been central to seeing various change initiatives in higher education through the social movement perspective, particularly among student groups, but also among faculty.

Research on How It Leads to Change and Scale

The research that exists on social movements within the academy suggests these efforts have been successful in creating significant and scaled up changes (Rojas 2012). Because social movements tend to be grassroots oriented and organic, there are fewer formal studies that can be provided than is the case with professional networks, communities of practice, and learning communities that are all more organizationally supported and the subject of study. Thus, while we have information to document social movements and their impact on the academy, we have less research about the process of change involved that would help to inform leaders who want to scale up change using a social movement perspective.

The literature on social movements suggests the importance of gathering people and creating networks, providing avenues for deliberation and discussion, fostering a sense of common purpose, and ensuring that resources are mobilized to support the movement as it expands (Hollander and Hartley 2000). One recent study by Kezar and Lester (2011) documents the work of 170 bottom-up or grassroots leaders, including faculty and staff, on five different campuses. These change agents are engaged in a variety of change initiatives from sustainability to diversity to pedagogical innovations, all using social movement approaches to creating change. The study found that the key levers for change in a social movement approach are the creation and spread of a shared vision, the development of coalitions and networks, and utilizing powerful partners such as community groups and media (see Chapter 6 for more details on grassroots strategies for change).

How This Approach Addresses Traditional Critiques of Scale Models

How do social movements address the traditional critiques to scale-up related to ownership, sustainability, depth of adoption, and spread? In this approach, change agents are engaged in shaping an innovation from the bottom up. A social movement approach also facilitates ownership because it is created by local change agents. Achieving broad implementation of an innovation through a social movement approach is context based, as it emerges within individual campuses and is shaped to the specific context. Thus, it also responds to local culture and structures. This approach also allows for flexibility for local leaders and their needs because it is not driven by ideals or values from the top down. Further, it fosters deliberation as like-minded people find each other and come together in informal groups to discuss ideas and interests through networks. A social movements approach is based on the assumption that motivation is best achieved internally and innovations are best developed, or at least modified, in particular settings. The ownership, spread, and depth typically lead to greater sustainability. Social movements work well when there is already a set of willing champions within the academy and when the reform is largely internal.

Current examples of social movements

Campus Compact

Campus Compact is an example of an organization that has worked to create change through a social movement perspective. By reviewing its website, including its strategies, network of members, shared interests, and vision, the social movement approach in practice becomes apparent, as well as how it can be used to impact change in higher education.[5] Campus Compact provides key documents about its vision for higher education that includes a greater focus on community engagement and civic education. For example, the President's Declaration on the Civic Responsibility of Higher Education is a key document for the movement. Campus Compact has state affiliates so that individuals in each state can meet regionally as well as at the national meetings. It provides resources for faculty, students, presidents, and service learning and community engagement professionals helping to network these subgroups. Campus Compact has a variety of initiatives to connect people with similar interests ranging from global citizenship to community/economic development to service learning. It also posts featured articles that help the members to create a greater shared understanding and hosts many different events to bring movement leaders together on a regular basis.

Change.org

Change.org is an example of a website that is attempting to foster a broad range of social movements by connecting people with shared purpose, helping them to identify the opponents, and creating networks. Through the website, people can create petitions that other people can sign in order to mobilize support for an issue or idea. Increasingly, higher education issues are being added to the website and education has become one of the 12 areas the site highlights as top causes.

Professional and Social Networks

Characteristics and Examples of Networks

Professional networks are loosely connected groups of individuals that focus on common professional values, goals, and ideas. While social movements include networks, the development of social networks does not always have to be around a common purpose or against a particular opponent. Also, professional networks may be more informal than groupings that form within social movements.

Recently, policymakers and foundations have begun to fund and create networks to activate education reforms (Lumina Foundation 2010). Leaders who have attempted to address complex problems realize that multiple stakeholders need to be engaged to address problems that are multi-faceted and require the input of people and groups with different expertise (Spillane et al. 2010). The Lumina Foundation, for example, has invested in a variety of statewide and national networks to help improve access to higher education. The foundation recognizes that its goal of increasing access in higher education to 60 percent by 2025 will not be met unless a variety of groups are connected and work together (Lumina Foundation 2010). Networks have also been used to scale up change in science disciplines. The National Science Foundation has invested in networks to connect STEM faculty to solve complex problems, improve the nature of undergraduate teaching and learning, and help transform K-12 teachers' knowledge and preparation so they can improve and expand the pipeline of students going into science (Fairweather 2009).

Many studies have linked the existence of social networks with the success of change initiatives (Daly 2010a, 2010b; Hartley 2009a, 2009b). As Alan Daly notes, the social network perspective provides proof that "relationships within a system matter to enacting change" (Daly 2010a: 2). He goes on to note that all reforms may begin as ideas or visions, but that they eventually need to be engaged by people who work in social structures and relationships. Therefore, webs of relationships are often the chief determinant of how well and quickly change efforts take hold, diffuse, and are sustained (Daly 2010c). Informal networks of relationships have a significant impact on whether individuals decide to engage in change or reform behavior. Networks also challenge the notion that only overarching norms (i.e. those of the society, organizations, institutions) impact behavior, instead noting the influence of close peers or even distant contacts over choices and attitude (Kilduff and Tsai 2003). The social networks literature describes more fluid relationships that cross organizational boundaries; scholars look, for example, at collaboratives, online communities, or informal collectives.

Research on How It Leads to Change and Scale

Researchers identify several key ways that social networks lead to change. First, social networks offer a set of mechanisms that enable change—through communication systems, knowledge transfer, alteration of schemas or mindsets, shaping of attitudes, increasing problem solving, and accountability (Ahuja 2000; Borgatti and Foster 2003; Kraatz 1998; McGrath and Krackhardt 2003; Szulanski 1996; Wasserman and Faust 1994). Change agents should be aware that well-formed networks create the conditions identified with successful change.

Second, two outcomes of social networks have been related to change—learning and social capital (Borgatti and Foster 2003; Burt 2000; Kilduff and Tsai 2003; Tenkasi and Chesmore 2003). Many researchers have found a strong linkage between learning and social networks, and learning has been strongly linked to changes in behavior (Tenkasi and Chesmore 2003). Networks also provide social capital that facilitates the change process (Burt 2000). While different definitions of social capital exist, underlying most of the theoretical discussions is the assumption that social capital includes the resources embedded in social relations and social structures, which can be mobilized by an actor to increase the likelihood of success in purposive action (Daly and Finnigan 2008). This resource can vary from knowledge of an organization's internal workings, to how to influence key people, to information on finances. The learning and social capital that are central to networks reflect key principles of change from *social cognition theories.*

Third, change often involves risk taking, which can be less perilous if it is done collectively, rather than individually (Valente 1995). If change agents know many of their peers are going to engage in a particular behavior, they are more likely to also engage in this behavior (Rogers 1962). If we know that social networks can facilitate change, how can it best be harnessed for serving this role?

Various studies have identified how the design of networks impacts positive outcomes such as social capital or learning, as outlined above. The most commonly identified design characteristics are strong and weak ties, heterophily and homophily, subgroups, connectedness, and opinion leaders. Strong ties are most useful for communication of tacit, non-routine, and complex knowledge, whereas weak or less dense networks are better suited for communication of simple and routine information (Nelson 1989; Tenkasi and Chesmore 2003). Strong ties are characterized by three defining characteristics; they are frequent interaction, an extended history, and intimacy or mutual confiding between parties (Kraatz 1998). Most studies of change find strong ties more conducive to deep or second-order changes (Balkundi and Harrison 2006; Tenkasi and Chesmore 2003). Strong ties are more likely to promote in-depth, two-way communication and an exchange of detailed information. Networks that are created for the purpose of innovation or reform may be less likely to have extended histories or intimacy; however, they can create opportunities for frequent interaction. Weak ties are typified by distance and infrequent relationships that may be casual, less intimate, and non-reciprocal in nature. However, for the diffusion of ideas and public information, weak ties can be extremely helpful. Also, weak links can provide important external ideas that promote a more robust change idea for the purpose of obtaining ideas for change. Thus, there may be times and circumstances where weak links are important for creating specific types of change or in certain phases of the change process.

Another area of design found to shape outcomes is the diversity or homogeneity of ties. Diversity of ties or heterophily leads to more complex thinking about change processes, but homophily (i.e. homogenous ties) can lead to quicker adoption of change and stronger relationship development, leading to strong ties (Borgatti and Foster 2003; Moody and White 2003). Homophily might also lead to greater engagement and participation of network members. The development of subgroups (i.e. cliques) within networks has been identified as a strong lever for moving changes forward (Freeman 1979; Reagans and McEvily 2003). Another concept, called connectedness, is a measure of how much exposure an individual receives to the innovation. Individuals surrounded by many people who have adopted a change, even when a change is not common across the profession or campuses, can be influenced to alter their behavior. The existence of opinion leaders is the last aspect of design identified as being critical to creating scaled up change. If a network can attract major opinion leaders to its membership and they become vocal and active, this can help to speed up change by drawing upon the influence of these individuals. As change agents create networks, they should be aware of these features and capitalize on them to shape their network to meet its goals.

How This Approach Addresses Traditional Critiques of Scale-up

Because people join professional networks out of an interest they have, they typically have a great degree of ownership for the change initiatives that are a part of these networks. Social networks are voluntary and build on people's inherent interests. They also facilitate the spread of change initiatives because social networks are broad, spanning institutional, regional, and state boundaries. Social and professional networks have a very broad spread. They can reach across organizations, regions, and nations. If well designed, social networks have proven to be sustainable and can support changes over decades. Some of the examples provided below (pp. 191–192) have been around for several decades. Yet, we do know that social networks are susceptible to not being sustainable. The design principles reviewed in the last section emerged from research about the fragility of social networks and how they often dissipate. Social networks typically do not achieve depth, which is a problem shared with traditional models of scale. People come in and out of social networks, and because they are often not part of members' day-to-day experience, they can sometimes lack the power to create an alteration in consciousness when this is necessary for change to occur. Thus, one of the main critiques of social networks related to change and scale is their lack of depth.

Examples of social networks

The New England Resource Center for Higher Education (NERCHE) Think Tanks

NERCHE Think Tanks bring together campus practitioners (e.g. chief academic officers, associate academic deans, department chairs, and multicultural officers) in similar fields to discuss issues associated with technology, diversity, legal matters, or fiscal management in difficult times and implement meaningful changes. These networks are very loosely designed; there is not usually a plan for holding ongoing meetings, but informal connections are encouraged after think tank meetings.[6]

The American Council on Educations' (ACE) Fellows Program

The American Council on Educations' Fellows Program helps provide professional development opportunities for future leaders in higher education. While it was established as a training program for academic affairs administrators, individuals who participate become part of a group that often stays in contact for years. Individuals who have gone through training later serve as mentors and role models for new members entering the program. ACE hosts events that bring fellows back together, maintains a listserv, and informal communication also occurs among individuals who participate. While the ACE fellows do not have an explicit agenda around change, many individual leaders have used the network to support change.

Science Education for New Civic Engagements and Responsibilities (SENCER)

Science Education for New Civic Engagements and Responsibilities is a faculty development and STEM education reform initiative initiated in 2001 under the National Science Foundation's course curriculum and laboratory improvement (CCLI) national dissemination track. SENCER offers an approach to STEM education that teaches through complex, capacious, contemporary, and contested civic challenges to basic canonical STEM knowledge and methods. It encourages using context to engage interest, make science real and relevant, and stimulate memorable learning. The project has expanded from focusing on single courses to smaller course modules, course intersections, learning communities, major curricular reforms, pre-medical and graduate education, new certificates, and degree-granting programs. The SENCER community includes thousands of faculty members, academic leaders, and students from more than 400 two- and four-year colleges and universities in 46 states and nine foreign nations. The organization's goals are to get more students interested and engaged in learning in STEM courses, help students connect STEM learning to their other studies, and strengthen students' understanding of science and their capacity for responsible work and citizenship by having faculty rethink their teaching practices.

Communities of Practice/Learning Communities

Characteristics and Examples of Communities of Practice/ Learning Communities

A community of practice is a group of people who share a concern or a passion for something they do and learn how to do it (Allee 2000; Lave 1988; Wenger 1998, 2006). Communities of practice are also professional networks, but they tend to be more geographically bound, as these groups have lots of regular social interaction. While there are virtual communities of practice, research on communities of practice emerged out of studies of geographically located professionals who were working together in apprenticeships and learned with each other. Lave and Wenger (1991) studied how newcomers or novices to informal groups become established members of those and participate in apprenticeships in order to better understand how learning occurs beyond formal classroom settings (Lave and Wenger 1991). A community of practice is essentially a way that people learn through participation in practice in their day-to-day lives, typically in the workplace. In terms of widespread change processes, if change agents can affect the socialization, norm setting, and learning among participants within organizations and systems, then they can shape how work gets done and create more widespread and scaled up changes.

In more recent years, organizations have begun to systematically create communities of practice to help channel further learning and development, which they then see as creating change (McDermott and Archibald 2010). In fact, communities of practice in business are now tasked with knowledge creation and dissemination activities that were formerly covered by more formal organizational structures, including planning, training, or research offices. Organizations believe that by sponsoring formal and informal communities of practice, they will create greater shared knowledge, which typically leads to greater innovation and effectiveness (Wenger 2004). Also, communities of practice rely on tacit knowledge that organizations typically have no way of systematically capturing and thus have a knowledge management function. Most of the research conducted by Lave and Wenger was on existing communities of practice, not structured or created ones. However, emerging research suggests that non-organic or created communities of practice can develop similar outcomes to organic ones (Lesser and Storck 2001).

The communities of practice approach operates from internal motivations and studies about what makes individual members successful in creating change—commitment, social presence, and an interest in collaborating with and enjoying interacting with others within the community. These types of organic qualities are hard to create organizationally, which is why communities of practice tend to be developed through professional organizations and informally around shared interests. Within higher education settings, communities of practice have typically been established to work with faculty on their teaching practices, which makes sense given these communities' orientation towards bringing together professionals so they can reflect on their practices. Often, centers for teaching and learning have been advocates for the creation of communities of practice for faculty. The community of practice vehicle has more traction internationally and tends to be used to describe ways people work together toward changes. However, communities of practice are also being advocated among professionals in higher education. For example, those interested in sustainability in higher education have created communities of practice based on their shared interest in environmentalism. Also, virtual communities of practice that can connect faculty with similar interests across institutions are becoming increasingly prevalent. For example, a faculty member may have a strong interest in interdisciplinarity, but work at an institution where very few faculty do interdisciplinary work. In cases such as these, communities of practice can be highly beneficial.

In the United States, the term learning communities is typically used. A learning community is similar to communities of practices, but varies slightly in that it is intentionally designed, whereas the communities of practice are usually more organic. The literature provides multiple definitions of learning communities but a common definition is that a learning community is a group of people who share common emotions, values, or beliefs, and are actively engaged in learning together, from each other, and through routine interaction (Smith et al. 2004). A learning community design is most commonly associated with interdisciplinary pedagogical techniques in higher education. Whereas communities of practice emerged from studies of informal learning within organizations and day-to-day social practice, learning communities evolved from constructivist views of learning in which individuals were successful in learning when they constructed knowledge together, rather than by trying to learn individually. This approach has been spurred on by studies that suggest participation in learning communities is associated with a number of positive outcomes, including gains on a range of developmental measures such as personal and social development, practical competence, and diversity awareness, as well as standard outcome measures such as retention and academic performance. Further, change agents considered whether learning communities could also serve as vehicles for change outcomes (Pascarella and Terenzini 2005; Smith et al. 2004).

Given the underpinnings of learning communities as a pedagogical technique, rather than a change strategy, why are they included in a book about change? Like communities of practice and social networks, campus change agents have been searching for levers for connecting people who are interested in similar ideas, as well as tapping into the various studies about organizational learning and sensemaking for deep change, as noted in earlier chapters. Many change agents use both communities of practice and learning communities as vehicles for achieving organizational learning, which has been elusive, through cross-campus teams formed by individuals in positions of authority.

Research on How Communities of Practice and Learning Communities Create Change and Scale

There is minimal research documenting how communities of practice or learn-ing communities have created scalability for changes in higher education. These vehicles are being used more often, but very few studies have examined their effi-cacy. Yet, anecdotal reports suggest that individual campuses, campus systems, and consortia have used learning communities to achieve greater attention to teaching and adoption of particular teaching practices, student outcomes assess-ment, technology adoption, diversity initiatives, and changes in promotion and tenure requirements (Cox 2004). In terms of scaling up initiatives, several states or national reform initiatives have used cross-campus learning communities in order to facilitate a focus on teaching within individual campuses. For example, Project Kaleidoscope has created regional communities of practice to advance hands-on learning in the sciences. Also, disciplinary societies have also used this model to scale up change within particular disciplines or fields. Studies of comprehensive school reform found that presence of formal and informal learning communities helped to improve schools and implement innovations needed for student success (Daly 2011a).

For change agents that are interested in creating or capitalizing on existing com-munities of practice for change, it is important to be familiar with some of the principles about what makes a community of practice successful or how it can be best designed. One of the major findings about communities of practice, though, is that their design varies according to their distinct goals. There are many differ-ent types of communities of practice, so no one design can be offered for ensuring the model's effectiveness, but there are several design principles that can enable a community to meet its specific goals (Wenger et al. 2002). Change agents can use these principles to design a community for scaling up a change. The following are some general principles and practices identified as being important for creating learning that leads to change:

1. Design the community to evolve naturally: Because the nature of a commu-nity of practice is dynamic, in that the interests, goals, and members are sub-ject to change, they should be designed to support shifts in focus. Therefore, ongoing surveying of individuals and the community is important to see how their perspectives and needs change.
2. Create opportunities for open dialogue within and with outside perspectives: While the members and their knowledge are a community of practice's most valuable resource, it is also beneficial to look outside of the community of practice to understand the different possibilities for achieving their learning goals.
3. Welcome and allow different levels of participation: Wenger et al. (2002) identifies three main levels of participation. First, there is the core group of individuals who participate intensely in the community through discussions

and projects. This group typically takes on leadership roles in guiding the group. Second, is the active group, whose members attend and participate regularly, but not to the level of the leaders. Third, there is the peripheral group, which includes members who, while passive participants in the community, still learn from their level of involvement. Wenger notes the third group typically represents the majority of the community.

4. Develop both public and private community spaces: While communities of practice typically operate in public spaces, where all members share, discuss, and explore ideas, they should also offer private exchanges. Different members of a community of practice could coordinate relationships among members and resources in an individualized approach based on specific needs. Creating member subgroups around particular tasks or interests is a way to capitalize on smaller group work to benefit the larger, public group.

5. Focus on the value of the community: Communities of practice should create opportunities for participants to explicitly discuss the value and productivity of their participation in the group.

6. Combine familiarity and excitement: Communities of practice should offer the expected learning opportunities as part of their structure, as well as opportunities for members to shape their learning experience together by brainstorming and examining the conventional and radical wisdom related to their topic. Key thought leaders should be brought into the community to help drive innovation in the discussion.

7. Find and nurture a regular rhythm for the community: Communities of practice should coordinate a thriving cycle of activities and events that allow for the members to regularly meet, reflect, and evolve. The rhythm, or pace, should maintain an anticipated level of engagement to sustain the vibrancy of the community, yet not be so fast-paced that it becomes unwieldy and overwhelming in its intensity. Throughout many of the steps there is emphasis on the building of relationships, but the community building aspect of this last recommendation focuses on the coordination of activities that help connect and maintain the enthusiasm of the members of the community.

(Wenger et al. 2002)

The design principles for learning communities are not vastly different from those of communities of practice. However, communities of practice emphasize more organic qualities, allowing participants to exercise more or less involvement, acknowledging that people will come in and out, and involve processes focused more on the inherent work, area of interest, and relationships that develop as a part of the process.

Cox (2004) used research specifically about faculty learning communities to develop the following characteristics for promoting their success:

1. Safety and trust: In order for participants to connect with one another, they must have a sense of safety and trust. This is especially true when

participants reveal weaknesses in their teaching or ignorance of teaching processes or literature.

2. Openness: In an atmosphere of openness, participants can feel free to share thoughts and feelings, without fear of retribution.

3. Respect: In order to coalesce as a learning community, members need to feel that they are valued and respected as people. It is important for the university to acknowledge their participation by financially supporting community projects and participation at faculty learning communities' topic-related conferences.

4. Responsiveness: Members must respond respectfully to one another and facilitators must respond quickly to participants. The facilitator should welcome the expression of concerns and preferences and, when appropriate, share these with individuals and the entire faculty learning community.

5. Collaboration: The importance of collaboration in consultation and group discussion on individual members' projects and on achieving community learning outcomes hinges on group members' ability to work with and respond to one another. In addition to individual projects, joint projects and presentations should be welcomed.

6. Relevance: Learning outcomes are enhanced by relating the subject matter of the faculty learning communities to the participants' teaching, courses, scholarship, professional interests, and life experiences. All participants should be encouraged to seek out and share teaching and other real-life examples to illustrate these outcomes.

7. Challenge: Expectations for the quality of faculty learning communities' outcomes should be high, engendering a sense of progress, scholarship, value, and accomplishment. Sessions should include, for example, some in which individuals share syllabi and report on their individual projects.

8. Enjoyment: Activities must include social opportunities to lighten up and bond and should take place in invigorating environments. For example, a retreat can take place off-campus at a nearby country inn, state park, historic site, or the like.

9. Esprit de corps: Sharing individual and community outcomes with colleagues in the academy should generate pride and loyalty. For example, when the community makes a campus presentation, participants strive to provide an excellent session.

10. Empowerment: A sense of empowerment is both a crucial element and a desired outcome of participation in a faculty learning community. In the construction of a transformative learning environment, the participants gain a new view of themselves and a new sense of confidence in their abilities. Faculty members leave their year of participation with better courses and a clearer understanding of themselves and their students. Key outcomes include scholarly teaching and contributions to the scholarship of teaching.

Both communities of practice and learning communities are seen as following through stages of formation, implementation, and sustaining. While they may not be identical, certain issues are important at their formation, such as defining and articulating the purpose of the group, creating an active core group, and building strong relationships that lead to open communication and learning. During the implementation phase, change agents can focus on involving thought leaders, collecting and using feedback from the group to create professional development, generating content, and building personal relationships among the group. As the group moves into the sustaining mode, members spend more time reinforcing the value of the community to individuals, fostering leadership, and facilitating member-run subgroups. Both literatures also emphasize the importance of understanding the institutional context and how it might shape the interactions and effectiveness of a learning community's or community of practice's efforts to create change. For example, organizational politics, stability of leadership, characteristics of the campus stakeholders, and other issues can shape the ability of change agents to develop the characteristics (e.g. deliberation or respect and support for members) which are needed for establishing functional learning communities and communities of practice.

How Communities of Practice and Learning Communities Address Traditional Scale-up Critiques

Communities of practice typically have strong ownership among members because people choose to belong and have a passion for the work they are engaged in as a part of the group. However, learning communities have often been formed or shaped by organizational leaders, rather than being organically created like communities of practice. There may be less of a sense of ownership within learning communities if they are not organic. Both communities of practice and learning communities are well designed for achieving depth, leading members to examine their values and norms and involving them in a process of schema change and learning. One of the primary advantages of either model is its ability to help change agents to rethink their views and engage with innovation. Communities of practice and learning communities might facilitate spread, but they also can be relatively contained. Often, a learning community will be created within a single unit or organization. Some national organizations, such as student affairs organizations like NASPA or NASFA (for international educators), have created nationwide communities of practice that help to connect people far beyond the boundaries of a single institution. Yet, most of the research and documented benefits have been conducted on smaller-scale communities of practice and learning communities.

We have little knowledge about whether large-scale learning communities create systemic and broad change. In terms of sustainability, communities of practice are typically sustainable because they are created organically within workplaces among people who do common work. In the examples provided below, faculty working at particular universities comprise the membership of the communities of practice. Given the longevity of faculty working for particular institutions, it is likely that these communities will be sustained for a long time. The sustainability of learning communities is based more on leadership, careful design, and other characteristics described in the section on research (pp. 195–196). Thus, we can create learning communities that have the capability of being sustainable, but this feature is not built into the model itself.

Example of a Community of Practice

The University of Southern Queensland

The University of Southern Queensland has established communities of practice for faculty to work together and improve their teaching.[7] They have established many different communities of practice, ranging from: administration coordinators, for tablet PC and Pen enabled technologies; faculty of arts; first-year experience; learning and teaching support; research supervisors; student equity; as well as other areas. The center host events for various communities, such as invited speakers. They connect people through a teaching fellows program, a toolkit for certain groups, such as those supporting students in their first year, provides publications on key educational challenges and perspectives, and has guidance for starting a new community of practice, including links to Wenger's work on communities of practice.

The Center described its mission and focus as the following:

> A community of practice approach to teaching and learning in higher education provides a space for staff to collaboratively reflect, review, and regenerate their current teaching and learning practices. Within higher education, the organizational structures and culture of individualism produce a situation where individuals are often isolated and unaware of practices that are followed by others. While initiatives to overcome this individualism within research endeavors such as research centers and research networks are well advanced, these are less common in relation to teaching in higher education.
>
> The consequences of a lack of formal or informal structures for the sharing of learning and teaching practices include a lack of institutional memory regarding innovations, little acknowledgement or recognition of the diversity of good practices outside formal award mechanisms, and little support for individuals in need of mentoring or guidance in reforming, improving, or reflecting on their practices.
>
> (http://www.usq.edu.au/cops/higher-education)

Examples of Learning Communities

National Resource Center for Learning Communities

Detailed resources for learning communities in higher education are available through the Washington Center at the Evergreen State College.[8] As the National Resource Center for Learning Communities, they believe that learning communities—done well—create a collaborative environment where students thrive, faculty and staff do their best work, and learning fosters the habits of mind and skills to tackle complex real-world issues. In order to foster learning communities they have created regional networks, a summer institute, a library of resources, including a student survey and assessment instruments, a journal of research and practice, a listserv to connect people and allow individuals in the network to help trouble shoot issues in building learning communities. They also offer technical assistance to institutions interested in building learning communities. Furthermore, they have engaged in research about the efficacy of learning communities and have collected an assortment of models and examples. The center focuses on learning communities as a means to foster student success and less so as a way to create change.

Center for the Integration of Research, Teaching, and Learning

The Center for the Integration of Research, Teaching, and Learning (CIRTL) is a learning community of institutions founded by the University of Wisconsin, Michigan State University, and the Pennsylvania State University, through which innovation and learning have occurred as member institutions interact around their shared aims to strengthen the professional development of STEM doctoral students.[9] The CIRTL network supports the mutual exchange of successful strategies and programs based on the CIRTL pillars. The collegiality and respect inherent in this learning community approach have naturally led to mutual support in program development across the network. There are now more than 20 institutions participating.

The goals of CIRTL are to:

1. Establish interdisciplinary learning communities at every network university, each founded on the CIRTL core ideas and each effectively preparing graduates-through-faculty to use and improve best practices in STEM teaching and learning with attention to diverse student audiences;
2. Establish a cross-network learning community by which graduates-through-faculty across the network are better prepared for teaching as a consequence of the diversity of the universities;
3. Foster transitions from the network learning communities into faculty positions that sustain the concepts, practices, and attitudes developed while graduate students or postdocs;

4.   Enhance graduate education in teaching and learning at universities beyond the CIRTL Network.

(CIRTL n.d.)

The long-range goal of the network is to produce a national cohort of STEM graduate students and postdoctoral researchers who are launching new faculty careers at diverse institutions, demonstrably succeeding in promoting STEM learning for all, and actively engaging in improving teaching and learning practice.

Miami University

Miami University has created faculty learning communities (FLCs), which are cross-disciplinary faculty and staff groups of as many as 12 members that engage in an active, collaborative, yearlong program with a curriculum about enhancing teaching and learning. Frequent seminars and activities provide opportunities for learning, development, interdisciplinarity, the scholarship of teaching and learning, and community building. In the literature about student learning communities, the word *student* usually can be replaced with *faculty* and still make the same point.

There are two types of faculty learning communities, cohort based and topic based. Cohort-based learning communities address the teaching, learning, and developmental needs of an important cohort of faculty that has been particularly affected by the isolation, fragmentation, or chilly climate in the academy. The curriculum of such a yearlong community is shaped by the participants to include a broad range of teaching and learning areas and topics of interest to them. These communities will make a positive impact on the culture of the institution over the years if given multi-year support. The examples of cohort-based communities at Miami are the Alumni Teaching Scholars Community for early-career faculty and the Senior Faculty Learning Community for Teaching Excellence for mid-career and senior faculty.

Each topic-based learning community is yearlong and has a curriculum designed to address a special campus teaching and learning issue, for example diversity, technology, or cooperative learning. These communities offer membership to and provide opportunities for learning across all faculty ranks and cohorts, but with a focus on a particular theme. A topic-focused faculty learning community ends when the teaching opportunity or issue of concern has been satisfactorily addressed. Examples of topic-based communities at Miami are discussed elsewhere in this book.

The long-term goals of a faculty learning communities program for the University are to:

- Build university-wide community through teaching and learning, essentially to create a learning organization;
- Increase faculty interest in undergraduate teaching and learning;

- Investigate and incorporate ways that difference can enhance teaching and learning;
- Nourish scholarly teaching and the scholarship of teaching and its application to student learning;
- Broaden the evaluation of teaching and the assessment of learning;
- Increase faculty collaboration across disciplines;
- Encourage reflection about liberal education and coherence of learning across disciplines;
- Increase the rewards for and prestige of excellent teaching;
- Increase financial support for teaching and learning initiatives; and,
- Create an awareness of the complexity of teaching and learning.

(Miami University n.d.)

Each faculty learning community has its own specific goals and objectives, which the facilitator and members determine.

The university also hosts an annual conference to help other institutions in developing faculty learning communities.[10]

Summary

Social movements, networks, and communities of practice/learning communities are some important vehicles that can be used to scale up change in higher education, fitting within its traditionally decentralized, autonomous, and professional structure and culture. While there may be other models that can be used to scale up change, each of these three vehicles has had success in scaling up changes and works with mechanisms that have proven to facilitate change, such as networks, deliberation, and the creation of external support for individuals who might be working within contexts where there is little or no support for the changes for which they advocate. These approaches have just begun to be used, so their potential is not fully understood, but would appear to be significant.

ten
The Ethics of Change

Liz and Mary work on a campus where changes are constantly occurring, but they do not see the connection to student learning. In fact, all the focus seems to be on marketing, branding, and advertising. Each month brings announcements of new policies or programs aimed at unclear goals that Liz and Mary can never seem to identify. They feel the campus is adrift.

Every change process is value and interest laden, and fraught with ethical choices and dilemmas. When proposing a change or trying to garner support for an effort, leaders need to examine the beneficiaries of the proposed change and whose interests are served. Change agents need to be vigilant about identifying ethical situations so they can make choices that support the greater good. In addition, recent research literature has identified a variety of processes that can be integrated into change initiatives in order to better ensure ethical outcomes. Scholars examining ethics in relationship to organizational change bemoan the paucity of research, even though studies of change routinely point to the importance of ethics in change processes (Sturdy and Grey 2003). Furthermore, research identifies that failed change efforts are often linked to resistance and cynicism resulting from earlier, unethical change processes. In the end, all propositions for change represent an ethical position. Change agents must be cognizant of this and think carefully about the implications of their proposed agenda, vision, or direction.

Still, resisting a misguided change can be seen as an ethical response and an act of leadership. Sturdy and Grey (2003) argue that those who hold positions of power have often embraced a mantra of change and are usually rewarded for creating changes within their organizations. The authors comically present an advertisement for a manager, asking for the individual to embrace stability and learn to manage continuity for the survival of the organization. Their point in arguing for continuity and critiquing the bias toward change among management is that change advocated by managers serves the interests of elites, while the broader concerns of other organizational stakeholders are usually unimportant in managers' agendas. Sturdy and Grey note the ethical problems with the pro-change orientation, which often lacks a sense of reflection, critique, or inclusion. Given the unexamined pro-change orientation of many who hold positions of power, resistance to change may be needed to protect non-elites' and broader stakeholders' interests and ethical considerations.

It is important to note that this chapter does not take a philosophical approach to discussing ethics. In fact, most philosophers would call this a technical perspective, in which I draw largely on social science studies about ethics, rather than drawing upon normative arguments from philosophy. Certainly, there are many important ethicists (e.g. Rawls, Aristotle, Habermas) and ethical traditions (e.g. teleological, deontological, pragmatism) that can be drawn upon to shape particular moral positions. Ethical principles provide perspective on fixed positions for guiding decisions such as whether a proposed change is just, fair, and honorable. Many of these principles are represented in this chapter, embedded in the social science constructs reviewed. For example, the calls for broad stakeholder involvement reflect Habermas's appeals for democratic discussion of principles; the importance of organizational justice reflects Rawls's theory of justice. So, while the chapter does not draw strongly from philosophy, the social science studies that have been drawn upon have these notions embedded within them. And, certainly, all of these philosophers provide important guideposts for any change agent and recommend the further study of ethics.

It is also important to note that most studies examining the ethics of change have focused on individuals in positions of authority and ways they may engage in ethical lapses through change processes. There is, however, little research on bottom-up change initiatives and ethical lapses that emerge within these processes. Many of the ideas described below can be applied to bottom-up change processes, as well, but there is little empirical data to draw upon to inform them. However, throughout the chapter I will make reference to the way that bottom-up change agents also need to think about ethical issues in their work.

This chapter will proceed as follows. First, I examine the challenge of the plurality of ethical positions that exist in a global societal context, which often paralyzes leaders from acting. I also introduce the notion of ethical fitness as a metaphor for leaders to engage in ethical practice, drawing on Rushworth Kidder's work. Next, I reflect on the ethics of the types of change and the overabundance of changes that reflect how managers' (e.g., administrators) interests are being pursued on campuses. I review common dilemmas encountered in change processes that help change agents to also see the necessity of engaging in ethical change processes. I note how resistance and cynicism might be profitably engaged to enhance change processes and can be an important indicator of problems. I also suggest how resistance may be a form of change agency. The focus of this chapter is on the processes that leaders can use to help enhance an ethical approach to change. The chapter ends by applying the principles reviewed throughout the chapter to two of the cases presented in Chapter 7.

Whose Ethics?

We live in a global society, where various cultures holding different and sometimes conflicting values interact on a daily basis. Our college campuses are filled with individuals from all over the world, who may draw upon very different traditions when determining what are the appropriate values in a given situation. Most people avoid ethics because it gets into the murky territory of values, morals, and religion, with few perceived universal or agreed-upon values. Yet, some ethicists underscore how certain qualities, such as honesty or justice, transcend almost every culture, emphasizing that we can speak about some level of human values or ethics (Kidder 1995). In fact, most human rights organizations that exist worldwide draw upon these more universal sets of principles. Kidder (1995) explains that you can look at different religious texts, secular codes, military regulations, business codes of ethics, centers for corporate responsibility, and various organizational creeds and find that they contain many of the same principles. These common principles include truth, fairness, loyalty, integrity, respect, goodwill, cooperation, kindness, appreciation for diversity, and the like. While there may be ethical distinctions in particular cultures and situations, there is much more that we share in terms of our values than there are differences.

But the question of "whose ethics" may prevent change agents from considering important ethical issues as they think about daily decisions. Most ethicists agree it is better to struggle with "whose ethics" than to not examine the ethical underpinnings of decisions that we make. Therefore, we may not be able to make decisions that are aligned with everybody's values, but we are more likely to make sound decisions when we at least examine the ethical consequences of our decisions. Also, change agents can engage in ethical processes or practices that unearth varying values among subgroups within organizations and that help groups have discussions to arrive at community decisions. For example, if one is in a position of power, it is important to recognize that people might be afraid to question their judgment or bring up concerns, even if they see that the proposed change might be unethical. The way that change agents in positions of power can better ensure that questionable ethical dilemmas are open for debate is by prompting the questioning of a proposed change initiative and demonstrating an openness to examining other sets of values.

Ethical Fitness

Kidder (1995) suggests that change agents should think about ethics the way they think about physical fitness. One cannot run the marathon without working out every day. Similarly, one is unlikely to make ethical decisions in a crisis when they do not routinely think about or discuss the ethics of decision-making. Instead, leaders need to consider ethics everyday and develop their ethical fitness in order to make sound decisions, particularly when there are crises, more challenging situations, or major change initiatives at hand. The process of developing ethical fitness begins by familiarizing oneself with the three most often used ethical approaches, as well as the criticisms of each approach. Next, change agents need to apply these ethical approaches in their work life.

Kidder (1995) also notes that decisions where the choice is between right or wrong (right versus wrong) require less reflection and are generally easier to make. Decisions where either course of action is viewed as right (right versus right) necessitate ethical fitness. They also require an individual to be able to identify the dilemma, sort out the information supporting each side, and use resolution principles, which are reviewed below to better understand how to best make a decision. Kidder reviews in detail what he calls right versus right dilemmas that require much more extensive ethical reflection. There are four dilemma paradigms that routinely emerge in human experience. They are truth versus loyalty, individual versus community, short term versus long term, and justice versus mercy. His book is based on interviews with hundreds of leaders making ethical decisions and these ethical dilemmas emerged consistently across different cultural contexts.

Ends-based or Teleological Thinking

This approach to ethics suggests following the maxim *the greatest good for the greatest number* (Kidder 1995). This principle relies heavily on assessing the consequences or ends of action. This requires change agents to be able to clearly think about the outcomes of a particular action and to be able to play that out in various decision scenarios. The dilemma with this approach is that serving the broader good often can hurt a minority group. Furthermore, humans are notoriously poor at speculating about the full range of possible consequences. So, if this process of thinking is not properly enacted, change agents may not end up with the ethical results they desire.

Rules-based Thinking

Based on some of the objections to the ends-based form of ethics, rule-based ethics emerged, focusing on having us act on our highest sense of inner conscience, based on universal principles (Kidder 1995). This approach suggests that we should never act in ways that do not conform to universal laws of honesty or justice. This approach suggests that you stick to a set of principles and let the consequences fall where they may. The consequences of our actions or situations should not dictate our ethical approach or opinions. The main criticism of the rule-based approach is that it may be overly rigid and strict. Also, given the vast variety of human individuality and circumstances, this may lead to making problematic choices by not allowing context to affect an ethical decision.

Care-based Thinking

This approach to ethics asks us to care enough about others, to put ourselves in their shoes, and to make ethical choices based on that understanding (Kidder 1995). It reflects the Golden Rule, that we should do unto others as we want done unto us. So, the test of rightness or wrongness of action is to imagine yourself as the object affected by the change, rather than the agent of action, and consider your own feelings emerging from this exercise. Criticisms of this perspective suggest that, out of empathy, this perspective can lead individuals to act in unethical ways according to the rule-based perspective. For example, a person may decide it is best to lie in a situation in order to protect someone from another person who might abuse them. Others suggest that situational dynamics dilute and make ethical choices more problematic, not easier to understand.

Kidder (1995) recommends applying all three of these approaches to situations and allowing them to help guide action by providing different ethical lenses for situations. He sees that all have their advantages, as well as downsides. So, by combining them, leaders are better able to create a multi-faceted solution. In his book *How Good People Make Tough Choices: Resolving the Dilemmas of Ethical Living*, he provides specific case examples where he guides leaders through the application of these different ethical frameworks on difficult ethical choices. He also helps demonstrate how the three principles can be reconciled, which may seem difficult for readers. I recommend this book as a way for change agents to develop their ethical fitness. By learning about and applying multiple ethical principles, change agents begin to advance toward being ethical change agents.

The Ethics of the Type of Change and the Overabundance of Top-down Change that Serve Management's Interest

Almost all of the literature on ethics and organizational change notes the dilemma that most change initiatives tend to come from the top down and serve managerial or elite interests. Whether these interests are ethical or not is rarely held up for examination. Instead, there's been a neutral orientation to whose or which values are represented in change initiatives. This value-neutral stance has hidden suspect ethical positions that are often adopted. Many scholars and commentators are now critiquing change initiatives undertaken by corporate entities in the 1980s and 1990s, including restructuring efforts, quality improvement, outsourcing, and other efforts under the title of new managerialism (McKendall 1993). Restructuring efforts resulted in downsizing many companies for the purpose of creating efficiencies and many individuals losing their jobs, with remaining staff having significantly increased workloads. Quality improvement initiatives often resulted in people losing their positions. As processes were re-examined, positions were restructured and people currently in positions no longer had needed expertise and were therefore unqualified and fired. New managerialism is another management approach that is results oriented and uses data to establish indicators of effectiveness and efficiency. In order to conduct this increased data collection, the management of the organization is becoming larger and larger at the expense of the lower levels of the organization. Since these lower levels are shrinking, people must work harder because there are fewer workers in place. There are always more and more offices and bureaucracies being created at the top of many organizations. Each successive change initiative focuses on creating efficiencies and saving organizations money, but often occurs at the expense of employees.

The same blind and neutral eye has been taken to many change initiatives on college campuses. As I noted in Chapter 1, in recent years, many leaders in positions of authority on college campuses have pursued prestige (e.g. increasing rankings), rather than focusing on the institutional mission. In addition, campuses have adopted corporate management practices ranging from responsibility-centered budgeting, to centralized governance, to outsourcing, which have been presented as political necessities or more advanced managerial techniques that would benefit the institution. Campus stakeholders have not asked questions (or been allowed to raise questions) about whether the pursuit of prestige undermines the institutional goals of student learning or intellectual engagement. The question of whose interests are served by a change and who loses out needs very careful consideration from change agents. Rawls would suggest changes that put undue stress on those in marginalized positions or work against their interests should be viewed with suspicion, compared to those that might decrease the interest of those in power. In my 20 years on college campuses, I have heard almost no discussion about the ethics of change initiatives pursued and whose interests they serve.

Over the years, a number of scholars have documented how changes that have been initiated overwhelmingly favor managerial interests and tend to have negative impacts on the remainder of the individuals in organizations. Birnbaum (2000) documented this trend in his book *Management Fads in Higher Education*. He describes leaders' propensity to implement change initiatives that serve managerial efficiency and business values for decade after decade in higher education. He reviews the emergence of management by objectives, re-engineering, quality management, and a variety of other management fads. He labels them fads because they come and go over the years and are typically not changes with staying power. He underscores how they have some benefits, but are largely a misuse of institutional energy, time, and resources. His findings are similar to other studies conducted in business about the impact of management fads (McKendall 1993). His work documenting these trends in higher education serves as a cautionary tale for leaders, particularly administrators, advocating for changes that do not consider broader interests and tend to focus more on managerial interests.

Diefenbach (2006) also provides case study data about an institution undergoing changes that were primarily oriented toward increasing management control and entrepreneurial prestige seeking, which was disguised by the administrators as a functional response to external pressures for survival to compete. The institution adopts practices aimed at being more efficient and accountable. The study demonstrates how this similar pattern is imitated by administrators on different campuses without regard to whose interests are served by centralizing power and limiting institutional voice. Diefenbach identifies how campuses pursue prestige and revenue generation in similar ways and campus constituencies are not able to question the new direction.

Yet, it is always important to consider whether a change ultimately benefits the client—customers in business, community members in government, and students in higher education institutions. In fact, students' interests should be the ultimate interest served through any change initiative because they are the primary beneficiaries and main focus of educational institutions. For example, a faculty member may be hesitant to move from the lecture method to a new pedagogy or method for teaching. However, if there is research that suggests that a new pedagogical style is far more beneficial for students, then it may be justified to override the faculty member's concern. Therefore, change initiatives that serve the interests of managers may be justified if they also serve the interests of students, but this interest needs to be balanced with the impact on organizational stakeholders such as faculty and staff. If a manager says that a change is being made to create efficiencies to save students money, then the administrators should be able to demonstrate the cost saving to students. Often, efficiency is pursued, but cost savings are never seen by students. Unfortunately, weighing the impact of change initiatives in this way is uncommon.

Furthermore, some ethicists suggest that change initiatives cause such fear, confusion, frustration, and vulnerability for many stakeholders that they need to be engaged only when there is sufficient evidence of their value and increased effectiveness for an organization or group (McKendall 1993). These scholars suggest that more evidence needs to be provided upfront about the efficacy of a particular change initiative before it is pursued. Also, as will be described on pp. 210–212, pursuing change initiatives that have little support for their efficacy has resulted in cynicism and resentment among employees (Dean et al. 1998). Therefore, it is important for change agents to explore the efficacy of their ideas to ensure that they are directions worth pursuing.

Let's take a specific example in higher education. The American Association of Colleges and Universities has been advocating for the use of high-impact practices such as service learning, undergraduate research, intergroup dialogues, learning communities, and active and experiential learning in a national campaign to improve undergraduate education. Yet, before it advocated for these high-impact practices, it conducted a detailed analysis of research studies examining teaching and learning initiatives. Its support for these particular changes for teaching and learning are grounded in significant data and research. It has synthesized this research to make it available to local change agents, who can make use of it to help others understand the efficacy of these approaches. However, many other change initiatives are not based on data, research, and thorough analysis. It is part of one's ethical obligation to conduct this type of analysis to ensure that the outcome is worth the ambiguity, confusion, and difficulties that change initiatives often cause on campus.

Common Dilemmas

Various scholars have identified a range of ethical dilemmas and problems that emerge as the change process unfolds. While the following discussion is not meant to be fully inclusive, it does provide a range of types of ethical issues that emerge over the entire process of change. It also provides reasoning for why change agents might want to adopt an ethical process for approaching change. I have already mentioned that the pure pursuit of managerial interests is an ethical dilemma that needs consideration. More dilemmas that occur during the process of change are reviewed next.

At the beginning of the change process many change agents oversell the value of the change or its benefits. Later, stakeholders are let down when the change does not live up to the promise. Another ethical dilemma is the misuse of data. Again, in the interest of selling a change initiative, data may be distorted, certain data are sometimes left out, and other manipulations take place that are dishonest. The dilemma of lack of full disclosure continues from the beginning of an initiative through its implementation, where the consequences and outcomes become apparent. Studies have found that the known outcomes of change initiatives, for example many people losing their jobs, have sometimes been hidden from individuals to try to mitigate resistance (White and Rhodeback 1992).

In fact, much of the management literature describes purposefully concealing the nature of a change, as well as corresponding data, as a strategy for moving changes forward when individuals within the institution might pose resistance. Gilley, Godek and Gilley (2009) use the medical analogy of concealing a foreign body (transplanted organ) so that the patient's body (or in this case social system) will not reject the transplanted organ. Concealing information is not even considered dishonest or inappropriate and is a commonplace strategy advocated within the management literature.

Another common dilemma is that change agents try to exclude individuals who they believe will be resistant or raise challenges by pointing out problems with a proposed change initiative, allowing time to begin implementing changes before criticism is allowed to emerge. Communication and information is often highly controlled to prevent others from possessing full knowledge. Change processes also create uncertainty and ambiguity because individuals often do not know or understand what a change will mean for their role or future with the organization. Uncertainty leads to stress, which can be crippling to employees. Again, by holding back information, organizations can create an unhealthy level of stress among employees and other stakeholders.

Those in positions of authority sometimes collect data about people's perceptions of a change initiative, as well. At times, this information has not been kept anonymous, causing employees who do not favor the change to experience backlash—sometimes resulting in their being fired. In efforts to squelch resistance, ethical violations of anonymity have emerged within many organizations (White and Rhodeback 1992). While the ethical violations can vary from extremely overt, such as violating promises of anonymity, to more subtle issues of not fully disclosing information, creating stress for employees, both subtle and overt actions can negatively impact individuals, but also the overall organization. With a sense of some of the ethical issues that commonly emerge, it is not surprising that change results in resistance. But, resistance can be an important indicator that efforts may be unethical.

Resistance and Cynicism—Indicators of Suspect Ethical Positions

How might a change agent determine when they have ignored ethical considerations? One way is to listen to stakeholders to identify the sources of resistance and cynicism. While all resistance and cynicism is certainly not a reflection of ethical violations, it can be an indicator that leaders can use to assess their processes.

A plethora of studies have identified how lack of attention to ethical issues in the change process results in resistance and cynicism, eventually resulting in a failed change process. As Dean at al. (1998) note, "Organizational change and quality improvement efforts particularly seem to engender cynicism" (p. 341). They point out that the cynicism has influenced the creation of comic strips such as *Dilbert* that routinely characterize organizational change initiatives as ludicrous endeavors. In the preface to this book, I noted how 70 percent of change processes fail and that many scholars who have recently examined ethics and organizational change suggest a strong link between the lack of ethical attention and the failure of change processes. Top-down leaders are prone to see change initiatives as value neutral. By ignoring the key ethical and value dimensions, they miss opportunities for creating buy-in and avoiding resistance and cynicism. Understanding more about resistance and cynicism, which is a growing topic of scholarship, can help change agents be more attentive to these responses, as well as learn how to engage resistant stakeholders and cynics effectively. Next, I review some of the research on resistance and cynicism to inform readers about how to use these as meaningful sources of feedback in the change process.

Perhaps the most cited obstacle to organizational change is resistance. Three of the main sources of resistance are related to ethical issues. They are a lack of belief in the efficacy of the idea, lack of trustworthiness on the part of the change agents, and the existence of prior, failed change processes that result in cynicism. First, not believing in the efficacy of an idea is usually an indication that the proposed change is connected to an overly narrow set of interests or interests that have a negative impact on a particular group. Second, those who register resistance often note a lack of trust in the people or groups that are proposing changes, sometimes because they have prior experience encountering change initiatives that have served those change agents, but not the rest of the organization. This fosters a lack of trust. Third, individuals who have experienced poorly conceived and executed change processes are more likely to be resistors that are less functional in terms of offering critique aimed at shaping the change in positive ways. Instead these resisters become dedicated to fully eradicate the change effort and act in unconstructive ways. Essentially, their experience with an unethical change can turn people who might have provided constructive criticism and help with modifying plans into more active resisters (Erwin and Garman 2010). A cynic provides helpful critique of changes and aims at the health of the overall organization; an active resister is not acting in good faith for the overall organization anymore and is merely focused on stopping the change at all costs.

Of course, there is research that suggests there are individuals whose personalities naturally make them more resistant to change. So, their resistance may not be the result of poor past performance or current unethical behaviors or directions. But, the only way to separate these two types of resistance is to engage in discussions that include those who might oppose a change. In order to engage stakeholders who might resist a proposed change, change agents can conduct anonymous surveys, allowing people to provide feedback without having to worry about backlash. Organizations have had success with placing boxes in areas for people to provide anonymous ideas and communicate any concerns that they have (Erwin and Garman 2010).

Cynics are a particular type of resister, that are helpful to learn more about. A variety of scholars have identified how employees sometimes develop cynicism toward change processes either through a history of less-than-successful attempts at change or by watching change initiatives emerge that are unethical or represent very narrow interests (Folger and Skarlicki 1999). A cynic is a person who has a disposition to disbelieve in the sincerity or goodness of human motives and actions, so they are likely to question intentions and actions (Dean et al. 1998). A cynic believes that an organization and its leaders often lack integrity. They also perceive that the organizational direction and change initiatives tend to be based on the self-interests of those in power. Studies within organizations have found that approximately 48 percent of employees register high levels of cynicism (Reichers et al. 1997). While a variety of factors impact individuals' cynicism, including organizational layoffs and increasing wage differentials, failed or poor organizational change efforts have been found to be high on the list of conditions that affect its rise within organizations. Some scholars suggest that the cynicism rising within organizations creates a sort of built-in, ingrained resistance to change because of the low level of trust that forms with regard to management and the readiness to disparage their efforts (Dean et al. 1998).

Research demonstrates that leaders who want to have a stronger ethical core will seek out cynics, who might provide a necessary check on misguided change initiatives. Some scholars note that cynics can act as the conscience for an organization, as they are usually still willing to speak out when others are afraid to or are apathetic (Dean et al. 1998). Cynics, more so than active resisters, may be willing to engage in dialogue. The studies point to the value of cynics within organizations to provide a moral compass, serving to question motives, values, and interests (Dean et al. 1998; Reichers et al. 1997).

Resistance as Ethical: Embracing Resistance

It may be ethical for a change agent to prevent a poor change from being implemented. It is surprising that resistance has not usually been seen as a potentially positive and functional response within organizations until relatively recently (Mabin et al. 2001). Prior to the last decade, resistance was almost universally seen as problematic, as something that needed to be overcome, without attention to understanding its sources or concerns. Various scholars have highlighted how most of the literature is biased toward a view of resistance as something negative, rather than a generative source for organizations (Bommer et al. 2005). Resistance is typically spoken about when reflecting on employees' reactions to managers' plans for change: "Researchers have assumed that resistance is largely a product of pessimistic reactionary employees representing obstacles to positive organizational progress" (Bommer et al. 2005: 748). Another line of research demonstrates how resisters often care deeply about the organization and are worried about the direction proposed by those in positions of authority (Reichers et al. 1997). Studies that follow leaders who obtain input from resisters and cynics demonstrate that they are better able to modify their plans to be stronger, obtain more buy-in, and abandon poor change initiatives (Mabin et al. 2001). While not all leaders change or abandon their initiatives, by engaging resisters they are able to demonstrate integrity in their process.

Many times, the role of change agents is to block or try to modify a poorly conceived change initiative. Most change agents do not see this as their role; they are usually working toward proactively creating changes. Imagine that you are on a campus that has decided to move all remedial education courses online, getting rid of all in-person instruction and support for these courses as a cost-saving measure. You have been involved with a task force that has been helping to inform the work of the campus remediation center. You know from surveys of students that they highly value the in-person support, ranking it as one of the key items to their success. If you were to find yourself in this situation, as an ethical change agent it would be your duty to make the information known about the downsides of the proposed change and the way it is wrongheaded in terms of serving the best interests of students. You can argue for the development of a cost–benefit analysis examining the cost savings to move the program online, as compared with the potential negative effects on student success. Every year on campuses there are changes, like this one, that are proposed and need our input—and likely, our resistance.

Diefenbach (2006) documents how resisters, often faculty and staff, are characterized by management as having no logic behind their opposition. This perspective is evidence of why administrators are often found centralizing power and facilitating growing managerialism; because faculty and staff are seen as being inherently resistant to any changes. Consideration for why faculty and staff might be resistant is often not acknowledged by administrators on campuses.

The most recent theorizing about organizational change describes resistance as a positive force that change agents need to engage in ongoing dialogue, rather than circumventing or overcoming it, as has been emphasized in the prior literature (Thomas et al. 2011). Negotiation of different views is emphasized as natural; critiquing and questioning a change direction is encouraged, rather than discouraged. Thomas et al. (2011) present a new model for resistance engagement and communication during change processes. This is an alternative to the more typical response of calculated engagement, wherein senior managers attempt to dismiss resistance by deploying authority and hierarchy, polarizing the environment and leaving employees feeling ignored and alienated. Under calculated engagement, administrators and staff take defensive stands that lead to conceptual closure, where no new ideas emerge to contribute to negotiation. This sort of standoff often results in changes that are imposed; knowledge is merely reproduced and larger goals are not reached because there is no real buy-in for changes among the staff. Instead, through their proposed model of communicative practices based on research, Thomas et al. recommend that senior managers invite feedback, ask for alternate proposals, clarify, and affirm criticism. This leads to more generative forms of dialogue and collaborative ideas—the change process itself takes on new meaning. Instead of power–resistance relations emerging, concepts and ideas are allowed to expand and develop, and more innovative, synergistic change occurs. The outcomes may not look exactly as planned in the original proposal for change, but the change moves forward. Also, the new change is aligned with broader stakeholders' interests and has greater buy-in.

The research of Thomas et al. (2011) underscores the facilitative and productive role of resistance in change processes for developing better outcomes, challenging conventional wisdom. They do note that this process occurs only when resistance is constructive in orientation; there are forms of resistance that do not lead to better outcomes. When people are not constructive in their resistance, they have become unilateral and are often no longer willing to listen or to engage in two-way communication. The authors caution that many poor change processes can leave organizations depleted and incapable of engaging in this type of positive dialogue. Still, the generative dialogue and communication may help with creating a better atmosphere that can foster change down the line, even if the current initiative fails.

Processes that Enhance Ethical Approaches

While individual change agents should develop their ethical fitness, understand ethical dilemmas, and engage resistance and cynics, they also need to become familiar with processes that help to create an ethical approach to change from the beginning. Many of the processes that help enhance the ethics of change processes will seem as if they overlap or relate to each other. While I discuss them separately, there is a strong synergy between these various concepts:

- Stakeholder participation;
- Broad information sharing;
- Full disclosure of direction and vision;
- Trust and acknowledgment of differing interests;
- Co-creation through ongoing dialogue;
- Transformational leadership; and,
- Organizational justice.

In a meta-analysis of the change literature, participation, open communication, trust, and transformational leadership were all identified as consistently helping to reduce resistance and lead to greater success in changes (Erwin and Garman 2010). I review each of these processes and end with examples that apply to these approaches.

Stakeholder Participation and Input

The most frequently cited process for increasing the ethical stance of a change proposal is broad participation among various stakeholders in the change process (Collier and Esteban 2000). Scholars emphasize that broad participation needs to be fostered from the beginning of the process, when the change initiative is designed. This way, the inherent interests and values undergirding the change initiative are more likely to represent shared interests, rather than those of elites or managers exclusively. For example, in studies of state public welfare agencies to implement new policies and procedures, employees were found to feel that the process was much more ethical and gained trust for managers when employees were allowed to participate in the change process, from defining the agenda through implementation (Bruhn et al. 2001). In fact, most of the current ethical frameworks for organizations, as well as in society, operate from the notion of the importance of deliberative stakeholder processes. One study in higher education found that college presidents that engage regularly with and learn from students of color are better able to advance diversity agendas because they receive regular input (Kezar 2007b).

Broad participation should continue as broad interests are turned into more specific goals in the change process and implementation has begun. Some argue that stakeholder participation can even be argued to be a right of employees, considering it as their duty under deontological models of ethics (Zajac and Bruhn 1999). Zajac and Bruhn note how colleges and universities have many different committees, but this does not necessarily ensure broad participation. Participation on committees is tightly controlled and administrators often choose who is to be included. While faculty may be voted into roles within the academic senate, this body is very limited in terms of its authority. The majority of decisions are made in non-participatory groups. Strategic planning processes are often broad in terms of input, but there is no accountability for which voices are ultimately included in the planning process. Therefore, Zajac and Bruhn note that mechanisms established for broad participation must be carefully examined to determine whether or not they are truly serving this purpose or whether they are more ceremonial or symbolic, which they find is common in higher education. Stakeholder participation needs to be authentic. Those in positions of power truly need to listen to stakeholders' perspectives and include this feedback in plans moving forward. If feedback is not included, then those in positions of authority need to explain why feedback is ignored.

Broad Information Sharing

One of the most basic principles for ensuring that a broad range of interests and values are considered is to make sure that information about change initiatives is broadly shared. While it is important to have participatory processes, if information is not shared broadly stakeholders are not able to be informed and to participate in evaluating the initiative itself or the discussion (Nielsen et al. 1991). Broad information sharing involves change agents providing stakeholders with all the knowledge or data informing their choice about taking on a particular change initiative, as well as information that is collected over time. This also means sharing information about the evaluation and assessment of innovative programs, new policies, and other change initiatives. While evaluation and assessment are becoming more common in education, the data are often highly controlled. Any negative assessments are typically not shared with stakeholders. This withholding of information can lead to cynicism and may also harm future change initiatives.

Full Disclosure of Direction and Vision, Including Pluses and Minuses

Related to broader information sharing is the notion of fully explaining what a change initiative involves, including the pros and cons. For example, in Ken's efforts to open a branch campus in Saudi Arabia (Chapter 7), it would be important for stakeholders to know if there is a plan for the branch campus to eventually have its own decision-making processes, potentially giving it significant independence from the home campus that might make certain people nervous about supporting the proposal. However, leaders need to provide full disclosure about their plans in order to avoid the development of cynics and growing resistance. When leaders do not provide information or garner input from members of the campus, people tend to become cynical about change. Also, campus stakeholders should understand the pros and cons associated with a change as completely as possible before moving forward. So, for example, if there is risk of monetary loss associated with Ken's proposed branch campus, this information should be shared with stakeholders. While people are often hesitant to share information that might make others question the change initiative and may decrease the momentum they gained, these lapses in disclosure will likely result in resistance down the line anyway, feeding into organizational cynicism (Nielsen et al. 1991).

Trust and Open Communication

A history of trust among groups on a campus enhances open communication, which is likely to identify any ethical problems undergirding proposed change initiatives. In addition to identifying problems, communication might also help to clarify misunderstandings that demonstrate there was only a perception of ethical problems. Therefore, providing communication forums, avenues, and vehicles is a key way to ensure an ethical process. Many of these processes are linked, since information sharing can be facilitated through communication vehicles, as well as broad participation, which is itself dependent on communication for inviting and informing people about change.

In terms of trust, Oreg (2006) found that employees' lack of trust in management was highly related to resistance. In Oreg's study, employees registered concern about their confidence in management's ability to carry out the change, so it's not enough to trust a leader, but there must also be confidence in their abilities to execute change. So, a lack of faith or trust had to do with people's confidence in leaders' skills. Lack of trust can lead to anger, frustration, and anxiety because employees sense that a change initiative may not be successful or could result in an incredible amount of uncertainty. Oreg also found that employees believe that managers do not conceive of meaningful change initiatives, so register that the changes are not actually needed, and this also contributed to their lack of trust. Employees hope that managers will much more carefully evaluate the need for and content of change up front. Studies also find a strong relationship between lack of trust and growing skepticism and cynicism within organizations; as distrust grows, so do measures of cynicism and skepticism (Erwin and Garman 2010).

While trust is an important mechanism for creating an ethical change process, it is often missing on many college campuses. Therefore, change agents who are interested in fostering trust in order to create more ethical change processes will need to examine relationships among groups, patterns of decision-making, the history of various programs and departments, and other fairly intensive practices. While it is beyond the scope of this book to describe all the ways that leaders can foster greater trust, an issue that has been the topic of entire books, a recent book by William Tierney (2006), *Trust and the Public Good*, describes how trust can be considered and fostered within higher education institutions.

Acknowledgment of Differing Values and Interests

Through full disclosure and the sharing of information, it is much easier for stakeholders to determine which or whose interests are represented in change proposals.

Ethical decisions are difficult to make if the underlying values and interests cannot be determined. Opportunities to participate in discussions about a change initiative also help to facilitate understanding and flesh out differing values and interests, which can lead to more profitable discussions and have the potential for bringing about more ethical outcomes. Rather than fearing different perspectives, change agents can use this knowledge to create a more inclusive dialogue. Oftentimes in organizational development efforts aimed at change, change agents will conduct surveys of organizational stakeholders to determine their opinions and perspectives in order to register or understand differing values that may exist. And, while congruence of values is not necessarily a goal in ethical processes, studies have found that organizations that have greater value congruence can move more quickly and deeply into change processes. The same studies demonstrate that acknowledging and working through varying values and interests can help with ultimately reaching congruence (Amis et al. 2002).

Co-creation through Ongoing Dialogue

One of the more radical ideas advanced, which breaks with traditional organizational processes and structures and can help to enhance the ethical underpinnings of change processes is the co-creation of change (Ford 1999). Some scholars suggest that one of the reasons that resistance to change exists is that so many proposals for change are not created out of shared interests and understanding about the organization. In order to move toward having more shared interests, organizational stakeholders need to engage with one another in conversation and dialogue on a more continuous basis. Thus, instead of isolated individuals, specifically those in positions of power, being the ones to create agendas for change, within this model different stakeholders can come together to negotiate around change initiatives that emerge from shared concerns, problems, or notions for improvement on an ongoing basis. If administrators, faculty, staff, and students sat down more regularly to talk about campus operations and needed improvements, ideas for change would emerge organically and benefit from greater buy-in. These ideas would also be more ethically grounded and would better represent the principles of organizational fairness and justice that are often violated through changes initiated from the top down. In higher education, shared governance could serve this purpose but is declining on many campuses. Historically it served the role of allowing ongoing dialogue between and among groups oriented toward change.

Transformational not Charismatic Leadership

Charismatic leaders are often received with some suspicion by ethicists who have focused on change (Howell and Avolio 1992). Charismatic leaders often believe so strongly in their cause or issue that they are unlikely to engage in ethical practices that help ensure broader input into change processes. Also, they are more likely to engage followers in ways that discourage questioning and examining the underlying values of a change initiative. While they might be very effective as change agents, their ethics often go unexamined. As Howell and Avolio note,

> The risks involved in charismatic leadership are at least as large as the promises. What is missing from current discussions about charisma are considerations of its darker side. Charisma can lead to blind fanaticism in the service of megalomaniacs and dangerous values.
>
> (Howell and Avolio 1992: 43)

Charismatic leaders are likely to censor critical or opposing views, demand followers accept their decisions without question, engage in one-way communication, be insensitive to followers needs, and rely on convenient, external moral standards to satisfy their self-interests.

While not all charismatic leadership is based on a strong personal interest or vision, it is much more common than what scholars have labeled *ethical charismatics*, who incorporate followers' hopes, dreams, and aspirations, use power in socially constructive ways, and genuinely care about the welfare of the community. An ethical charismatic leader considers and learns from criticism and provides opportunities for criticism to emerge; they also stimulate their followers to think independently and question views. They operate with more open communication to ensure a better understanding of the varying interests and values that exist and inform decision-making. The characteristics of an ethical charismatic leader are similar to those qualities of leadership advocated for within transformational theories of leadership. These leaders should be oriented toward serving a common purpose, two-way communication, productive uses of power, and support of followers, as well as their development and growth. The notion of transformational leadership was developed within an ethical framework and scholars within this tradition note that leadership and ethics are inseparable. All of the dimensions of transformational leadership—the behaviors and characteristics—are oriented toward acting in ways that demonstrate a more ethical process with the goal of producing more ethical outcomes. Transformational leadership has also been identified as helping employees to overcome cynicism about organizational change developed when employees have observed or experienced failed change efforts created to serve narrow, managerial interests (Bommer et al. 2005).

Interestingly, studies at the intersection of organizational change and leadership suggest that 75 percent of employees consider their leaders poor at advancing change. They also perceive leaders to be one of the reasons for their resistance to changes and a barrier to moving forward effectively (Gilley, McMillan and Gilley 2009). Gilley, McMillan and Gilley (2009) demonstrate a relationship between employees' documenting of leaders' positive transformational qualities and success within organizations in creating changes (Gilley, McMillan and Gilley 2009). Furthermore, studies of employees' impressions of leaders attempting to create changes suggest what is usually a relatively negative view. One study found 40 percent of employees thought managers were coercive and power oriented, 43 percent considered them rational empirical leaders focused on facts (although they found this had some advantages), and only 6 percent considered leaders to be collaborative and involved with individuals in decision-making, the qualities associated with ethically driven transformational leadership (Erwin and Garman 2010).

Organizational Justice

One of the major areas of organizational inquiry that has grown in recent years focuses on issues of organizational justice. More recently, the interest in organizational justice has been connected to organizational change. Several recent studies have examined whether employees' perceptions of organizational justice as they relate to a particular change initiative can actually enhance its implementation and overcome traditional resistance that emerges (Shapiro and Kirkman 1999). Within studies of justice, organizational justice is conceived in three ways: procedural justice, distributive justice, and interactional justice. Procedural justice is when employees perceive that processes or the actions of organizational actors are fair, reflecting honesty, integrity, consistency, bias suppression, accuracy, and ethicality. Individuals are more likely to accept a change if the procedures are fair, even if they perceive the change as unwanted. Distributive justice exists when employees receive outcomes they perceive as being fair. Interactional justice is focused on employees' perceptions of the quality of the interpersonal treatment received during the enactment of organizational procedures. That might include phenomena such as social sensitivity, respect, dignity, or behaviors such as listening to concerns or providing adequate explanations for decisions.

All three forms of justice have been found to be critical for helping support change initiatives and to demonstrate a more ethical orientation. For example, studies have found that when employees anticipate distributive injustice, they are more likely to be resistant to change and less committed to the overall organization. Conversely, when they experience distributive justice, they are more likely to accept the change (Shapiro and Kirkman 1999). Another interesting finding is that if procedural justice is in place, employees may not resist a change they feel does not reflect distributive justice or has outcomes with which they are disappointed (Folger and Skarlicki 1999). So, while all three are important, they do not all need to be present in order for employees to consider that an ethical process has been followed. Therefore, providing an explanation and rationale for needed changes, even if they have unfair outcomes, can help decrease resistance. Studies have even found that employees that are under stress, have experienced loss, or other conditions of adversity will be much more open to change if they feel that they are being treated fairly and that the organization is just (Folger and Skarlicki 1999). In the end, all of the studies suggest that perceptions of fairness have significant implications for whether changes are resisted and for the likely degree of support.

Therefore, change agents need to consider carefully their ethical conduct throughout the change process as it unfolds and how this will shape the ultimate success of this change initiative. In many ways, organizational justice can be used as a meta-framework to guide change agents because it encompasses the process elements through procedural and interactional justice, while also examining outcomes through distributive justice.

Gioia (1992) warns us that without using these intentional ethical processes, there are many blinders for organizations that can lead us to ethical lapses. In his analysis of the lack of a recall for Ford Motor Company's Pinto, which resulted in catastrophic deaths, Gioia demonstrates how organizations reinforce the schema of neutrality and particular values that lead away from ethically oriented decisions and changes. Schemas within organizations blind us to ethical questions by focusing on decisions as being neutral, but they may be driven by business principles of efficiency and effectiveness over other values, such as safety. Organizations, over time, create blinders within their leaders that mask personal values that might otherwise lead them or change agents in other situations to see ethical lapses. These capabilities often become absent within organizational situations. So, change agents must be extremely vigilant because organizations actually create blindness that ends up impeding ethical decision-making.

Ethics and Our Change Initiatives

One way to apply these ethical concepts is to examine the cases addressed in this book in chapter 7. Let's take the example of Ken, with his branch campus in Saudi Arabia, and Jeff, who wants to introduce more family-friendly policies. In these cases, we can examine several of the principles described in this chapter, including whose interests are represented in the change, what ethical process they followed, how resistance was handled, and the degree of openness to ethical concerns.

Whose interests were served when Ken proposed the creation of the branch campus in Saudi Arabia? We know that he felt it was important to take this action in order to remain competitive as an innovative international business program. We also know that his program is aligned to calls for his campus to be on the forefront of international education. However, we don't know if there is a strong student demand for a program in this country, whether this type of program will serve to advance the goals of the education system in Saudi Arabia, and we do not know what are the costs for faculty or other missed opportunities the institution might otherwise take. There likely needs to be a more thorough examination of whose interests are served, particularly as Ken's initiative has been encountering a great deal of resistance. Faculty in the humanities have been worried about human rights issues in Saudi Arabia, the legislature was worried about money being spent on international students, and support among alumni was lacking. These various forms of resistance are not engaged from an ethical perspective, but only from the perspective of expediency and how to mitigate resistance.

Even though there is formidable resistance, Ken has not considered if there are any problematic aspects to his plan. While he invites the humanities faculty onto the task force, it is unclear whether he will legitimately listen to their concerns. Also, he is prepared to bargain with the state, but seems to not be willing to examine their concerns about state funding going to international students. And, he is not engaging the alumni concerns at all because he feels that the administration will not be persuaded by them, so he does not feel the need to try to understand their resistance. Also, Ken is not engaged in a second-order change initiative, so the level of resistance should have been a red flag for him to spend more time attending to the resistance and thinking about whether there are any ethical underpinnings. Ken shows little concern for potential ethical dilemmas.

In terms of his process, Ken has broad involvement with stakeholders who have registered resistance, which the administration is worried about, but has done very little to arrange for other forms of stakeholder involvement. He has engaged in information sharing by providing data and research from the Association to Advance Collegiate Schools of Business, but he has done so only in ways that provide information that supports this decision and direction. He engages in no self-analysis about the potential downsides, nor does he engage in conversations with individuals about the pros and cons of the initiative. The moral imperatives raised by faculty members or cost concerns raised by the legislature are never engaged with data or through discussions. Also, the movement forward is aimed at one-way, rather than two-way communication. Other stakeholders lacking awareness of the faculty's or legislators' concerns would not receive information about these issues from Ken. In other words, Ken is not acknowledging the differing interests and what they might represent in relation to this change.

None of his actions reflect transformational leadership, epitomized by two-way communication, the creation of a shared vision with benefits for the common good, or concern for and support of campus stakeholders. It would seem that Ken's change initiative would violate distributive justice, in that most stakeholders' interests are not served by the proposal (although it is hard to make a clear determination at this point). He is not an overt violator of procedural justice in that he is not acting in dishonest ways or being unfair. His single-mindedness in trying to move his agenda forward may be blinding him from acting in more ethical ways. We don't get a good insight into his interactions with people on campus and it is difficult to understand the level at which he is engaging in interactional justice, but the lack of two-way communication and focus on his own vision suggest it is lacking. Ken's activities suggest there is no awareness of an ethical dimension to his change initiative; nor do they suggest an interest in engaging in an ethical process toward change. In fact, all of these efforts suggest that Ken may be moving into an area that increasingly is ethically precarious.

Let's consider Jeff's family-friendly policy initiative now (Chapter 7). First, Jeff's interest in this topic does not come from any personal or self-serving interest. It is not tied to his career advancement; rather it emerged out of watching others within his community deal with inequities. Therefore, the initiative itself is based on broader concerns. However, Jeff did not seek out women to talk with about his idea as it was emerging. As he finds out later in the process, they had important and valuable input that could have helped him with shaping the initiative from a focus on family-friendly policies to include other concerns such as hiring practices, mentoring, and committee work. With more input from stakeholders, he would have framed the change initiative more broadly from the beginning. While this did not necessarily represent an ethical violation, the narrower-than-ideal interests represented in his change demonstrate the limitations of operating from one's own observations. But his choice of change initiative was itself ethically grounded.

Jeff, being a savvy change agent, anticipated resistance, particularly as this is a second-order change penetrating people's sense of identity and underlying assumptions about how the institution should be run. In this case, the institution has typically not been supportive of family and a balanced work environment. Jeff has considered who might be resistant to the change initiative and witnessed resistance to prior family-friendly initiatives that emerged. He has been able understand this resistance as coming from sexism and fear among those with long-standing power that change will reshape norms, threatening their status quo. However, Jeff can draw on Rawls's work to defend a change that will support a marginalized group even at the perceived expense of the group with power. Jeff also has evaluated the issue and recognizes that the male faculty on campus will not really suffer or lose out if this change is implemented. But, rather than move forward, he decides that providing an opportunity for long-standing members of the campus to become acquainted with this new value system is important. So, he spends a year bringing in speakers to try to educate his male colleagues and make them more comfortable with the idea. While he recognizes that many of them may never be convinced, he feels that broader information sharing and full disclosure about the proposed changes is important in having it be accepted in the end. Many of the speakers who come to campus describe not only the advantages of family-friendly policies, but also some of the problems they've had in instituting them. For example, one speaker talked about how their campus has the policies in place but no one uses them because of fear that they will affect their success in the tenure and promotion process.

The task force that is assembled includes several people who are resistant to or have been questioning the direction of the family-friendly initiative. However, both Jeff and the provost recognize the need to acknowledge different interests on campus and to respect them as part of the process. So, this begins to demonstrate the way that Jeff uses broad stakeholder participation by including resistors on the task force and through the speaker series, where people have conversations and can talk about the change initiative prior to its implementation. Many people feel like they have the opportunity to consider and shape the initiative before it is fully implemented. Jeff also provides opportunities for ongoing dialogue that can ensure ethical issues are raised. Not only does he create the speaker series and hold individual conversations with task force members, as well as the full task force, he also slows down the task force formation and process. The ongoing conversations went on for three years and expanded the initiative and ensured that questions and concerns were addressed. Also, Jeff has established trust through his relationships and support for women faculty over the years. He has developed good relationships with both the administration as well as his faculty colleagues so that they are likely to begin their interactions with him from a place of trust. He continues this trust building process by his open communication throughout the change process.

Jeff also demonstrated transformational leadership in that his communication was two-way and the change initiative was broadened by listening to the suggestions of women on the task force about important changes that needed to be made to include more than just family-friendly policies. He helped to inspire and create a shared vision, which was informed by the community and not created in isolation. He helped to facilitate the development of others on campus through the speaker series, professional development, and by engaging multiple perspectives within all of the processes, including the task force. Throughout the process he fostered collaboration and self-development.

Jeff's initiative led to distributive justice because the broader community's interests were not diminished in any way and a group that had been marginalized can be treated in more just and fair ways. The many activities that he engaged in reflect procedural justice in that he was acting with integrity, honesty, and accuracy. For example, Jeff did not oversell the family-friendly policies and the speakers he invited speak about the pros and cons of such policies. He also expressed interactional justice through two-way communication, taking time for many individual meetings and conversations, being open to being critiqued, and providing people with the full rationale and information about the change initiative through the yearlong pre-planning process. In the end, Jeff's change initiative and process represented an ethically grounded approach.

Summary

While many leaders feel it is difficult to engage in ethical change processes, hopefully the literature presented in this chapter and the case examples demonstrate some touchstone points for change agents to consider, including the importance of examining:

- Whose interests are represented in the change initiative;
- Whether the initiative meets the standards of distributive justice;
- Ethical dilemmas that might emerge in this change process;
- Resistance and what type of feedback this is providing about the ethical basis of this change;
- Which ethical processes to incorporate; and,
- An examination of leadership style.

Conclusion

Having ventured through the swamps, deserts, and chasms of change implementation that were noted in the Preface, we should now revisit the key goals and ideas presented in the book.

The goal of this book is to improve the efficacy of change processes in higher education by highlighting the problematic assumptions that leaders bring to change processes, providing a macro framework for helping leaders to design a change strategy suited to their planned initiative and context, helping leaders to consider the challenges of deep change and scaling up innovations, and by examining the ethical underpinnings of change processes that can often lead to failure. It is only appropriate to end with a discussion of ethics because it is inattention to ethics that has perhaps created the greatest amount of resistance and problems related to change. Certainly, as I reviewed the literature on organizational learning and sensemaking, readers should have developed an appreciation that when resistance occurs it is often because of a lack of understanding about changes. But, just as often, resistance is a result of inattention to feedback or problems that are a result of a weak change idea or poorly analyzed and executed change process. I want to raise inattention to a thoughtful change process to the same level of importance as ethical concerns for leaders involved in change processes. Continuing to treat change as an intuitive process, when there are thousands of studies to guide leaders and a great deal of consensus about meta-principles that can be used to frame a strategy within a particular context, seems careless.

Another goal of this book is to make readers aware of the continuous change processes that will shape their efficacy as leaders. Lack of attention to the ongoing flow of changes makes organizations reactive, rather than proactive in responding to changes in ways that are in the best interests of the organization. These changes may not be of change agents' own making; sometimes they are the result of events in the external environment, the actions of other stakeholders, or even institutional devolution. Declining budgets, calls for greater accountability and transparency, affordability concerns, mission drift, and prestige-seeking activity can erode the quality, effectiveness, and mission-centered nature of educational institutions if they are not engaged by campus leaders and stakeholders promptly.

Change processes need to involve collaboration, the examination or formation of shared interests, and collective leadership. The bad faith created through unethical change processes; a continuing erosion of trust between faculty, administrators, and staff through unilateral campus decision-making processes; a lack of vision for multi-level leadership; and limited empowerment among employees; all continue to create a context unfavorable to true or authentic change. While some leaders can suggest they have dictated a change process, it is more likely that, when digging deeper, a lack of buy-in will be found among stakeholders on campus, causing their mandates to not be fully realized or to go nowhere.

There remain a plethora of exciting ideas at various levels of implementation across the academy, whether they are civic engagement initiatives, forms of undergraduate research, or interdisciplinary research programs. The degree to which they will take hold depends on individual change agents and their ability to better understand the system in which change takes place and the process for implementing change outlined in this book. My hope is that more change agents will be willing to embark on this journey—to deeply reflect on the changes they are proposing, to systematically analyze and design a change process that fits the institutional context in which they are located, and to engage in the challenges of creating deep change, as well as scaling up changes across the academy, in an ethical manner that maintains—and perhaps enhances—the integrity of the enterprise.

Notes

Preface

1 Throughout the book, I will use change agent and leader interchangeably as individuals that move changes forward.

1 Why Change?

1 See, for example, high impact practices encouraged by the Association of American Colleges and Universities: http://www.aacu.org/leap/hip.cfm.
2 Christensen, Horn, Caldera and Soares (2011) suggest that higher education is now in a position to be disrupted by technology (online learning) and that change is likely inevitable as higher education may be unable to buffer itself.
3 Kerr reminds us, though, that campuses have long had a complex web of stakeholders, but the number continues to increase and they have greater investments in outcomes than in the past.
4 See Kezar (2010) for a description of the deep changes needed to support low-income students.
5 For good resources for engaging diverse populations, see Bensimon and Neumann (1993).
6 Competition and hierarchies have always been present in traditional higher education institutions, but the for-profit model has made market-based competition (e.g. marketing, branding, and competing for students) more prevalent.
7 Information about the Tuning Project can be found online at http://www.unideusto.org/tuning/.
8 A more complete discussion of the issue of campus leaders pursuing revenue generating changes at the expense of mission-centered change can be found in Kezar (2008).

2 Theories of Change: Change Agent Guides

1 This chapter draws heavily on the ideas developed in an earlier book focused on change theories: Kezar, A. (2001) *Understanding and Facilitating Organizational Change in the 21st Century: Recent Research and Conceptualizations*, Washington, D.C.: ASHE-ERIC Higher Education Reports.
2 Essentially, many of the concepts from institutional entrepreneurship mirror literature from social movement theory, particularly around grassroots leadership, and the ways that individuals from the bottom up can make change against formidable forces. The main difference is that institutional theory suggests the difficulty of making bottom-up changes and agency is seen as more constrained than in theories of grassroots leadership.

3 Type of Change

1 Double-loop learning occurs when a change challenges underlying assumptions; individuals must question and change their underlying assumptions in order for the change to take place.

4 Creating Deep Change

1 For detailed case studies of campuses undergoing sensemaking, see Eckel and Kezar (2003b).
2 The resource kit for the project can be found at: http://www.aacu.org/irvinediveval/ evaluationresources.cfm.

5 Context of Change

1 See Bergquist (2007) for a detailed description of each cultural archetype.
2 For detailed examples of institutions that have aligned their change approach to the institutional culture, please see Kezar and Eckel (2002a) or Eckel and Kezar (2003b).
3 For additional details, see Toma (2010).

6 Leadership and Agency of Change

1 This book, overall, is very much aligned with contingency theories of leadership that suggest leaders need to alter their strategies based on the situation, particularly by being informed by the organizational context or their own agency. It is also aligned with cognitive theories of leadership in which leaders need to be attentive to their mental models and develop complex ways to think about organizations to be successful. The attention to the six different change theories aligns with creating complex mental models for leading change advocated for by cognitive models of leadership. Some readers may be familiar with Bolman and Deal's (1991) approach to multi-frame leadership. This book is similar in providing a multi-theory approach to change, like their four frames of leadership. Therefore, there is a great deal of synergy between the framework offered in this book and the most recent conceptualization of leadership.
2 A detailed description of the power conditions bottom-up leaders face can be found in Kezar and Lester (2011).
3 For more details about the lone ranger view of leadership, see Kezar et al. (2006).
4 For more detailed information on skills with which change agents should be familiar, please see Bensimon and Neumann (1993), Pearce and Conger (2003), Kezar et al. (2006), and Komives et al. (1998).

5 For more information on shared leadership skills, see Pearce and Conger (2003) and Spillane (2006).
6 Detailed examples of each of the strategies for bottom-up leaders and other advice to help grassroots leaders converge with top-down leaders can be found in Kezar and Lester (2011).

8 Change Implementation: Encounters with Resistance and Obstacles

1 For examples, see Kezar (2007d).

9 Scaling Up Changes Beyond the Institutional Level

1 Certainly there are more nuanced definitions of scale, which examine the level at which the reforms are undertaken (classroom, school, district) and the breadth of impact of what is scaled up—the structures, programs, strategy, or resource base, for example (Samoff et al. 2003). Yet, this general definition holds among many studies across policy and development circles.
2 For a detailed discussion of a critique of traditional scale-up models, please see Kezar 2011.
3 A learning community[0][0] is similar to communities of practices, but varies slightly in that it is intentionally designed, whereas the communities of practice are usually more organic.
4 Not all definitions of social movements include the last item of infrastructure and rewards.
5 Detailed information about Campus Compact's initiatives is available online at http://www.compact.org/initiatives/.
6 Additional details about NERCHE Think Tanks can be found at http://www.nerche.org/index.php?option=com_contentandview=articleandid=192andItemid=85.
7 Information about the University of Southern Queensland's goals and other aspects of their communities of practice are available on their website at http://www.usq.edu.au/cops/about/highered.
8 Detailed resources for learning communities in higher education are available through the National Resource Center for Learning Communities at http://www.evergreen.edu/washcenter/lcfaq.htm.
9 For more information on the Center for the Integration of Teaching, Research, and Learning, please go to http://www.citrl.net.
10 Information about Miami University's Faculty Learning Communities can be found online at http://www.units.muohio.edu/flc/.

Bibliography

Ahuja, G. (2000) "Collaboration networks: structural holes, and innovation: a longitudinal study," *Administrative Science Quarterly*, 45(3): 425–55.

Albert, S. and Whetten, D. (1985) "Organizational identity," *Research in Organizational Behavior*, 7: 263–95.

Allee, V. (2000) "Knowledge networks and communities of learning," *OD Practitioner*, 32(4): 1–15. Online. Available HTTP: <http://www.vernaallee.com/images/VAA-KnowledgeNetworksAndCommunitiesOfPractice.pdf> (accessed 21 January 2013).

Altbach, P., Berdahl, R., and Gumport, P.J. (eds.) (2011) *American Higher Education in the 21st Century: Social, Political, and Economic Challenges*, Baltimore, MD: Johns Hopkins University Press.

Amis, J., Slack, T., and Hinings, C. (2002) "Values and organizational change," *Journal of Applied Behavioral Science*, 38(4): 436–65.

Andrews, J., Cameron, H., and Harris, M. (2008) "All change? managers' experience of organizational change in theory and practice," *Journal of Organizational Change Management*, 21(3): 300–14.

Argyris, C. (1982) "How learning and reasoning processes affect organizational change," in P.S. Goodman (ed.) *Change in Organizations*, San Francisco: Jossey-Bass.

——. (1991) "Teaching Smart People How to Learn," *Harvard Business Review*, 69(3): 99–109.

——. (1994; 2nd edn. 1999) *On Organizational Learning*, Oxford: Blackwell.

Astin, H.S. and Leland, C. (1991) *Women of Influence, Women of Vision: A Cross Generational Study of Leaders and Social Change*, San Francisco: Jossey-Bass.

Baldridge, J.V. (1971) *Power and Conflict in the University*, New York: Wiley.

Baldridge, J.V., Curtis, D.V., Ecker, G.P., and Riley, G.L. (1977) "Alternative models of governance in higher education," in G.L. Riley and J.V. Baldridge (eds.) *Governing Academic Organizations*, Berkeley, CA: McCutchan.

Balkundi, P. and Harrison, D. (2006) "Ties, leaders, and time in teams: strong inference about network structure's effects on team viability and performance," *Academy of Management Journal*, 49(1): 49–68.

Bassett, R.M. and Maldonado-Maldonado, A. (2009) *International Organizations and Higher Education Policy: Thinking Globally, Acting Locally?*, New York: Routledge.

Bauman, G. (2005) "Promoting organizational learning in higher education to achieve equity in educational outcomes," in A. Kezar (ed.) *Organizational Learning in Higher Education*, San Francisco: Jossey-Bass. New Directions in Higher Education 131.

Becker, K.L. (2007) *Unlearning in the Workplace: A Mixed Methods Study*. Online. Available HTTP: <http://eprints.qut.edu.au/16574/1/Karen_Louise_Becker_Thesis.pdf> (accessed 4 April 2011).

Bensimon, E. and Neumann, A. (1993) *Redesigning Collegiate Leadership: Teams and Teamwork in Higher Education*, Baltimore, MD: Johns Hopkins University Press.

Berdahl, R.O. (1991) "Shared governance and external constraints," in M.W. Peterson, E.E. Chaffee, and T.H. White (eds.) *Organization and Governance in Higher Education*, Needham Heights, MA: Ginn Press.

Bergquist, W. (1992) *The Four Cultures of the Academy: Insights and Strategies for Improving Leadership in Collegiate Organizations*, San Francisco: Jossey-Bass.

——. (2007) *The Six Cultures of the Academy*, San Francisco: Jossey-Bass.

Birnbaum, R. (1991; 2nd edn. 1999) *How Colleges Work: The Cybernetics of Academic Organization and Leadership*, San Francisco: Jossey-Bass.

——. (2000) *Management Fads in Higher Education*, San Francisco: Jossey-Bass.

Bolman, L.G. and Deal, T.E. (1991) *Reframing Organizations: Artistry, Choice, and Leadership*, San Francisco: Jossey-Bass.

——. and Deal, T.E. (2007) "Reframing change: training, realigning, negotiating, grieving and moving on," in J.V. Gallos (ed.) *Organization Development*, San Francisco: Jossey-Bass.

Bommer, W., Rich, G., and Rubin, R. (2005) "Changing attitudes about change: longitudinal effects of transformational leader behavior on employee cynicism about organizational change," *Journal of Organizational Behavior*, 26: 733–53.

Borden, V.M.H. and Kezar, A. (2012) "Institutional research and collaborative organizational learning," in R.D. Howard, G.W. McLaughlin, and W.E. Knight (eds.) *The Handbook of Institutional Research*, San Francisco: John Wiley & Sons.

Borgatti, S.P. and Foster, P.C. (2003) "The new paradigm of organizational research: a review and typology," *Journal of Management*, 29(6): 991–1013.

Boyce, M.E. (2003) "Organizational learning is essential to achieving and sustaining change in higher education," *Innovative Higher Education*, 28(2): 119–35.

Brill, P.L. and Worth, R. (1997) *The Four Levers of Corporate Change*, New York: American Management Association.

Brown, J.S. and Duguid, P. (2000) "Balancing act: how to capture knowledge without killing it," *Harvard Buisness Review*, 78(3): 73–80.

Bruhn, J., Zajac, G., and Al-Kazemi, A. (2001) "Ethical perspectives on employee participation in planned organizational change: a survey of two state public welfare agencies," *Public Performance and Management Review*, 25(2): 208–28.

Burgan, M. (2006) *What Happened to Faculty Governance*, Baltimore, MD: Johns Hopkins University Press.

Burke, C.S., Stagl, K.C., Salas, E., Pierce, L., and Kendall, D. (2006) "Understanding team adaptation: a conceptual analysis and model," *Journal of Applied Psychology*, 91(6): 1189–207.

Burnes, B. (1996) *Managing Change: A Strategic Approach to Organizational Dynamics*, London: Pitman Publishing.

———. (2011) "Introduction: why does change fail and what can we do about it?," *Journal of Organizational Change Management*, 11(4): 445–51.

Burt, R. (1992) *Structural Holes: The Structure of Competition*, Cambridge, MA: Harvard University Press.

———. (2000) "The network structure of social capital,"in R. Sutton and B. Staw (eds.) *Research in Organizational Behavior*, Greenwich, CT: JAI Press.

Bushe, G and Shani, A. (1991) *Parallel Learning Structure: Increasing Innovation in Bureaucracies*, Workingham, MA: Addison-Wesley.

Cameron, K.S. (1991) "Organizational adaptation and higher education," in M.W. Peterson, E.E. Chaffee, and T.H. White (eds.) *Organization and Governance in Higher Education*, 4th edn., Needham Heights, MA: Ginn Press.

———. (2008) "Paradox in positive organizational change," *Journal of Applied Behavioral Science*, 44(1): 7–24.

Cameron, K.S. and Quinn, R.E. (1988) "Organizational paradox and transformation," in K. Cameron and R.E. Quinn (eds.) *Paradox and Transformation*, New York: Bellinger.

Cameron, K.S. and Smart, J. (1998) "Maintaining effectiveness amid downsizing and decline in institutions of higher education," *Research in Higher Education*, 39(1): 65–86.

Carlson-Dakes, C. and Sanders, K. (1998) "A movement approach to organizational change: Understanding the influences of a collaborative faculty development program," paper presented at Annual Meeting of the Association for the Study of Higher Education, Miami, FL, November 1998.

Carnall, C.A. (1995) *Managing Change in Organizations*, London: Prentice Hall.

Carr, C. (1996) *Choice, Chance, and Organizational Change: Practical Insights from Evolution for Business Leaders and Thinkers*, New York: AMACOM.

Carr, D., Hard, K., and Trahant, W. (1996) *Managing the Change Process: A Field Book for Change Agents, Consultants, Team Leaders, and Reengineering Managers*, New York: McGraw-Hill.

Center for the Integration of Research, Teaching, and Learning (CITRL) (n.d.) CITRL Network. Online. Available HTTP: <http://www.cirtl.net/> (accessed 21 January 2013).

Center for Urban Education (n.d.) *The Equity Scorecard*. Online. Available HTTP: <http://cue.usc.edu/our_tools/the_equity_scorecard.html> (accessed 21 January 2013).

Chaffee, E. (1983) "Three models of strategy," *Academy of Management Review*, 10(1): 89–98.

Chermak, G.L.D. (1990) "Cultural dynamics: principles to guide change in higher education," *CUPA Journal*, 41(3): 25–7.

Childers, M.E. (1981) "What is political about bureaucratic-collegial decision-making?," *Review of Higher Education*, 5(1): 25–45.

Christensen, C., Horn, M., Caldera, L., and Soares, L. (2011) *Disrupting College*, Washington, D.C.: Center for American Progress.

Clark, B.R. (1983) "The contradictions of change in academic systems," *Higher Education*, 12(1): 101–16.

———. (1998a) *Creating Entrepreneurial Universities: Organizational Pathways of Transformation*, Oxford: Pergamon Press.

———. (1998b) "The entrepreneurial university: demand and response," *Tertiary Education and Management*, 4(1): 5–16.

Coburn, C. (2003) "Rethinking scale: moving beyond the numbers to deep and lasting change," *Educational Researcher*, 32(6): 3–12.

Cohen, M.D. and March, J.G. (1974) *Leadership and Ambiguity: The American College President*, Boston: Harvard Business School Press.

——. (1991) "Leadership in an organized anarchy," in M.W. Peterson, E.E. Chaffee, and T.H. White (eds.) *Organization and Governance in Higher Education*, Needham Heights, MA: Ginn Press.

Collier, J. and Esteban, R. (2000) "Systemic leadership: ethical and effective," *Leadership & Organization Development Journal*, 21(4): 207–15.

Collins, D. (1998) *Organizational Change: Sociological Perspectives*, London: Routledge.

Conrad, C.F. (1978) "A grounded theory of academic change," *Sociology of Education*, 51(2): 101–12.

Cox, M.D. (2003) "Proven faculty development tools that foster the scholarship of teaching in faculty learning communities," *To Improve the Academy*, 21: 109–42.

——. (2004) *Faculty Learning Community Program Director's and Facilitator's Handbook*, Oxford, OH: Miami University.

Cross, J.G. and Goldenberg, E.N. (2009) *Off-Track Profs: Non-Tenured Teachers in Higher Education*, Cambridge, MA: MIT Press.

Curry, B.K. (1992) *Instituting Enduring Innovations: Achieving Continuity of Change in Higher Education*, Washington, D.C.: George Washington University, School of Education and Human Development. ASHE-ERIC Higher Education Report No. 7.

Daly, A. (2010a) "Mapping the terrain: social network theory and educational change," in A.J. Daly (ed.) *Social Network Theory and Educational Change*, Cambridge, MA: Harvard Education Press.

——. (ed.) (2010b) *Social Network Theory and Educational Change*, Cambridge, MA: Harvard Education Press.

——. (2010c) "Surveying the terrain ahead: social network theory and educational change," in A.J. Daly (ed.) *Social Network Theory and Educational Change*, Cambridge, MA: Harvard Education Press.

Daly, A., and Finnigan, K. (2008) "A bridge between worlds: understanding network structure to understand change strategy," *Journal of Educational Change*, 11(2): 111–38.

Daly, C.J. (2011) "Faculty learning communities: addressing the professional development needs of faculty and the learning needs of students," *Currents in Teaching and Learning*, 4(1): 3–16.

Damasio, A.R. (1994) *Descartes' Error: Emotion, Reason, and the Human Brain*, New York: Grosset/Putnam.

Datnow, A. (2005) "The sustainability of comprehensive school reform models in changing district and state contexts," *Educational Administration Quarterly*, 41(1): 121–53.

Dawson, P. (1994) *Organizational Change: A Procedural Approach*, London: Paul Chapman Publishing.

Dean, J., Brandes, P., and Dharwadkar, R. (1998) "Organizational cynicism," *Academy of Management Review*, 23(2): 341–52.

Dede, C. (2006) "Scaling-up: evolving innovations beyond ideal settings to challenging contexts of practice," in R. Sawyer (ed.) *Cambridge Handbook of the Learning Sciences*, Cambridge: Cambridge University Press.

Diefenbach, T. (2006) "Intangible resources: a categorical system of knowledge and other intangible assets," *Journal of Intellectual Capital*, 7(3): 406–20.

Dill, D.D. (1999) "Academic accountability and university adaptation: the architecture of an academic learning organization," *Higher Education*, 38(2): 127–54.

Dill, D. and Sporn, B. (eds.) (1995) *Emerging Patterns of Social Demand and University Reform: Through a Glass Darkly*, Trowbridge, UK: Redwood Books.

DiMaggio, P.J. and Powell, W.W. (1983) "The iron cage revisited: institutional isomorphism and collective rationality in organizational fields," *American Sociological Review*, 48(2): 147–60.

Dorado, S. (2005) "Institutional entrepreneurship, partaking, and convening," *Organization Studies*, 26(3): 385–414.

Eckel, P., Hill, B., Green, M., and Mallon, B. (1999) *Taking Charge of Change: A Primer for Colleges and Universities*, Washington, D.C.: American Council on Education. On Change Occasional Paper 3.

Eckel, P. and Kezar, A. (2003a) "Key strategies for making new institutional sense: ingredients to higher education transformation," *Higher Education Policy*, 16(1): 39–53.

——. (2003b) *Taking the Reins: Institutional Transformation in Higher Education*, Phoenix, AZ: ACE-ORYX Press.

El-Khawas, E. (2000) "The impetus for organisational change: an exploration," *Tertiary Education and Management*, 6(1): 37–46.

Elmore, R. (1996) "Getting to scale with good educational practice," *Harvard Educational Journal*, 66(1): 1–26.

Erwin, D.G. and Garman, A.N. (2010) "Resistance to organizational change: linking research and practice," *Leadership and Organization Development Journal*, 31(1): 39–56.

Fairweather, J. (2009) *Linking Evidence and Promising Practices in Science, Technology, Engineering and Mathematics (STEM) Undergraduate Education*, Washington, D.C.: National Academies. Paper for the National Academies National Research Council Board of Science Education.

Feldman, M.S. (1991) "The meanings of ambiguity: learning from stories and metaphors," in P.J. Frost, L.F. Moore, M.R. Louis, C.C. Lundberg, and J. Martin (eds.) *Reframing Organizational Culture*, Newbury Park, CA: Sage.

Fiol, C.M. and Lyles, M. (1985) "Organizational learning," *Academy of Management Review*, 10: 803–13.

Folger, R. and Skarlicki, D. (1999) "Unfairness and resistance to change: hardship as mistreatment," *Journal of Organizational Change Management*, 12(1): 35–50.

Ford, J. (1999) "Organizational change as shifting conversation," *Journal of Organizational Change Management*, 12(6): 480–500.

Freeman, L.C. (1979) "Centrality in social networks: conceptual clarification," *Social Networks*, 1(3): 215–39.

Fullan, M. (1989) "Managing curriculum change," in M. Preedy (ed.) *Approaches to Curriculum Management*, New York: Open University Press.

Garvin, D. (1993) "Building a learning organization," *Harvard Business Review*, 71(4): 78–91.

Gersick, C.J.G. (1991) "Revolutionary change theories: a multilevel exploration of the punctuated equilibrium paradigm," *Academy of Management Review*, 16(1): 10–36.

Gilley, A., Godek, M., and Gilley, J.W. (2009) "Change, resistance, and the organizational immune system," *SAM Advanced Management Journal*, 74(4): 1–20.

Gilley, A., McMillan, H.S., and Gilley, J.W. (2009) "Organizational change and characteristics of leadership effectiveness," *Journal of Leadership and Organizational Studies*, 16(1): 38–47.

Gioia, D.A. (1992) "Pinto fires and personal ethics: a script analysis of missed opportunities," *Journal of Business Ethics*, 11(5): 379–89.

Gioia, D.A., Schultz, M., and Corley, K.G. (2000) "Organizational identity, image, and adaptive instability," *Academy of Management Journal*, 25(1): 63–81.

Gioia, D.A., and Thomas, J.B. (1996) "Identity, image, and issue interpretation: sensemaking during strategic change in academia," *Administrative Science Quarterly*, 41(3): 370–403.

Gioia, D.A., Thomas, J.B., Clark, S.M., and Chittipeddi, K. (1996) "Symbolism and strategic change in academia: the dynamics of sensemaking and influence," in J.R. Meindl, C. Stubbart, and J.F. Poroc (eds.) *Cognition in Groups and Organizations*, London: Sage.

Golembiewski, R.T. (1989) *Ironies in Organizational Development*, London: Transaction Publishers.

Goodman, P.S. (1982) *Change in Organizations: New Perspectives on Theory, Research and Practice*, San Francisco: Jossey-Bass.

Gumport, P.J. (1993) "Contested terrain of academic program reduction," *Journal of Higher Education*, 64(3): 283–311.

——. (2012) "Strategic thinking in higher education research," in M. Bastedo (ed.) *The Organization of Higher Education: Managing Colleges for a New Era*, Baltimore, MD: Johns Hopkins University Press.

Gumport, P.J. and Pusser, B. (1995) "A case of bureaucratic accretion: context and consequences," *Journal of Higher Education*, 66(5): 493–520.

——. (1999) "University restructuring: the role of economic and political contexts," in J.C. Smart (ed.) *Higher Education: Handbook of Theory and Research*, New York: Agathon Press.

Gumport, P.J. and Sporn, B. (1999) "Institutional adaptation: demands for management reform and university administration," in J.C. Smart (ed.) *Higher Education: Handbook of Theory and Research*, New York: Agathon Press.

Guskin, A. (1996) "Facing the future: the change process in restructuring universities," *Change*, 28(4): 27–37.

Harris, S.G. (1996) "Organizational culture and individual sensemaking: a schema-based perspective," in J.R. Meindl, C. Stubbart, and J.F. Poroc (eds.) *Cognition in Groups and Organizations*, London: Sage.

Hartley, M. (2009a) "Leading grassroots change in the academy: strategic and ideological adaptation in the civic engagement movement," *Journal of Change Management*, 9(3): 323–38.

——. (2009b) "Reclaiming the democratic purpose of American higher education: tracing the trajectory of the civic engagement movement," *Learning and Teaching*, 2(3): 11–30.

Healy, F. and DeStefano, J. (1997) *Education Reform Support: A Framework for Scaling-Up School Reform*, Raleigh, NC: Research Triangle Institute.Paper prepared for USAID, Advancing Basic Education and Literacy Project.

Hearn, J.C. (1996) "Transforming U.S. higher education: an organizational perspective," *Innovative Higher Education*, 21(2): 141–54.

Hedberg, B. (1981) "How organizations learn and unlearn," in P.C. Nystrom and W.H. Starbuck (eds.) *Handbook of Organizational Design*, New York: Oxford University Press.

Hollander, E. and Hartley, M. (2000) "Civic renewal in higher education: the state of the movement and the need for a national network," in T. Ehrlich (ed.) *Civic Responsibility and Higher Education*, Westport, CT: The American Council on Education and Oryx Press.

Howell, J.M. and Avolio, B.J. (1992) "The ethics of charismatic leadership: submission or liberation?," *Academy of Management Executive*, 6(2): 43–54.

Hrebiniak, L.G. and Joyce, W.F. (1985) "Organizational adaptation: Strategic choice and environmental determinism," *Administrative Science Quarterly*, 30(3): 336–49.

Huber, G.P. and Glick, W.H. (1993) *Organizational Change and Redesign: Ideas and Insights for Improving Performance*, New York: Oxford University Press.

Hurtado, S., Milem, J., Clayon-Pederson, A., and Allen, W. (1999) *Enacting Diverse Learning Environments*, Washington, D.C.: George Washington University. Association for the Study of Higher Education Report 26.

Kanter. R.M. (1983) *The Change Masters*, New York: Simon and Schuster.

——. (1990) *When Giants Learn to Dance*, London: Allen & Unwin.

——. (2000) *Evolve: Succeeding in the Digital Culture Tomorrow*, Boston: Harvard Business School Press.

Keller, G. (1983) "Shaping an academic strategy," in G. Keller (ed.) *Academic Strategy: The Management Revolution in American Higher Education*, Baltimore, MD: Johns Hopkins University Press.

——. (1997) "Examining what works in strategic planning," in M. Peterson, D. Dill, and L. Mets (eds.) *Planning and Management for a Changing Environment*, San Francisco: Jossey-Bass.

Kennedy, D. (1994) "Making choices in the research university,"in J.R. Cole, E.G. Barber, and S.R. Graubard (eds.) *The Research University in a Time of Discontent*, Baltimore, MD: Johns Hopkins University Press.

Kenny, J. (2006) "Strategy and the learning organization: a maturity model for the formation of strategy," *Learning Organization*, 13(4): 353–68.

Kerr, C. (2001) *The Uses of the University*, Cambridge, MA: Harvard University Press.

Kezar, A. (2001) *Understanding and Facilitating Organizational Change in the 21st Century: Recent Research and Conceptualizations*, Washington, D.C.: George Washington University School of Education and Human Development. ASHE-ERIC Higher Education Report.

——. (ed.) (2005a) *Higher Education as a Learning Organization: Promising Concepts and Approaches*, San Francisco: Jossey-Bass. New Directions for Higher Education 131.

——. (2005b) "Redesigning for collaboration with higher education institutions: an exploration into the developmental process," *Research in Higher Education*, 46(7): 831–60.

——. (2007a) "A tale of two cultures: universities and schools working together," *Metropolitan University Journal*, 18(4): 28–47.

——. (2007b) "Learning from and with students: college presidents creating organizational learning to advance diversity agendas," *NASPA Journal*, 44(3): 578–610.

——. (2007c) "Learning to ensure the success for students of color: a systemic approach to effecting change," *Change*, 39(4): 19–25.

——. (2007d) "Tools for a time and place: phased leadership strategies for advancing campus diversity," *Review of Higher Education*, 30(4): 413–39.

——. (2007e) "Successful student engagement: aligning and fostering institutional ethos," *About Campus*, 3(6): 13–19.

——. (2008) "Is there a way out? Examining the commercialization of higher education," *Journal of Higher Education*, 79(4): 473–82.

——. (ed.) (2010) *Recognizing and Serving Low-income Students in Postsecondary Education: An Examination of Institutional Policies, Practices, and Culture*, New York: Routledge.

——. (2011) "What is the best way to achieve reach of improved practices in education," *Innovative Higher Education*, 36(11), 235–49.

——. (forthcoming) "Organizational conditions that shape the implementation of student learning outcomes assessment," *Innovative Higher Education*.

Kezar, A., Chambers, T., and Burkhardt, J. (eds.) (2005) *Higher Education for the Public Good: Emerging Voices from a National Movement*, San Francisco: Jossey-Bass.

Kezar, A., Contreras-McGavin, M., and Carducci, R. (2006) *Rethinking the "L" Word in Leadership: The Revolution of Research on Leadership*, San Francisco: Jossey-Bass.

Kezar, A. and Eckel, P. (2002a) "The effect of institutional culture on change strategies in higher education: universal principles or culturally responsive concepts?," *Journal of Higher Education*, 73(4): 435–60.

——. (2002b) "Examining the institutional transformation process: the importance of sensemaking, inter-related strategies and balance," *Research in Higher Education*, 43(4): 295–328.

Kezar, A. and Lester, J. (2009) Organizing for Collaboration in Higher Education: A Guide for Campus Leaders, San Francisco: Jossey-Bass.

———. (2011) *Enhancing Campus Capacity for Leadership: An Examination of Grassroots Leaders*, Stanford, CA: Stanford University Press.

Kezar, A. and Sam, C. (2010) *Understanding the New Majority: Contingent Faculty in Higher Education*, San Francisco: Jossey-Bass. ASHE Higher Education Report Series.

Kidder, R. (1995) *How Good People Make Tough Choices: Resolving the Dilemmas of Ethical Living*, New York: HarperCollins.

Kilduff, M. and Tsai, W. (2003) *Social Networks and Organizations*, Thousand Oaks, CA: Sage.

Kinser, K. (2011) "The rise and fall of for-profit higher education," paper presented at the Association for the Study of Higher Education Annual Meeting, Charlotte, NC, November 2011.

Knight, D., Pearce, C.L., Smith, K.G., Olian, J.D., Sims, H.P., Smith, K.A., and Flood, P. (1999) "Top management team diversity, group process, and strategic consensus," *Strategic Management Journal*, 20(5): 445–65.

Komives, S.R., Lucas, N., and McMahon, T.R. (1998) *Exploring Leadership: For College Students Who Want to Make a Difference*, San Francisco: Jossey-Bass.

Komives, S.R. and Wagner, W. (eds.) (2009) *Leadership for a Better World: Understanding the Social Change Model of Leadership Development*, San Francisco: Jossey-Bass.

Kotter, J.P. (1985) *Power and Influence: Beyond Formal Authority*, New York: Free Press.

———. (1988) *The Leadership Factor*, New York: Free Press.

———. (1996) *Leading Change*, Boston: Harvard Business School Press.

Kraatz, M. (1998) "Learning by association? Interorganizational networks and adaptation to environmental change," *Academy of Management Journal*, 41(6): 621–43.

Kramer, M. (2000) *Make It Last Forever: The Institutionalization of Service Learning in America*, Washington, D.C.: Corporation for National Service.

Lave, J. (1988) *Cognition in Practice: Mind, Mathematics and Culture in Everyday Life*, New York: Cambridge University Press.

Lave, J. and Wenger, E. (1991) *Situated Learning: Legitimate Peripheral Participation*, New York: Cambridge University Press.

Leicht, K.T. and Fennell, M.L. (2008) "Who staffs the US leaning tower? Organizational change and diversity," *Equal Opportunities International*, 27(1): 88–105.

Leslie, D. and Fretwell, L. (1996) *Wise Moves in Hard Times*, San Francisco: Jossey-Bass.

Lesser, E.L. and Storck, J. (2001) "Communities of practice and organizational performance," *IBM Systems Journal*, (40)4: 831–41.

Levy, A. and Merry, U. (1986) *Organizational Transformation: Approaches, Strategies, Theories*, New York: Praeger.

Lieberman, D. (2005) "Beyond faculty development: how centers for teaching and learning can be laboratories for learning," in A. Kezar (ed.) *Organizational Learning in Higher Education*, San Francisco: Jossey-Bass. New Directions for Higher Education 131.

Lincoln (2012) motion picture, DreamWorks Pictures, United States.

Lindquist, J. (1978) *Strategies of Change*, Washington, D.C.: Council of Independent Colleges.

Lucas, A.F. (ed.) (2000) *Leading Academic Change: Essential Roles for Department Chairs*, San Francisco: Jossey-Bass.

Lumina Foundation (2010) *Lessons: When Networks Build a Platform Students Step Up*, Indianapolis, IN: Lumina Foundation Press.

Mabin, V., Forgeson, S., and Green, L. (2001) "Harnessing resistance: using the theory of constraints to assist change management," *Journal of European Industrial Training*, 25(2–4): 168–91.

McDermott, R. and Archibald, D. (2010) "Harnessing your staff's informal networks," *Harvard Business Review*, 88(3): 82–9.

McGrath, C. and Krackhardt, D. (2003) "Network conditions for organizational change," *Journal of Applied Behavioral Science*, 39(3): 324–36.

McKendall, M. (1993) "The tyranny of change: organizational development revisited," *Journal of Business Ethics*, 12(2): 93–104.

McMahon, J.D. and Caret, R.L. (1997) "Redesigning the faculty roles and rewards structure," *Metropolitan Universities*, 7(4): 11–22.

McNulty, S.K. and Enjeti, P. (2010) "Connecting campuses and building international competencies with study abroad programs: the Texas A&M University at Qatar experience," paper presented at Transforming Engineering Education: Creating Interdisciplinary Skills for Complex Global Environments, Dublin, April 2010.

McRoy, I. and Gibbs, P. (2009) "Leading change in higher education," *Educational Management Administration and Leadership*, 37(5): 687–704.

Magala, S. (2000) "Critical complexities: from marginal paradigms to learning networks," *Journal of Organizational Change Management*, 13(4): 312–33.

March, J.G. (1991) "Exploration and exploitation in organizational learning," *Organizational Science*, 2(1): 71–87.

——. (1994) "The evolution of evolution," in J.A.C. Baum and J.V. Singh (eds.) *Evolutionary Dynamics of Organizations*, New York: Cambridge University Press.

Martin, J. (1992) *Cultures in Organizations: Three Perspectives*, New York: Oxford University Press.

Meyerson, D. (2003) *Tempered Radicals*, Cambridge, MA: Harvard Business School Press.

Miami University (n.d.) *Website for Developing Faculty and Professional Learning Communities (FLCs): Communities of Practice in Higher Education*. Online. Available HTTP: <http://www.units.muohio.edu/flc/> (accessed 20 January 2013).

Moody, J. and White, D.R. (2003) "Structural cohesion and embeddedness: a hierarchical concept of social groups," *American Sociological Review*, 68(1): 103–27.

Morgan, G. (1986) *Images of Organization*, Newbury Park, CA: Sage.

——. (1997) *Imaginization: New Mindsets for Seeing, Organizing and Managing*, San Francisco: Berrett-Koehler.

Morphew, C.C. (2009) "Conceptualizing change in the institutional diversity of U.S. colleges and universities," *Journal of Higher Education*, 80(3): 243–69.

Neill, J. (2004) *Field Theory – Kurt Lewin*. Online. Available HTTP: <http://wilderdom.com/theory/FieldTheory.html> (accessed 5 April 2011).

Nelson, R. (1989) "The strength of strong ties: social networks and intergroup conflict in organizations," *Academy of Management Journal*, 32(2): 377–401.

Neumann, A. (1993) "College planning: a cultural perspective," *Journal of Higher Education Management*, 8(2): 31–41.

Nevis, E.C., Lancourt, J., and Vassallo, H.G. (1996) *Intentional Revolutions: A Seven-point Strategy for Transforming Organizations*, San Francisco: Jossey-Bass.

Nielsen, W., Nykodym, N., and Brown, D. (1991) "Ethics and organizational change," *Asia Pacific Journal of Human Resources*, 29(1): 82–93.

Oreg, S. (2006) "Personality, context, and resistance to organizational change," *European Journal of Work and Organizational Psychology*, 15(1): 73–101.

Palmer, P. (1992) "Divided no more: a movement approach to educational reform," *Change*, 24(2): 10–17.

Pascarella, E.T. and Terenzini, P.T. (2005) *How College Affects Students: A Third Decade of Research*, San Francisco: Jossey-Bass.

Pearce, C. and Conger, J. (2003) *Shared Leadership*, Thousand Oaks, CA: Sage.

Peterson, M.W. (1995) "Images of university structure, governance, and leadership: adaptive strategies for the new environment," in D. Dill and B. Sporn (eds.) *Emerging Patterns of Social Demand and University Reform: Through a Glass Darkly*, Oxford: Pergamon Press.

——. (1997) "Using contextual planning to transform institutions," in M. Peterson, D. Dill, and L. Mets (eds.) *Planning and Management for a Changing Environment*, San Francisco: Jossey-Bass.

Peterson, M.W., Dill, D.D., and Mets, L.A. (1997) *Planning and Management for a Changing Environment: A Handbook on Redesigning Postsecondary Institutions*, San Francisco: Jossey-Bass.

Phillips, R. and Duran, C. (1992) "Effecting strategic change: biological analogues and emerging organizational structures," in R.L. Phillips and J.G. Hunt (eds.) *Strategic Leadership: A Multiorganizational-level Perspective*, Westport, CT: Quorum Books.

Poole, M.S. and Van de Ven, A.H. (2004) *Handbook of Organizational Change and Innovation*, New York: Oxford University Press.

Powell, P.J. and DiMaggio, W.W. (eds.) (1991) *The New Institutionalism in Organizational Analysis*, Chicago: Chicago University Press.

Pusser, B. and Marginson, S. (2012) "The elephant in the room: power, politics, and global rankings in higher education," in M. Bastedo (ed.) *The Organization of Higher Education: Managing Colleges for a New Era*, Baltimore, MD: Johns Hopkins University Press.

Ramaley, J.A. and Holland, B.A. (2005) "Modeling learning: the role of leaders," in A. Kezar (ed.) *Organizational Learning in Higher Education*, San Francisco: Jossey-Bass. New Directions for Higher Education 131.

Reagans, R. and McEvily, B. (2003) "Network structure and knowledge transfer: the effects of cohesion and range," *Administrative Science Quarterly*, 48(2): 240–67.

Reichers, A.E., Wanous, J.P., and Austin, J.T. (1997) "Understanding and managing cynicism about organizational change," *Academy of Management Journal*, 11(1): 148–59.

Rhoades, G. (1995) "Rethinking and restructuring universities," *Journal of Higher Education Management*, 10(2): 17–23.

——. (1996) "Reorganizing the workforce for flexibility: part-time professional labor," *Journal of Higher Education*, 67(6): 626–59.

Rhoades, G.R. and Slaughter S. (1997) "Academic capitalism, managed professionals, and supply-side higher education," *Social Text 51*, 15(2): 9–38.

Rhoads, R.A. (2005) "Student activism in the contemporary context: lessons from the research," *Concepts and Connections*, 13(1): 3–4.

Roberts, A.O., Wergin, J.F., and Adam, B.E. (1993) *Institutional Approaches to the Issues of Reward and Scholarship*, San Francisco: Jossey-Bass. New Directions in Higher Education 81.

Rogers, E.M. (1962; 4th edn. 1995) *Diffusion of Innovations*, New York: Free Press.

Rojas, F. (2012) "Social movements and the university," in M. Bastedo (ed.) *The Organization of Higher Education: Managing Colleges for a New Era*, Baltimore, MD: Johns Hopkins University Press.

St. John, E.P. (1991) "The transformation of private liberal arts colleges," *Review of Higher Education*, 15(1): 83–106.

Salipante, P. and Golden-Biddle, K. (1996) "Managing traditionality and strategic change in nonprofit organizations," *Nonprofit Management and Leadership*, 6(1): 3–19.

Samoff, J., Sebatane, E.M., and Dembélé, M. (2001) "Scaling up by focusing down: creating space to expand education reform," paper revised for inclusion in the publication resulting from the Biennal Meeting of the Association for the Development of Education in Africa held in Arusha, Tanzania, October 2001, pp. 7–11.

Schein, E.H. (1985; 3rd edn. 2004) *Organizational Culture and Leadership: A Dynamic View*, San Francisco: Jossey-Bass.

Schon, D. (1983) *The Reflective Practitioner*, New York: Basic Books.

Scott, W.R. (1995) *Institutions and organizations*, London: Sage.

Senge, P. (1990) *The Fifth Discipline: The Art and Practice of the Learning Organization*, New York: Doubleday.

Seo, M. and Creed, W.E.D. (2002) "Institutional contradictions, praxis, and institutional change: a dialectical perspective," *Academy of Management Review*, 27(2): 222–47.

Shapiro, D. and Kirkman, B. (1999) "Employee's reaction to the change to work teams: the influence of anticipatory injustice," *Journal of Organizational Change Management*, 12(1): 51–67.

Shaw, K.A. and Lee, K.E. (1997) "Effecting change at Syracuse University: the importance of values, missions, and vision," *Metropolitan Universities: An International Forum*, 7(4): 23–30.

Simsek, H. (1997) "Metaphorical images of an organization: the power of symbolic constructs in reading change in higher education organizations," *Higher Education*, 33(3): 283–307.

Simsek, H. and Louis, K.S. (1994) "Organizational change as paradigm shift: analysis of the change process in a large, public university," *Journal of Higher Education*, 65(6): 670–95.

Slaughter, S. and Rhoades, G. (2004) *Academic Capitalism and the New Economy: Markets, State, and Higher Education*, Baltimore, MD: Johns Hopkins University Press.

Slowey, M. (1995) *Implementing Change from within Universities and Colleges: Ten Personal Accounts*, London: Kogan Page.

Smircich, L. (1983) "Organizations as shared meanings," in L.R. Pondy, P.J. Frost, G. Morgan, and T.C. Dandridge (eds.) *Organizational Symbolism*, Greenwich, CT: JAI Press.

Smircich, L. and Calás, M. (1982) "Organizational culture: a critical assessment," in M. Peterson (ed.) *ASHE Reader on Organization and Governance*, Needham Heights, MA: Ginn Press.

Smith, B.L., MacGregor, J., Matthews, R.S., and Gabelnick, F. (2004) *Learning Communities: Reforming Undergraduate Education*, San Francisco: Jossey-Bass.

Sohail, M. S., Daud, S., and Rajadurai, J. (2006) "Restructuring a higher education institution: a case study from a developing country," *International Journal of Educational Management*, 20(4): 279–90.

Solem, M.N. (2000) "Differential adoption of internet-based teaching practices in college geography," *Journal of Geography*, 99(5): 219–27.

Spillane, J.P. (2006) *Distributed Leadership*, San Francisco: Jossey-Bass.

Spillane, J.P., Healey, K., and Kim, C.M. (2010) "Leading and managing instruction: formal and informal aspects of the elementary school organization," in A.J. Daly (ed.) *Social Network Theory and Educational Change*, Cambridge, MA: Harvard Education Press.

Sporn, B. (1999) *Adaptive University Structures: An Analysis of Adaptation to Socioeconomic Environments of U.S. and European Universities*, London: Jessica Kingsley Publishers.

Stake, R. (1995) *The Art of Case Study Research*, Thousand Oaks, CA: Sage.

Steeples, D.W. (1990) *Managing Change in Higher Education*, San Francisco: Jossey-Bass.

Stoll, L., Bolam, R., McMahon, A., Wallace, M., and Thomas, S. (2006) "Professional learning communities: a review of the literature, *Journal of Educational Change*, 7(4): 221–58.

Stragalas, N. (2010) "Improving change implementation," *OD Practitioner*, 42(1): 31–8.

Stuckey, B. (2004) "Making the most of the good advice: meta-analysis of guidelines for establishing an internet-mediated community of practice," paper presented at the IADIS Web-based Communities Conference, Lisbon, Portugal, March 2004.

Sturdy, A. and Grey, C. (2003) "Beneath and beyond organizational change management: exploring alternatives," *Organization*, 10(4): 651–62.

Szulanski, G. (1996) "Internal stickiness: impediments to the transfer of best practices within the firm," *Strategic Management Journal*, 17: 27–43.

Tenkasi, R. and Chesmore, M. (2003) "Social networks and planned change: the impact of strong ties on effective change implementation and use," *Journal of Applied Behavioral Science*, 39(3): 281–300.

Thomas, J.B., Clark, S.M., and Gioia, D.A. (1993) "Strategic sensemaking and organizational performance: linkages among scanning, interpretation, action, and outcomes," *Academy of Management Journal*, 36: 239–70.

Thomas, R., Sargent, L.D., and Hardy, C. (2011) "Managing organizational change: negotiating meaning and power-resistance relations," *Organizational Science*, 22(1): 22–41.

——. (1991) "Organizational culture in higher education: defining the essentials," in M. Peterson (ed.) *ASHE Reader on Organization and Governance*, Needham Heights, MA: Ginn Press.

——. (2006) *Trust and the Public Good*, New York: Peter Lang.

——. (2012) "Creativity and organizational culture," in M. Bastedo (ed.) *The Organization of Higher Education: Managing Colleges for a New Era*, Baltimore, MD: Johns Hopkins University Press.

Tierney, W.G. and Rhoads, R.A. (1993) *Enhancing Promotion and Tenure: Faculty Socialization as a Cultural Process*, Washington, D.C.: Association for the Study of Higher Education. Association for the Study of Higher Education-ERIC Higher Education Report 6.

Toma, J.D. (2010) *Building Organizational Capacity*, Baltimore, MD: Johns Hopkins University Press.

——. (2011) *Managing the Entrepreneurial University: Legal Issues and Commercial Realities*, New York: Routledge.

——. (2012) "Institutional strategy: positioning for prestige," in M. Bastedo (ed.) *The Organization of Higher Education: Managing Colleges for a New Era*, Baltimore, MD: Johns Hopkins University Press.

Touchton, J., Musil C.M., and Campbell, K.P. (2008) *A Measure of Equity: Women's Progress in Higher Education*, Washington, D.C.: Association of American Colleges and Universities.

Trowler, P.R. (1998) *Academics Responding to Change: New Higher Education Frameworks and Academic Cultures*, Philadelphia: Open University.

——. (2009) "Beyond epistemological essentialism: academic tribes in the 21st century," in C. Kreber (ed.) *The University and Its Disciplines: Teaching and Learning within and beyond Disciplinary Boundaries*, London: Routledge.

Tsoukas, H. and Chia, R. (2002) "On organizational becoming: rethinking organizational change," *Organizational Science*, 13(5): 567–82.

Valente, T. (1995) *Network Models of the Diffusion of Innovations*, Cresskill, NJ: Hampton Press.

Van de Ven, A.H. and Poole, M.S. (1995) "Explaining development and change in organizations," *Academy of Management Review*, 20(3): 510–40.

Wasserman, S. and Faust, K. (1994) *Social Network Analysis: Methods and Applications*, Cambridge: Cambridge University Press.

Weick, K.E. (1993) "The collapse of sensemaking in organizations: the Mann Gulch disaster," *Administrative Science Quarterly*, 38(4): 628–42.

——. (1995) *Sensemaking in Organizations*, Thousand Oaks, CA: Sage.

Wenger, E. (1998) "Communities of practice: learning as a social system," *Systems Thinker*, 9(5).

——. (2006) *Communities of Practice: A Brief Introduction.* Online. Available HTTP: <http://www.ewenger.com/theory> (accessed 14 January 2009).

Wenger, E., McDermott, R., and Snyder, W. (2002) *Cultivating Communities of Practice: A Guide to Managing Knowledge,* Cambridge, MA: Harvard Business School Press.

White, L. and Rhodeback, M. (1992) "Ethical dilemmas in organization development: a cross-cultural analysis," *Journal of Business Ethics,* 11(9): 663–70.

Zajac, G. and Bruhn, J. (1999) "The moral context of participation in planned organizational change and learning," *Administration and Society,* 30(6): 706–33.

Zemsky, R., Wegner, G.R., and Massy, W.P. (2005) *Remaking the American University: Market-smart and Mission-centered,* Piscataway, NJ: Rutgers University Press.

Zull, J. (2011) *From Brain to Mind: Using Neuroscience to Guide Change in Education,* Sterling, VA: Stylus.

Index

Page numbers in **bold** refer to figures, page numbers in *italic* refer to tables.